The WIN-WIN CLASSROOM

To Tony Lettieri, who by his example taught me the importance of caring about and connecting with kids.

JANE BLUESTEIN

The WIN-WIN CLASSROOM

A FRESH AND POSITIVE LOOK AT CLASSROOM MANAGEMENT

CORWIN PRESS
A SAGE Company
Thousand Oaks, CA 91320

For information:

Corwin Press
A SAGE Company
2455 Teller Road
Thousand Oaks, California 91320
www.corwinpress.com

SAGE Ltd.
1 Oliver's Yard
55 City Road
London EC1Y 1SP
United Kingdom

SAGE India Pvt. Ltd.
B 1/I 1 Mohan Cooperative Industrial Area
Mathura Road, New Delhi 110 044
India

SAGE Asia-Pacific Pte. Ltd.
33 Pekin Street #02-01
Far East Square
Singapore 048763

Printed in the United States of America

Library of Congress Cataloging-in-Publication Data

Bluestein, Jane.
The win-win classroom : a fresh and positive look at classroom management/Jane Bluestein.
    p. cm.
Includes bibliographical references and index.
ISBN 978-1-4129-5899-8 (cloth)
ISBN 978-1-4129-5900-1 (pbk.)
    1. Classroom management—Handbooks, manuals, etc. I. Title.

LB3013.B548 2008
371.102′4—dc22   2007023890

This book is printed on acid-free paper.

07   08   09   10   11   10 9 8 7 6 5 4 3 2 1

Acquisitions Editor:	Hudson Perigo
Editorial Assistant:	Cassandra Harris
Production Editor:	Catherine M. Chilton
Copy Editor:	Tina Hardy
Typesetter:	C&M Digitals (P) Ltd.
Proofreader:	Doris Hus
Indexer:	Molly Hall
Cover Designer:	Michael Dubowe
Graphic Designer:	Monique Hahn

Contents

Acknowledgments

Writing for other educators always seems to take me back through a great deal of my history, allowing me to relive not only my first weeks and years in the classroom, but also hundreds of subsequent classroom observations and visitations, as well as conversations with educators at all grade levels throughout the world. To be sure, each story and example presented here has faces and feelings attached; each of them is a part of who I am today, both personally and professionally. Much water, many bridges, as a friend once said.

Certain individuals bear mention, as their influence on my knowledge, beliefs, confidence, skills, and understanding of how people learn and interact successfully has been immense. I never would have survived my first year without the constant support of Marian Morris, the site coordinator of the intern program in which I was enrolled, as well as the other beginning teachers fumbling and stumbling along with me. I have had many opportunities to thank her personally over the years and am grateful that we are still in touch, although less frequently than I would like.

Various professors throughout my graduate training at the University of Pittsburgh also left their respective marks. My thanks to John Morgan, Horton Southworth, Jeanne Winsand, Janice Gibson, Dave Champagne, Larry Knolle, and Dave Campbell. All of these individuals could somehow see me beyond where I was when I came into their lives; each in his or her own way planted seeds for an unfoldment I could not have imagined. Many of these people are gone now and I've lost touch with the others, but each will remain a part of who I am, and who I have become, for the rest of my days.

I would also like to acknowledge the students and teachers with whom I worked at Arlington Heights, Sterrett School, and Chartiers Elementary in Pittsburgh, Pennsylvania, as well as the student teachers and interns I supervised at the University of New Mexico, students at several middle schools and at a day treatment program where I volunteered for a time here in Albuquerque, as well as students and teachers in classrooms I've visited around the world. Much of what I know I learned from them.

I also owe enormous thanks to Carla Hannaford, Aili Pogust, Terry Burik, Mary Sue Williams, and Sherry Shellenberger. These individuals have contributed greatly to my understanding of the role of the body and brain in student learning and behavior, knowledge acquired from their classes or books, and in some of the most stimulating conversations I've ever enjoyed.

I am also indebted to the thousands of workshop participants throughout the world who generously shared their stories and experiences with me. I would also like to thank my colleague and friend, Mark Ita, for his quote from Coach Dave Triplett, and who otherwise refuses to allow me to publicly attribute any of his terrific quotes and contributions, although they have become an important part of my work and show up throughout this book.

This book has also benefited from a peer review process, from which I received invaluable feedback and suggestions. I'd especially like to acknowledge and thank Naomi Drew, Lynn Collins, Susan Fitzell, Wendy Marshall, Stephen Haslam, Jo Ann Freiberg, Aili Pogust, Ken Fraser, Robert Reasoner, Keith Ward, Stephen Tipps, and Jared Scherz, whose painstaking notes and individual perspectives have added a great deal of clarity and continuity to this book.

And finally, an extra-special thank you to my husband, Jerry Tereszkiewicz, who came into my life as I was just starting out in my first classroom—and has hung with me ever since.

Corwin Press thanks the following reviewers for their contributions to this book:

Lynn Collins, President, Lynn Collins & Associates, Albuquerque, NM

Naomi Drew, Educational Consultant, Learning Peace, Lambertville, NJ

Susan A. Fitzell, Educational Consultant, AIMHI Educational Programs, Manchester, NH

Ken Fraser, Educational Consultant, Esteem Wizard, Canberra, Australia

Jo Ann Freiberg, Associate Educational Consultant, Bullying, School Climate and Character Education, Connecticut State Department of Education, Middletown, CT

Stephen Haslam, Managing Partner, Resource International, Houston, TX

Wendy J. Marshall, Armstrong Atlantic State University, Savannah, GA

Aili Pogust, Educational Consultant, The Pogust Group, Marlton, NJ

Robert Reasoner, President, International Council for Self-Esteem, Port Ludlow, WA

Jared Scherz, Director, Integrative Training and Consulting, Mt. Laurel, NJ

Stephen Tipps, Professor of Education (Retired), Flat Rock, NC

Keith Ward, Director, School Success Strategies, Doylestown, PA

About the Author

 **Jane Bluestein**, PhD, a dynamic and entertaining speaker, has worked with thousands of educators, counselors, health care professionals, parents, child care workers, and other community members worldwide. She has appeared internationally as a speaker and talk show guest, including several appearances as a guest expert on CNN, National Public Radio, and *The Oprah Winfrey Show*.

Dr. Bluestein specializes in programs and resources geared to provide practical and meaningful information, training, and hope in areas related to relationship building, effective instruction and guidance, and personal development, with a particular emphasis on positive interactions between adults and children. Her down-to-earth speaking style, practicality, sense of humor, and numerous stories and examples make her ideas clear and accessible to her audiences.

She is an award-winning author whose other books include *Creating Emotionally Safe Schools; Being a Successful Teacher; Parents in a Pressure Cooker; Parents, Teens, and Boundaries; The Parent's Little Book of Lists: Do's and Don'ts of Effective Parenting; Mentors, Masters, and Mrs. McGregor: Stories of Teachers Making a Difference; High School's Not Forever;* and *Daily Riches: A Journal of Gratitude and Awareness*. She has also produced a number of audio and video programs, as well as dozens of articles and stationery items for adults who live and work with children of all ages.

Formerly a classroom teacher, crisis intervention counselor, teacher training program coordinator, and volunteer with high-risk teens at a local day treatment program, Dr. Bluestein currently heads Instructional Support Services, Inc., a consulting and resource firm in Albuquerque, New Mexico.

To contact Dr. Bluestein, or for more information about her workshops, background, and resources, plus several hundred pages of free articles, excerpts, and handouts, visit Dr. Bluestein's Web site at http://www.janebluestein.com.

Preface

I t's hard for me to believe that it's been more than two decades since I first wrote about relationships between teachers and students. When I began, my work focused almost exclusively on discipline and classroom management, arising from the needs of the student teachers and first-year teaching interns charged to my care. Among my earliest works was a book entitled *21st Century Discipline,* written when the new millennium still seemed to be a long way off. As that book—and a subsequent revision ten years later—generated its own strange history, passing from one publisher to another, so did my work with this topic continue to evolve.

When Corwin Press asked me to revisit the manuscript, I realized that with all the additions and changes, the book really wasn't about discipline anymore.

As might be expected, my perceptions and feelings about student behavior has, over the years, instigated numerous shifts in the vocabulary and conceptual framework presented in my writing and teaching. What started as a book (and eventually a seminar) about discipline had come to embrace a far wider range of issues related to various dimensions of classroom climate, particularly the teacher-student interactions that influence behavior. Nowadays, whether I'm talking about discipline and student behavior, school safety, dropout prevention, or dealing with difficult students, I always seem to be addressing not only power dynamics, but academic and cognitive issues, social and emotional matters, feedback and encouragement, learning needs, and neurological and physiological concerns. So it really was no surprise to discover, as I went through the manuscript for a final revision, that with all the new material I had included, and all the changes I had made to the ideas that had appeared in previous editions of the discipline book, that I had an entirely new creation on my hands (although a few of the stories and examples hail from my earlier work).

The concerns expressed by teachers today are not much different than they were when I first started writing about them. Kids still come to class unprepared, forget to put materials away, don't turn their homework in on time, and lack skills needed to succeed with the curriculum we're supposed to teach them. Bad attitudes, lack of initiative, poor impulse control, passive learning, indifference, power struggles, and, in many instances, verbal or physical violence, are a reality in many classrooms. Over the years, I've seen increasing impatience and disillusionment with traditional practices and ineffective techniques that simply do not address the most fundamental component of any educational experience, that is, the relationship between teacher and student.

The good news is: There is a better way.

I've spent much of my career looking for strategies that help teachers connect with kids in positive ways. In this book, I've done my best to share the ideas that worked best for the teachers I've met and observed—and those that worked for me as well. In the time that I've been writing about these strategies, I've received feedback from countless teachers, counselors, administrators, and other school personnel who have made the changes suggested in this book. Although often attempted as a last resort, the enormous success they report continues to reassure me that the changes we say we want are not going to come from stricter enforcement of punitive discipline codes or increasing the number of rules. I am convinced that these changes will come, instead, from our efforts to develop relationships, structures, and a positive context within our classrooms that can indeed accommodate our students' needs, including their needs for autonomy and power within clear, definite limits in an emotionally safe environment.

As my work has evolved, I have concentrated my efforts on refining the language, conceptual foundation, and techniques of a win-win approach to dealing with student behavior and achievement. This revision incorporates research, observations, personal experiences, and information that account for several significant changes, any one of which can reduce stress and conflict in a school environment. I've borrowed from other fields and have learned much from educators throughout the world with whom I've worked. I've examined some of our most common and enduring practices, patterns, and policies and have found some simple, effective alternatives to the ones that aren't working, as well as the ones that are actually making things worse. I've broadened my understanding of how the brain works—and how brain- and body-related issues can contribute to student behavior—and have added these insights to my writing.

One of the most interesting updates in my work has come from changes in the technology that was available when I started teaching (and writing) and that which we currently find in schools. I'm well aware that my audiences are getting younger: I often find myself defining words like *ditto* for new teachers these days. I have attempted to eliminate all references to dittos,[1] as well as things like filmstrips, records, carbon paper, and film projectors, all of which were common references in my earlier work. Despite my passion for the latest technologies, writing about this makes me feel old.

Regardless of the focus of my work, putting a positive spin on negative student behavior has always been a challenge. Although *The Win-Win Classroom* has gotten away from the emphasis on discipline per se, many of the ideas presented here will have a positive impact on student behavior, eliminating many of the discipline problems teachers encounter. From my earliest work, I've tried to get away from equating discipline with punishment, or, at the very least, a negative reaction to a student's misbehavior, and to redefine the term to emphasize the development of relationships and classroom environments in which many typical discipline problems simply do not occur (or occur much more infrequently and much less disruptively).

While my earliest works included mention of rules and consequences (with the traditional negative orientation to dealing with misbehaviors), I simply couldn't get past the fact that there were just too many similarities, both in concept and implementation, to the dynamics of using punishments. Even the most positive spin on the pattern of using rules and negative consequences could not pull this approach out of its punitive and reactive tradition. As this work developed, I discovered the language and concepts that allowed me to shift from promoting rules and negative consequences to strategies for setting boundaries[2] and emphasizing contingent access to *positive* outcomes instead. I have found that this model afforded me a context, not only for intervening in disruptions and off-task behavior, but also for motivating and reinforcing cooperation without relying on power, anger, threats, or conditional teacher approval.

I believe that this shift to positive consequences lies at the heart of what *The Win-Win Classroom* is all about. The change is subtle but the difference is powerful. As a result, the relationship dynamics are a great deal cleaner and less power oriented, all without losing their effectiveness. While rules may persist as a fact of life in educational institutions, my preference for using boundaries stands, as well as my belief in their effectiveness and compatibility with win-win objectives, even in the most negative and reactive environment.

Another change was in the area of internal and external motivation. These terms seemed a lot less ambiguous when I first started writing about them. I've seen a lot of teachers upset or confused by these terms, and I have experienced a great deal of frustration with this language myself. What I've come to is this: *All motivation is internal.* Whether we do something for the joy of doing it, to please someone, to get it out of the way, to feel a sense of pride or accomplishment, to fulfill a commitment or responsibility, to avoid a penalty or punishment, to keep from disappointing or annoying someone, to get a grade or a paycheck, or so that we can do something we enjoy even more when we're done, we are satisfying some internal need. Always.

Nowadays, I attempt to clarify this point by differentiating between motivators and reinforcers that rely on the reaction of another person (or jeopardize emotional safety with conditional approval) and those that do not. As far as I'm concerned, doing what the teacher wants so you can do a fun enrichment activity, check off a task you've completed, or go help out in the library is just as internal (and, quite frankly, as reasonable) as cooperating because you happen to love a particular subject area. In creating a safe emotional environment, I'm far more troubled about motivators and reinforcers that teach kids to constantly look outside themselves, to base their decisions on anticipated reactions of other people or build dependence on outside approval. Regardless of what we call it, quite frankly, the need to avoid rejection or anger is just as internal as anything else.

Writing this book has allowed me to not only put the latest incarnation of these ideas into print, but also to share a wealth of very practical and effective strategies gleaned from the research, from conversations and visits with teachers over the years, and from my personal experiences as well. It is my hope that this material will make the creation of a productive, cooperative, enjoyable—and yes, win-win—learning environment clear and accessible, that it will put some fun and passion into your work, and that it will help you remember what brought you to this profession in the first place. I wish you joy and success in your journey.

—Jane Bluestein
April, 2007
Albuquerque, New Mexico

NOTES

1. In case you're not familiar with this medium, *dittos* are duplicated papers with purple imprints, run off on machines that left a subtle solvent residue smell my kids used to love.

2. I elaborate on the concept and use of boundaries in greater detail in later chapters. To introduce the term, I'm referring to a process that goes beyond simply setting limits. Therapist Jared Scherz suggests thinking of boundaries as "a meeting place for the transfer of ideas (as opposed to a fence)."

Introduction

On paper, I was a terrific teacher. I was getting great grades in all of my education classes, although my training—and confidence—were geared to things like sequencing content and creating gorgeous instructional materials. In terms of preparation, I could not have been outdone. Yet the thought of facing a roomful of children somehow wasn't relieved by my skill with the laminator. Throughout my methods courses, one question persistently nagged: What do I do with the *kids?*

I did not get many answers, and those I did hear were not particularly satisfying. More often than not my question was answered with a warning: "Keep them busy and make sure you look like you're in charge."

Great.

To make things more interesting, there appeared to be a contradiction between the priorities expressed in our teacher training programs and what the schools actually seemed to want. While the university was big on freedom, creativity, and democracy in the classroom, the undercurrent from the schools, where we would actually be working, warned that control was the goal. It didn't take long for my idealism to yield to this pressure. I remember meeting veterans who confessed to having their students copy their science books because, when observed, the kids were quiet and looked busy. But that certainly wasn't what drew me to teaching. Surely there was a way to actually create order and inspire productivity without policing my kids—or academically wasting their time just so I'd look like I knew what I was doing!

Hoping for the best, I started my career armed with the most beautiful bulletin boards in the district and a handful of clichés: *Be tough. Be consistent. Be clever. Don't smile before Christmas.* Nonetheless, my power was, for the most part, unimpressive and unheeded. The worst punishments I had at my disposal were generally met with a shrug. My students resisted cooperating on even the most reasonable requests, and despite all their street smarts and savvy, could not make simple decisions or get from one side of the room to the other without a problem. I spent so much time nagging, reminding, and monitoring them that I never seemed to do any teaching.

Those months were painful, to say the least. Nothing could have prepared me for the realization that all my dedication, enthusiasm, and creativity would not be enough to engage my students, keep them on task, or generate a passion for learning. And I was devastated to find that my expectations alone would not generate their cooperation. Kids were indifferent to me and mean to one another. Nothing I tried seemed to create anything resembling a sense of community.

For weeks, I cried at the end of every day. But every now and then, I'd stumble across something that worked. And over time, I discovered that the success of these strategies was closely tied to the quality of the classroom culture and the interactions that occur, things over which I had far more influence than I realized. I stopped blaming other teachers, the system, or parents, and eventually found ways to meet the students' needs without sacrificing my own.

Probably the most important lesson came from the discovery that the common thread among the most effective teachers I observed seemed to be the relationship and the connections that these teachers established with their students—and most often, with the students' parents and with other staff as well. While I may have implicitly understood the importance of these connections when I entered the profession, I had not a clue as to how to bring them about. And so the search began.

In recent years, I've had the pleasure of standing in the halls of a number of schools and watching teachers connect with kids between classes. I've seen the impact of a simple expression of interest or concern. I've heard of a teacher who greeted each of her first graders with an offer of a handshake or a hug.[1] I've sat in a class with an Algebra teacher who stayed after school until five o'clock to tutor her low-achieving kids, each of whom had voluntarily stayed or returned for help catching up. (Unfortunately, I've also walked down hallways and heard yelling and insults that would wither the most emotionally hardy adult, and sometimes wonder how things aren't actually worse than they are in some schools.)

The work I've done since I left the classroom has focused on developing a greater understanding of the dynamics of adult-child relationships and the power of connectedness, and how these contribute to learning, achievement, motivation, self-concept, and behavior in school. This book details what I've learned. My initial focus on discipline, which is still a major concern for educators worldwide, led me to the importance of honoring the need for everyone in a classroom to be valued, respected, and successful—in other words, the need for everyone, teacher and student, to "win."

I remember a conversation that occurred several years ago with my friend and colleague, Dr. Stephen Tipps. In discussing the problems with win-lose patterns so common in schools, he succinctly noted that whether we're talking about discipline or achievement or social interactions, "We cannot afford to have losers in education." Yet how many of our long-cherished traditions continue to put children in this very position. Whether insisting on a certain degree of failure to maintain the distribution of a bell-shaped curve, creating and imposing discipline policies that focus on punitive outcomes for misbehavior, or according privileges or status to certain individuals or groups of students,[2] when it comes to creating an environment with a high degree of commitment, self-management, and success in all students, we keep shooting ourselves in the foot.

Yet it's hard to let go of what we know. As author Alan Blankstein cautions, "Like the smoker who knows better or the gambler who occasionally wins, we can become wedded to what worked at one time or what works once in a while."[3] What I hope to do in this book is to present an alternative to the practices and policies that no longer help us reach our goals, and, in fact, may very well be getting in our way. It would be nice to imagine that the direction for the changes we need will come from the system itself, but it seems, more and more, that the most positive changes are happening *in spite of* established systems.

So here is a roadmap for change, presented with the power of the individual in mind. If you've questioned existing patterns but couldn't think of other options, you'll find them here. These ideas will help you match behaviors to intentions, enhancing the successes you're probably already experiencing. If your work environment is negative and toxic, you'll find some ways to create your own little corner of sanity and success, and maybe even turn the culture of your school around. With or without support, there are things you can do to make your work life a positive, productive, and enjoyable experience, one that will have a significant impact on the kids whose lives you inevitably touch. And in so doing, everyone wins.

NOTES

1. From a story by Michele Borba in *Mentors, Masters and Mrs. MacGregor: Stories of Teachers Making a Difference* by Jane Bluestein (Deerfield Beach, FL: Health Communications, 1995).

2. The most common prejudices in schools tend to favor kids with money, kids who dress well, and those with academic or athletic talent. From *Creating Emotionally Safe Schools* by Jane Bluestein (Deerfield Beach, FL: Health Communications, 2001).

3. Alan M. Blankstein, *Failure Is Not an Option* (Thousand Oaks, CA: Corwin Press, 2004).

PART I

The System, Your Students, and You

1

Drawing the Line

Years ago, after meeting the student teachers and first-year teaching interns I was to supervise, I asked about the topics and concerns they wanted to explore during the year we were to work together. Nearly all their responses had to do with student behavior and motivation. They had dozens of questions, mostly about how to get the kids to do something or stop doing something: "What if they don't listen?" "What if there's a fight?" "What if they won't do their work?" "What if . . . ?"

Since then, I've run across thousands of teachers whose primary concerns have sounded remarkably similar. But I've discovered few simple answers to questions about specific behaviors or misbehaviors. Over the years, any time I tried to address discipline issues in my teaching, presenting, or writing, I found myself backing up to explore seemingly unrelated issues—goals, intentions, needs, relationships, cooperation, motivation, success, classroom climate, and responsibility, to name a few. Without addressing these issues, most advice is short term, shortsighted, ineffective, and unrelated to the context of classroom relationships in which the problems occur.

> I've discovered few simple answers to questions about specific behaviors or misbehaviors.

We have a peculiar myopia when it comes to discipline, and I hope that this book takes consideration of the topic beyond the normal "student behavior–teacher reaction" paradigm through which we typically regard how kids act in class. Instead, I present discipline in the context of a much bigger picture. When we look at the academic, social, emotional, and physiological issues involved with simply being a student—and not just the behavioral concerns—we can see a lot of places where our traditions can create stress, as well as a host of survival responses to this stress, any one of which can look like a discipline problem.

In a context of creating healthy, positive, and mutually respectful relationships between teachers and students, we can take a wider range of issues into consideration and examine how our policies and practices contribute to student behavior, attitudes, and achievement. Discipline then becomes a set of proactive and preventive techniques that encourage student self-management and self-control while reducing the number of conflicts anticipated by the vast majority of the "what if" questions. In other words, rather than reacting to negative student behaviors, we focus instead on creating the kind of classroom environment in which these behaviors are not likely to occur in the first place.

For some, this is a hard sell. After years of traditions that require some negative or painful event to follow a misbehavior, any book or seminar that promises solutions to student behavior problems is bound to attract at least a few individuals who come looking for a bigger hammer with which to figuratively hit their unruly kids. But as many teachers know, some of the worst behaviors we see in classrooms are those exhibited by kids who are getting "hammered" pretty regularly outside the classroom. Looking for more effective punishments—in the hope of creating enough emotional, social, or in some cases, physical discomfort to discourage similar behaviors in the future—can be much like pouring gasoline on a fire.

So *The Win-Win Classroom* is not about better ways to punish kids, and it probably won't help much if you're simply searching for more effective negative consequences to student misbehavior. I am convinced that the lack of motivation, bad attitudes, and disruptions we see aren't happening because we don't have enough rules or bad enough punishments in our schools. And I'm less concerned with the specific reasons individual kids misbehave or shut down than I am with the things we can do to reduce the likelihood of these behaviors occurring in the first place. So any discussion of student behavior ultimately leads back to teacher behavior. Motivating cooperation from our students usually means modifying our own behaviors, learning new interaction skills, and letting go of ineffective or destructive policies and techniques. For better or worse, the kids don't change until we change. Whenever we're not happy with how students are behaving, the big question for us to consider is not about what we need to do to the kids, but instead what we can do differently in our behaviors and interactions with them to minimize the kinds of student behaviors we find most troublesome.

> Any discussion of student behavior ultimately leads back to teacher behavior.

This news can be rather disconcerting. To begin, the culture of schools and communities typically rewards "strict" or "tough" teachers, and that generally includes expectations for big-hammer approaches. It is my hope that this book will provide tools, strategies, and language to help teachers establish their authority, to draw the line, and, indeed, to be strict, even tough, in very positive and effective ways. Grasping the fact that these ideas are not mutually exclusive was an enormous challenge for me—and for many of the educators (and parents) with whom I work—and hopefully this middle ground will become clearer in the following pages.

Further, it will always be easier to want other people to change. For years, I've seen perfectly reasonable adults resist this proposition: "Why should *I* have to change? *I'm* not the one disrupting the class!" I'm sure most teachers agree that we shouldn't have to deal with half of what we inevitably confront, sometimes on a daily basis, in terms of student behaviors, language, or the quality (or absence) of their work. Let me urge you to do it anyhow. The alternative is the insanity of doing the same ineffective, frustrating things over and over and seeing nothing improve in the process.

> I'm sure most teachers agree that we shouldn't have to deal with half of what we inevitably confront, sometimes on a daily basis, in terms of student behaviors, language, or the quality (or absence) of their work.

Most often, this resistance to change simply reflects a lack of clear, practical, and usable alternatives to the patterns and policies with which we are most familiar. Even with firm commitments to positive interaction strategies, avoiding the pitfalls of our own negative programming is always a challenge. Not realizing that more positive options exist, much less knowing what these specific options look and sound like, severely limits our responses. We know what we know, and in some instances, it will serve us well to unlearn some of what we know, to clarify our intentions, and to actually think differently about how we approach issues like how we interact with our students. Certainly this is a process on every level, not just for us, but for our students as well.

2

Starting
Where You Are

As with any change, the prospect of restructuring relationships may seem a bit overwhelming, so let's start with where you are right now. A preassessment follows to help you identify the beliefs and behaviors you currently bring to your work. In each pair of statements below, mark the one that most closely represents your actual behavior, or the one you identify with most strongly.

The purpose of this activity is to establish a basis for setting goals and tracking your growth and to present a foundation for exploring different ways in which we approach our work with kids. The first statement in each pair reflects the philosophy and considerations described in this book. If you have checked a majority of these statements, this book will help you enhance what you're already doing.

The second statement in the pair reflects a more traditional, authoritarian approach to dealing with students. If you checked many of these statements, you're certainly in good company. This is the model most of us experienced as we were growing up and the way many of us were trained to work with children. Read on—you'll find more positive alternatives. If you had a difficult time choosing between two statements, this book can point out the differences between the two approaches, which are very different and generally exclusive of one another.

Preassessment Form

_____ I believe a positive emotional climate is a prerequisite for a strong learning environment.

_____ I prefer to focus on academics. The students are there to learn.

_____ I try to give each student a chance to feel successful by meeting his or her individual needs.

_____ All students have an opportunity to feel successful if they listen and stay caught up.

_____ The best negative consequence is the absence of a positive consequence.

_____ A negative consequence is more effective when it involves some degree of discomfort or embarrassment.

_____ Whether or not my students cooperate, I communicate my acceptance of them as people.

_____ When my students cooperate, I communicate my approval.

_____ I have a variety of classroom materials out and available for my students to take as needed.

_____ Most of the time, I dispense materials.

_____ I want my students to listen to me and I try to make it need fulfilling for them to do so.

_____ I want my students to listen to me and I punish them when they do not.

_____ "Johnny, you really got ready in a hurry today!"

_____ "I like the way Johnny got ready today!"

_____ My students can manage okay even if I'm not there.

_____ My students behave as long as I don't turn my back on them.

_____ I try to find something positive to say about every paper I get.

_____ I normally mark only mistakes or incorrect answers.

_____ My students know I care about them even if they are driving me crazy.

_____ I find it difficult to like them when they act up.

_____ "Now that your work is caught up, you can play this Saturday."
_____ "I'm so happy that you got all your work in."

_____ I like my job most of the time.
_____ My job is often more stressful than it is enjoyable.

_____ I use the state-mandated curriculum as a guideline, while I adjust my teaching according to my students' academic and cognitive needs.
_____ I follow the state-mandated curriculum as closely as I can, regardless of my students' academic and cognitive needs.

_____ I like to call parents when my students are doing well.
_____ I rarely call parents unless my students create a problem or fall behind.

_____ I work to earn my students' respect.
_____ Students should respect me because I'm their teacher.

_____ It's possible for students to have power in the classroom without disrupting the class or hurting anyone.
_____ Give them an inch and they'll take a yard.

_____ I immediately withdraw privileges when my students misbehave (or violate boundaries).
_____ I frequently give my students warnings and reminders when they misbehave (or violate boundaries).

_____ I know I'm doing a great job when I'm prepared and doing my best, even if my students don't respond.
_____ It's hard for me to feel successful or effective unless my students are busy learning and excited about their work.

_____ When my students behave, it is because they are working for positive consequences.
_____ When my students behave, it is because they want to avoid negative consequences.

_____ Everyone works better when there is a meaningful payoff.
_____ Good behavior should be expected, not rewarded.

_____ "You can get credit for your work if it's turned in by the end of the day."
_____ "I feel angry and frustrated when you forget your work."

_____ I want my students to care about me.
_____ I do not care if my students like me as long as they behave and do their work.

_____ My students sometimes choose which problems or assignments they want to do.
_____ I determine the assignments for my students.

_____ "You can take another library book home as soon as you return the one you borrowed last week."
_____ "If you don't return your library book, you can't take another one home."

_____ I sometimes ask my students to choose which assignments they would like to do first.
_____ My students do their work in a specific sequence, which I assign.

_____ "Please pick up those marbles so that no one will slip and fall."
_____ "Would you pick up those marbles for me, please?"

_____ I try very hard to treat my students with respect, even when I am responding to their negative behavior.
_____ It's sometimes necessary to criticize or humiliate a student. (Students who are misbehaving forfeit their right to be treated respectfully.)

_____ I have a number of unrelated, nondestructive diversions to relieve work-related stress.
_____ Most of my out-of-school time is devoted to my work.

3

Clarifying What You Want

Having identified the patterns in your teaching behaviors, we've got one more brief activity before talking about the whys and hows of establishing win-win classroom interactions. Let's look at your priorities, what's important to you, and what you need to make your teaching "work." I would also like to make sure we're headed in the same direction in terms of the results you're likely to achieve with the strategies presented in this book.

Right now, it's fantasy time. Imagine you have an ideal class of perfect students who behave exactly the way you want, all the time. How do they act? Think about those specific classroom behaviors that you perceive as ideal. Consider what you want and need as a classroom teacher and what your students need to succeed in your class.

Now total your ratings. If your score is low (that is, closer to 25 than 125), either your teaching goals are significantly different from those expressed in this book or your imagination was not adequately cranked. Try again. (Be good to yourself!) And if the aforementioned behaviors really aren't important to you, keep in mind that the more of these behaviors you see, the fewer problems you're likely to have, not just with student behavior but with achievement as well. When your students are demonstrating these behaviors, class time can be devoted to instruction and positive interactions, making your job significantly easier and more pleasant. Additionally, students who acquire these skills tend to be able to function more successfully in the classroom and out, during their school years and later in life.

> The more of these behaviors you see, the fewer problems you're likely to have, not just with student behavior but with achievement as well.

Student Behaviors I'd Like to See

Regardless of how your students actually behave, how strongly would you want to see the behaviors in each statement—for their benefit and yours? Use the following scale to complete the survey:

5 = Yes, very much! (Where do I sign up?)

3 = Not crucial, but would be nice

1 = No big deal

I want my students to

____ respect school (and classroom) limits, standards, and rules.

____ be good decision makers, be able to evaluate options and predict outcomes.

____ take care of materials, put things back, and keep the work area neat.

____ make cooperative choices within the limits I define.

____ be committed to their own learning.

____ take risks with their learning, try new things.

____ exhibit responsibility, accountability, and independence.

____ interact cooperatively and respectfully with each other.

____ solve their own problems constructively.

____ come to class prepared.

____ listen and follow directions—the first time.

____ participate enthusiastically in activities and discussions.

___ take initiative for their work and learning.

___ stay on task and make good use of class time.

___ turn in work on time (with their names on their papers).

___ demonstrate self-control, manage disruptive impulses.

___ feel confident about their ability to learn.

___ manage frustration or setbacks, keep trying even when something is difficult or challenging for them.

___ control aggression, disruptiveness, and rebelliousness.

___ try to make progress, regardless of where they start academically.

___ be able to learn and work in ways that are natural and comfortable for them without creating problems for me or other students.

___ respond to feedback (positive and negative) in respectful and appropriate ways.

___ accommodate their social and emotional needs in respectful and appropriate ways.

___ come to class clean and sober (and, ideally, with their nutritional needs met in healthy ways).

___ enjoy school and learning in general.

Reflection

Your own educational experiences play an important role in some of your teaching choices. To explore this connection, complete the following statements as you remember them:

1. My school experience was

2. Most of my teachers were

3. The thing I remember liking best about school was

4. The thing I remember disliking most about school was

5. The one thing I would have changed about my school experiences was

6. The kind of authority relationships (or discipline) I was most responsive to in school was

7. The kind of authority relationships (or discipline) I felt was most damaging to me was

8. What created a sense of emotional safety for me in school was

9. My sense of security and emotional safety in school was threatened by

10. The one thing I would now like to say to my teachers is

11. The part of my school experience that I would most like to share and pass on to my own students is

12. The part of what I learned from my school experiences I would most like to change for my own students is

13. In looking over your responses to Questions 1 through 12, what can you say about the behaviors you want to practice with your own students?

14. What do you want to do for or with your students that your teachers did for or with you?

15. What patterns do you want to change in your classroom?

SOURCE: Adapted from an activity in Jane Bluestein and Lynn Collins, *Parents in a Pressure Cooker, Teacher Workbook* (Rosemont, NJ: Modern Learning Press, 1990).

These behaviors do not evolve in a vacuum, however, and the remainder of this book is devoted to helping you create the kind of classroom environment in which students do what you ask, come prepared, interact cooperatively, act responsibly, feel confident, *and* remember to put the caps back on the markers! However, getting consensus on the value of the student behaviors listed earlier is generally easier than actually bringing them about. In fact, even teachers with the deepest devotion to achieving these goals may fall into patterns that actually prevent these skills from developing. To complicate matters, these teachers probably work in a system that supports, encourages, or even rewards those very teaching behaviors! Add to that the baggage and survival strategies many kids develop well before they ever set foot in a classroom, the politically motivated demands on teachers that often bear no resemblance to the reality of what they encounter in class every day, and changes in the workplace that have rendered many sacred school practices and priorities anachronistic, and you can see a few of the obstacles we face.

The next section examines these challenges and why we are where we are. The rest of the book shows the way out.

PART II

The Challenges

4

Behavior and the Brain

Imagine you are a student in my class. You and I have a good working relationship. You enjoy my class and the subject I'm teaching. I'm doing one of the best lessons I've ever done—creative, interesting, challenging, and academically and developmentally appropriate. But . . . you just broke up with your boyfriend or girlfriend last period. (Or you just found out your parents are getting a divorce, or you walked into my class right after a classmate threatened to "get you" after school.) How much attention are you giving to my spectacular presentation or the materials I so painstakingly prepared? What are you thinking about? How much are you likely to learn in class today?

Similarly, our students have more on their minds than our subject areas or what they're going to do in class today. The more stress going on in a young person's life, the more difficult it will be for him or her to learn, remember, retrieve stored information, or even "think straight." Under threat, whether real or imagined, the brain releases certain hormones that are biologically ideal for mobilizing our fight, flight, or freeze responses. Now some may argue that these survival behaviors are far better suited to the wild than the classroom; however, the brain doesn't distinguish between environments in which a stress response will or will not be convenient for teacher or classmates.

Many of the problems we see in school—whether they involve blatant oppositions to reasonable requests, distracting outbursts, bad attitudes, indifference, refusal to work, social conflicts, the tendency to fade into the woodwork, or even compulsive overachieving—are simply reflections of patterns children develop, often before they ever come to school, to accommodate their basic needs for things like safety, belonging, and survival. But survival responses not only make it difficult for a student to learn, they can also make it hard for us to teach and can interfere with other kids' learning as well. So to get a sense of what we're working with, and why this can be so challenging, here are a few things to keep in mind.

STRESS AFFECTS LEARNING

Have you ever gone into a test completely prepared and yet froze, practically forgetting everything you knew, as soon as the test paper landed in front of you? Under stress, we tend to operate from a more primitive, survival-oriented part of our brain.[1] And since survival always overrides more complex cerebral processes, things like problem solving, analyzing, remembering, pattern detection, and other rational processes can become nearly impossible when we are frightened, worried, or otherwise distracted.

Stress hormones affect the memory centers of the brain, inhibiting the growth of new brain cells, leading to decreased memory and learning. Excess cortisol, a chemical released under trauma and stress, can cause brain cells to die off, and can result in memory lapses, anxiety, and difficulty regulating attention and emotional outbursts. Kids who are feeling anxious, angry, or frightened, for example, are less able to "hear" what we say to them, and are likely to misunderstand or distort what they actually receive, which can result in a cycle of behavior problems, failure, and punishment, compounding the initial stress. When we can reduce stress in the classroom, we can increase the amount of learning that takes place there and decrease the number of stress response behaviors that result in discipline issues as well.

CONTEXT IS IMPORTANT

I often ask people in my workshops how they would feel if I handed out worksheets with, say, a number of advanced math problems for them to do. Responses are, at times, extreme. Some practically start gathering their things and glance nervously at the door. This query usually comes early in the presentation; the participants have barely known me for half an hour, if that, so it's probably not personal. Their admitted discomfort must derive from their previous experiences with math. The mere anticipation creates a great deal of anxiety for some individuals, even when they know that I'm simply making a point. At the same time, there are invariably others who light up at the thought. Clearly, their brains are releasing different chemicals than the brains of those who struggled with challenging math problems at some point in their lives.

The brain interprets new information in the context of things it has already experienced. Kids who have had good experiences in school will walk into your classroom with

> The brain interprets new information in the context of things it has already experienced.

an entirely different set of expectations and beliefs than students who have had negative or painful experiences in school. Recalling my first day as a teacher, standing in front of my classroom door, nearly shivering with excitement at the prospect of meeting my first class after a lifetime of preparing for this very moment, there was no way I could have anticipated the defenses I encountered as my kids filed in the room. A few were cautiously curious, but most were suspicious, prickly, or simply resigned to one more year in fifth grade. Before I had a chance to say a word, one girl greeted my outstretched hand with a warning: "I don't do reading."

Gee . . . what page is *that* on? How do I deal with kids who have not only given up, but are also encouraging me, upon meeting them, to do the same?

This is an example of the importance of context. Changing students' expectations—and their beliefs about what school is like and how successful they are likely to be—challenges us to change the types of experiences they will have, to create a different context from the one in which their defensive behaviors were formulated.

IF THE BRAIN THINKS IT'S REAL, IT'S REAL

I had the pleasure of visiting a friend in Southern California on the night of the Northridge earthquake. When the shaking awakened me in the middle of the night, my first thoughts attributed the movement to some heavy traffic on the freeway nearby—clearly a product of the East Coast "context" in which I grew up. Seconds later, when I realized what was going on, my survival response took over and I suddenly found myself standing in the doorway of the bedroom, heart pounding, body shaking—a common physiological response to what was a very frightening and disorienting experience.

For months after Northridge, I was extremely sensitive, even jumpy, whenever a strong wind or a big truck rattled any building I was in. In the most unlikely of places, I actually awoke standing in the doorway of a Midwestern motel bathroom when a train went by in the middle of the night. I do not remember going from the bed to the doorway. I was just *there.* Clearly, the emotional part of my brain, which was simply trying to protect me, worked a whole lot faster than the part of my brain that recognized I was not in danger, that it was just a train.

Perception is reality! Our interpretation of an event triggers the reaction in our brain. If a student interprets your glance as hostile, he will respond to the perceived hostility, even if you weren't consciously looking in his direction or feeling anything negative. (Lots of kids, especially students we consider to be most at risk, have a hard time interpreting social cues accurately. I've seen more than one fight break out when a student insisted another kid was "looking at me.") If math classes were painful for you—and I use this example only because math is the class most frequently mentioned by still-phobic adults—you will react to whatever anxiety you experienced in the past. Perhaps at some point you will realize that I'm actually a *fun* quadratic equations teacher. But until then, I'm going to have to help you understand that your defenses and protective mechanisms will not be necessary—at least not in this class.

SENSITIVITIES VARY

Have you ever lost your patience with a kid, really let him have it, only to have him respond to your fury by asking if your shoes are new? While your anger had no apparent impact on this particular student, you notice another child, someone who has never been in trouble or done anything wrong in your class, cringing on the other side of the room, reacting to your angry energy.

Some young people can deal with stress better than others, and what causes stress for one child can be a completely neutral experience, or even an exciting one, for others. Many, as a part of their survival repertoire, are hypersensitive to how others around them are feeling and can pick up on subtle cues we may not even be aware we are sending out. (Notice how often a teacher's angry words or behaviors have the strongest effect on the students behaving the best.) Some will be bothered by comments that others wouldn't even notice, or disturbed by things that wouldn't bother you or me. Additionally, sensitivities can vary from day to day and can be exaggerated by circumstances of which we may not be aware, things that have nothing to do with us. (I once had a student burst into tears over an offhand comment I made to her. This was a very different reaction than I would have expected based on our previous interactions and something about which, many years later, I still feel awful.) If kids' bodies are already flooded with stress hormones, it may not take much to set them off.

Survival responses can vary from one child to the next. They might include physical reactions, such as sweating, dry mouth, shallow breathing, headache, pounding pulse, intestinal distress, weakness, a lack of focus or coordination, or "freezing" or "going blank." Anxiety or stress can also provoke behavioral reactions such as panic, irritability, depression, agitation, worry, inattention, forgetfulness, and distractibility, not to mention disruptive and sometimes hurtful outbursts.

Even though stress may initiate outside of school, the climate of a classroom matters a great deal, and the energy we put out, in our voice, tone, or body language, can have a tremendous impact on how kids experience our classes. While we can't always anticipate a student's reaction to the things going on in a classroom at any given time, it is well worth noting that, as survival responses go, one size does not fit all.

NOTE

1. All these points and the information that follows include material adapted from my book, *Creating Emotionally Safe Schools* (Deerfield Beach, FL: Health Communications, 2001), Chapter 4.

5

Tripping
Over the System

I recently addressed a group of teachers in a school district that requires the posting of rules and punishments in each class. Now we know that after about three days, the materials we hang on our classroom walls generally stop registering with the kids, unless these materials have some particular significance or value to them.[1] It's also doubtful that many kids cooperate and apply themselves—or refrain from acting out—because the rules requiring these behaviors are posted on the wall. So why do so many districtwide policies insist on doing this? Perhaps, as one high-ranking administrator admitted, it's political, an effort to reassure the community and protect the

> It's doubtful that many kids cooperate and apply themselves—or refrain from acting out—because the rules requiring these behaviors are posted on the wall.

district from potential legal complications. This is only one of a number of policies and traditions that have long outlived their usefulness, and, in this case, is particularly dangerous because it creates a false sense of external power and expectations in teachers who truly believe that kids will (or at least should) behave because "it's a rule."

There are a lot of places where the system is broken, dysfunctional, if you will, and not likely to get better until we examine and replace the pieces that no longer serve us. Any one of these traditions can make it even harder to create the kind of learning environments in which so many of the most common discipline problems need not occur. Of course, it will always be easier to make a list of rules than it will be to restructure power dynamics, to look for a different "hammer" than to change the way we relate to students. But unless we break out of the current, traditional mind-set, we end up spinning our wheels, creating very similar—and similarly ineffective—versions of the same old stuff.

Here are a few of the patterns we will invariably encounter in our quest for "a better way." Some are so familiar, so well entrenched, that it may even be hard to recognize them as potential problems. Any one can present an obstacle to making positive changes in the culture of a classroom.

REACTIVITY

When we examine the hidden dangers in commonly used negative consequences, I am often asked, "Well, what do I do if I *don't* put their names on the board (or keep them in from recess)?" These kinds of questions come from a reactive point of view and are actually a request for a different kind of "hammer" or punishment. Looking instead at ways to change relationship patterns and perhaps increase the number of positive incentives we make available requires a very different way of thinking and a very different set of teacher behaviors.[2]

Discipline policies adopted by schools and school districts are nearly uniformly reactive. Examine any discipline code and it's a fair bet you'll find a list of unacceptable behaviors along with a list of increasingly negative consequences for multiple infractions of each. Even the most forward-thinking districts still feel the need to include some version of the familiar rules-and-punishment model. However, this model relies on the students' fear of the negative outcomes and forces an emphasis that takes us farther away from a more proactive, preventive approach—the things we might do instead to build self-management and to motivate cooperative, engaged behavior in more positive ways.

NEGATIVITY

We don't have to look far for examples of negativity in schools. The vast majority of all written feedback focuses on errors, flaws, and omissions. Our discipline and behavior management policies typically focus on dealing with misbehavior rather than encouraging or motivating a more cooperative alternative.

It seems our very culture has a rather negative focus. Did you know that on average, elementary students experience three negative comments (or other forms of feedback), either from adults or other students, for every positive comment they receive? By middle school, that ratio is nine to one; the numbers in high school are even worse.[3] And that's no guarantee that some positive feedback is universally obtainable. I'm sure we can all think of some unfortunate child who probably goes through an entire day without receiving any recognition, positive acknowledgement, or expression of appreciation. The good news is that these ratios are easy to upset, and there are many ways to bring a great deal more positivity into a school or classroom setting.

> The good news is that these ratios are easy to upset, and there are many ways to bring a great deal more positivity into a school or classroom setting.

PRODUCT OVER PROCESS

We see this emphasis everywhere! Whether we're talking about instruction and curriculum, social interactions, or personal behavior, we tend to focus our attention on a particular outcome, rather than on the value of how kids might arrive at that particular outcome. This emphasis is responsible for a great deal of perfectionism, oversimplification, and black-and-white thinking: Either you get it or you don't.

Growth and learning are processes, but we in education rarely leave any program or strategy in place long enough for it to actually work. Unfortunately, we rarely have the patience or the luxury of the time it takes for "do-overs," to allow kids to explore, make mistakes, try again, and get it right. We deduct points for something a child didn't understand rather than reexplaining or sending the child back to the library to fill in the blanks. We outlaw certain desirable items in school instead of making them available if used in an appropriate time, place, and manner. We withhold full credit for a child who has made enormous strides in reading because he or she is still not quite up to grade level. This issue will present a significant challenge when it comes to facing the choice between looking for ways to improve school climate and in-school relationships and looking for a quick fix for specific problems.

> We in education rarely leave any program or strategy in place long enough for it to actually work.

ALL-OR-NOTHING THINKING

Ask any group of adults to identify children's most basic needs and you'll hear about food, shelter, and clothing, as well as things like love, success, limits, belonging, and acceptance. Interestingly, no one ever seems to remember the need that typically emerges in developmentally normal kids sometime around their second birthday: the need for power and control. Mention this need and people get nervous. Seen in an all-or-nothing paradigm, the reality of children needing power can be extremely unnerving: "Wait a minute! If they have power, we *don't*!"

Sometimes called black-and-white thinking or dualism, an all-or-nothing approach can apply to just about anything, but most often it comes up in talks about power dynamics with kids (and other adults as well). This type of thinking represents a most pervasive form of oversimplification and ultimately limits our focus to either spending a lot of time and energy attempting to control kids or simply throwing up our hands in permissive surrender. In fact, people who can't get beyond the familiar win-lose model of relationships with kids—"Either I win or you win"—will generally see *anything* that doesn't look like a big-hammer, authoritarian approach to dealing with kids as permissive. Being able to see the gray area between empowering and permissiveness gives us a very effective way to be in charge, without needing to control or disempower anyone.

DOUBLE STANDARD

I once had a parent disclose an experience she had on a recent visit to her son's school. While pleased to see a variety of lovely Character posters extolling the virtue of things like caring, responsibility, and respect, she was taken aback by the number of teachers who failed to exhibit those same qualities in their interactions with the students (or one another). We've all seen—and probably experienced—similar inconsistencies between what we ask of kids and what we are willing to do ourselves. (Years ago, one of the defining moments that proved most helpful in my eventually successful efforts to quit smoking came when several of my seventh graders proudly announced that they had switched to my brand!)

How consistently do we model the behaviors we ask of our students, whether that be coming to class on time, speaking in respectful tones, or keeping our desk and work area neat? If we insist that they refrain from bringing food or drink into the room, are we willing to model those same behaviors? Walking the talk, as they say, is a very powerful way to demonstrate and inspire the kinds of self-discipline we hope our students will develop.

IMPRESSION MANAGEMENT

Any struggling teacher who's ever been told, "Well, *I* never had a problem with them last year," learns very quickly how unsafe it can be to admit to or appear to be having a hard time with the kids. Look at how much energy districts, schools, and individual teachers put into "looking good." Whether cheating on standardized tests to maintain a certain level of status in the community, rejecting a bully-proof curriculum because it would imply that the school had a bullying problem, or simply feeling the need to respond, "I'm fine," any time someone asks how things are going, we attempt to manage the impression someone has of us. The upshot becomes a resistance to seeking help or attempting to rectify situations for fear of having our competence called into question, having an agenda imposed on us, or being penalized in some way. It takes a very safe and supportive school community for teachers to admit to having a problem connecting with a student, or even just having a bad day, and get the support, acceptance, and encouragement they need.

Any of these patterns can create obstacles to creating positive classroom climates and establishing the kinds of relationships possible in a win-win school environment. Yet our awareness of these challenges can help us navigate unfamiliar territory and establish new patterns and traditions in their place. Having examined the role of the brain and its reaction to stressful situations in relation to learning, and the role of the cultural values and traditions that provide a context in which student and teacher interactions occur, now let's look at one more piece of the puzzle: the historic and economic realities that shape education and the reason schools exist in the first place.

NOTES

1. Our brains adjust to the familiar. We stop noticing things that remain constant for long periods of time. Only different and distinctive information will generate an emotional response and gain our attention. Gordon H. Bower, "How Might Emotions Affect Learning?" in *The Handbook of Emotion and Memory: Research and Theory*, ed. Sven-Ake Christianson (Hillsdale, NJ: Lawrence Erlbaum, 1992), 10; Richard Howell Allen, *Impact Teaching* (Boston: Allyn & Bacon, 2002), 212.

2. All of these points and the information that follows include material adapted from Jane Bluestein, *Creating Emotionally Safe Schools: A Guide for Educators and Parents* (Deerfield Beach, FL: Health Communications, 2001), Chapter 11.

3. Although my numerous attempts to locate the original studies from which these numbers were determined has not proved successful, my faith in their credibility comes from the variety of sources from which I've heard them, the consistency with which they've been reported, anecdotal feedback from adults and kids, and personal experience and observations as well. (In fact, in some cases, I've wondered if these ratios weren't rather generous.) Regardless of the numbers, my point here is that the amount of feedback kids receive is overwhelmingly negative, and it gets worse the older they get and the longer they stay in school.

6

Catching Up to the Twenty-First Century

I f you've ever watched any of the television family sitcoms of the 1950s, you may have noticed how the family structures and priorities were remarkably similar from one show to another. To a great extent, the values of suburban, middle-class America at the peak of the postwar industrial era were products of the current factory economy. During this period, as so clearly reflected in the television programming of the time, uniformity was the goal; innovation and initiative were viewed as odd or eccentric, if not downright threatening.

These values were clear in the workplace and the classroom, where authority relationships were typically power oriented and hierarchical. Competitive goal structures limited the number who could succeed, and behavior was governed by fairly rigid expectations. In the industrial era, success, recognition, and advancement, whether in school or in the workplace, depended on compliance, conformity, and the ability to avoid making waves.

> In the industrial era, success, recognition, and advancement, whether in school or in the workplace, depended on compliance, conformity, and the ability to avoid making waves.

But a gradual shift in economic realities was taking place and by 1956, for the first time in our history, there were more information- and service-oriented jobs than manufacturing.[1] With the continuing technological developments of the past few decades, manufacturing gave way to an information economy. I saw this firsthand as a resident of western Pennsylvania in the 1970s. When I started college there in 1969, the steel mills were running three shifts a day. By the end of the following decade, nearly all the mills in Pittsburgh had shut down, replaced by restaurants, theaters, and shopping complexes. Thousands of mill workers were faced with the need to retrain for the newly emerging white-collar economy.

It isn't just the type of available jobs that has changed. This new economy demands a different set of work skills than those required by a factory economy, particularly in areas such as interaction, innovation, negotiation, and communication. With a need for different work skills comes a gradual shift in what is valued and expected in the workplace. While the worker of the industrial age may have looked for security and permanence, workers in the current economy show a marked preference for individuality, autonomy, personal fulfillment, a sense of purpose, and potential for growth.[2]

That's the good news.

The bad news is that although our systems of education have generally made strides in curriculum and technological resources, they are still, behaviorally and philosophically, set up to crank out factory workers. I hear evidence of this discrepancy when I interview business leaders, who almost uniformly tell me that the last thing in the world they need are kids who are conditioned to simply listen well and follow orders. "Those kids are a liability to me. I need employees who can think and take initiative," one CEO told me. "I'm not always going to be there to tell them what to do." Perhaps the best indication of this shift is reflected in a comment from one executive who reported, "I need kids with vision and attitude. That's what will make my business grow."[3]

Well, vision and attitude are all well and good until we realize what actually happens to kids when these attributes show up in school. The skills and personal traits that our economy needs are often the very things that will land kids in detention or special-needs classes. (A teacher of gifted students recently told me that a large number of kids end up in his classes not because they are significantly more cognitively skilled than the other students but because they are behaviorally more manageable.) Nonetheless, present-day businesses, which lean more toward networking, cooperation, negotiation, flexibility, creativity, and divergence than their industrial-era counterparts, complain of having to fill openings with students schooled in a system that values—and is structured in the context of—factory-era skills.[4] Business leaders report that these students often have difficulty making the transition to an information-age workplace. Even when individual teachers recognize these needs and make a commitment to build toward the future, we are so much a product of factory-era traditions that our teaching and interaction skills may lack congruence between well-intentioned goals and our ability to carry them out.

How many of us have vowed, at one time or another, never to act or sound like an authoritarian teacher we did not like when we were in school? And how many of us have

> The skills and personal traits that our economy needs are often the very things that will land kids in detention or special-needs classes.

The Push Beyond Factory-Era Skills

By the late 1980s, it was clear that at the turn of the millennium, "even the least-skilled jobs will require a command of reading, computing, and thinking that was once necessary only for the professions."[5] While the number of factories—and factory jobs—are on the decline, the jobs that still exist require skill levels that are far beyond those demanded of previous generations, with a continuing need for the workers to keep up with the new technologies. "In today's factories, no worker is more than a boss's coffee break away from needing at least some computing skills."[6] Even the amount of information has changed so drastically that the notion of a "body of knowledge" is a thing of the past. "The amount of available information in all fields is growing at more than a billion times the rate it was in 1950" and is expected to continue to expand at an enormous rate.[7]

actually kept that promise? Regardless of how much we may have resented those behaviors when we were students, they are the very behaviors modeled by the adults who were in our lives at the time. These are the patterns we know best and at least some of our teaching behavior will reflect what is most familiar. Even the most conscientious teacher, when tired or angry or stressed, will revert to default behaviors, which are generally among the most primitive and negative in our repertoire.

The value system of the industrial era seeped into all authority relationships. These values shaped the behavior of our parents and teachers, who used strategies necessary to help us fit into a factory society. Perhaps by necessity, the model was rigid and power oriented, competitive and geared to win-lose outcomes; like it or not, this was how most factories operated. (Ask anyone who ever spent time working on an assembly line—myself included—how much creativity and initiative we were invited to bring to our jobs, or how welcome any comments would be that questioned authority or challenged the status quo.) There existed a generally undisputed "should" or "for-your-own-good" mentality in these workplaces and in society in general, as well as a belief that control and punishment were essential and ultimately effective, particularly with regard to raising and educating children.

It's doubtful that parents, teachers, or employers of this era were deliberately cruel; more likely, they had simply bought into the values and structures of the times and probably believed themselves to be short on options. Whether they actually liked the model, most people accepted it and followed the precedents set by their own parents, teachers, and bosses, probably without giving it much thought. In this context, it's easy to see how information-age priorities, such as individuality, independence, intrinsic motivation, and self-control, would pose quite a threat to any autocratic, conformity-oriented value system or institution.

Regardless of the models we grew up with, the behaviors we observed are the ones we tend to adopt. As society changes, however, the needs of society also change, which is why so many of the old ways, which characterized the factory economy, cannot work in today's information age.[8] Additionally, when we rely on industrial-age techniques for educating children, we interfere with our students' ability to develop the skills they will need in an economy structured on a different set of needs and values—often the very skills we claim we're trying to inspire. Therein lies much confusion and frustration.

When everything is going along well, we have no need to fear the demons of our upbringing. It is the conflict situation that elicits the words and behaviors we had sworn to avoid. And conflict situations are inevitable when we attempt to motivate or teach information-age children with industrial-age strategies. Yet discrepancies often exist between what we want and what we know best. The world has gotten considerably larger for children than it was even a few years ago. No longer do kids depend on a handful of significant adults to let them know what's going on. Simply regretting the simplicity of the typically idealized "good old days" will not help kids rise to the demands of contemporary realities. What worked for our teachers not only may not work for us, but it may also actually work against us. We need a new game plan.

Creating a win-win classroom means examining attitudes, beliefs, and behavior patterns that are generally automatic and solidly entrenched in our educational structures, demanding that we bring a greater degree of deliberate awareness and mindfulness to our work than perhaps has ever been asked of us. It means rethinking goals and priorities, and, in some instances, letting go of long-cherished values that no longer serve us. It involves reframing the concept of

> Creating a win-win classroom . . . involves reframing the concept of discipline from a set of punitive behaviors . . . to a set of preventive behaviors . . . so we can avoid conflicts and disruptions in the first place.

discipline from a set of punitive behaviors that emphasize reactions to what kids are doing wrong, to a set of preventive behaviors that emphasize relationship building so we can avoid conflicts and disruptions in the first place. It entails making the shift from labeling student behavior as "inappropriate," "irresponsible," or "disrespectful" to those teaching behaviors that will help them learn more appropriate, responsible, and respectful alternatives. It calls for taking time to learn new techniques to teach responsible learning skills and to restructure relationships in ways that will allow us to accomplish what we say we truly want to experience and achieve in our schools.

Fortunately, the means to reaching these goals are specific, learnable skills, strategies you probably already know and use in successful adult relationships. Now, in our well-established information economy, we have a context for applying them in the classroom (see Table 6.1).

Table 6.1 Comparison of (Win-Lose) and Win-Win Classrooms

Traditional Classroom (Win-Lose)	Win-Win Classroom
• Optimal for training students to go to work in factories or industrial environments that require a great deal of uniformity.	• Optimal for training students to work in information-age environments that require initiative, creativity, problem solving, communication, networking, and people skills.
• Most important priorities or values: uniformity, sameness (reflected in today's standards); fitting in; stability, permanence, security (rigid roles).	• Most important priorities or values: growth potential, personal fulfillment; diversity, personal unfoldment; flexibility, choices, personal control (variable roles, expectations).
• "Fair": Same (requirements, assignments, placements, etc., regardless of child's needs, experience, interests, skills).	• "Fair": Equally Appropriately Challenged (based on needs and progress of individual child).
• Rigidity and uniformity in assignments, rewards; placement and evaluation tends to be comparative (based on the performance of others).	• Diversity and flexibility in assignments, rewards; placement and evaluation based on individual performance and ability.
• Characterized by competition; ranking; personal worth judged by achievement, appearance, wealth, performance, etc.	• Characterized by cooperation, respect for individual differences; personal worth is unconditional.
• "Winning": Requires that others lose (zero-sum environment); others' needs are disregarded or devalued.	• "Winning": Possibility of everyone's needs being satisfied (non-zero-sum environment); others' needs are considered.
• Cooperates to please authority (seeks approval); avoid punishment, humiliation, rejection, disapproval; pleases others regardless of personal needs.	• Cooperates to satisfy curiosity or obtain positive outcomes that are unrelated to reaction of others; self-care with consideration for others.
• Outcome or product orientation.	• Process or person orientation.
• Low or no tolerance for mistakes or errors; perfectionism.	• Mistakes seen as a necessary and valuable part of growth.
• All-or-nothing thinking, dualism; tunnel vision	• Many options and alternatives, ability to see various points of view.
• Decisions referenced to past or future.	• Decisions based on present-time orientation.
• Encouragement and recognition for following orders, obedience, people pleasing, asking permission, compliance, dependence; not making waves; maintaining status quo; self-sacrifice, self-abandonment; putting others first even at cost to self.	• Encouragement and recognition for taking initiative; making decisions within limits of rules or boundaries; taking risks, trying new things; innovating; teamwork and networking; self-care; maintaining personal boundaries; service and consideration with respect to personal needs.
• Values the ability to listen, protect existing hierarchy or power structure.	• Values the ability to communicate, network, and negotiate.
• Support for ability to stuff feelings, appear "fine;" impression management; blaming, making others responsible for how you feel.	• Support for expressing feelings honestly, responsibly, and nondisruptively.
• Encouragement for following others (or orders), acceptance of imposed values without question.	• Encouragement for operating according to a personal value system as long as no one's rights or boundaries are violated.

(Continued)

Table 6.1   (Continued)

Traditional Classroom (Win-Lose)	Win-Win Classroom
• Expectation for learning the way the teacher teaches; teaching the way you teach.	• Tolerance for learning in a way that is natural (without disturbing others); teaching the way they learn.
• Discipline goal: controlling students, disempowerment.	• Discipline goal: student self-control.
• Independent decision making discouraged (threat to teacher's authority).	• Independent decision making encouraged.
• Positive behavior praised, connecting positive choices or accomplishments to student's worth (or value to teacher).	• Positive behavior recognized with emphasis on deed, not student (student's worth is not an issue), and value of student's choice to student.
• Focus on negative; critical, judgmental.	• Focus on positive; avoidance of negative judgments.
• Emphasis: Punishments, negative consequences.	• Emphasis: Positive consequences and outcomes.
• Responses to negative behavior include frequent warnings, threats, lectures, asking for excuses, delayed or meaningless negative consequences; labeling misbehavior; labeling misbehavior; identification of misbehavior as character flaw.	• Responses to negative behavior include immediate withdrawal or removal of privilege until behavior changes; identifying and requesting more desirable behavior and providing tools to help students make more positive choices (character is not an issue).
• Few opportunities for self-correction (changing behavior or doing work over correctly).	• Self-correction encouraged; objective is improved behavior and achievement.
• Problems with students often referred to outside authority for punishment (principal, counselor, coach, parent).	• Teacher takes personal responsibility for problems with students; may contact outside authority as a resource, for ideas or support, or to provide information.
• Authority relationships tend to be reactive, power oriented, punitive, win-lose (powering or permissive), command oriented, demanding; few choices are offered.	• Authority relationships tend to be proactive, preventive; goal or consequence oriented (positive or negative); win-win (cooperative); choice oriented; many choices may be offered; negotiation may be possible.
• Rules and boundaries are power based: "Because I said so"; not explained to students; established to protect teacher power.	• Rules and boundaries are consequence based; explained to students; established to protect everyone's rights, consider everyone's needs.
• Belief that students are always trying to get away with something and will behave only in presence of authority they fear.	• Belief that students will make responsible choices if given the opportunity (and reason) to do so; trust in students' ability to function even in absence of authority.
• Approval of students is conditional, based on students' cooperative, teacher-pleasing behavior.	• Acceptance of students is unconditional, regardless of their behavior.
• Arrogance, self-righteousness; focus on teacher needs, wrongness of students.	• No need to make student wrong for teacher to be right; respect for students' dignity.
• Double standards for adults and children; certain language, tone of voice, behaviors, or attitudes modeled by teachers are not tolerated (and are punished) when students do the same things.	• Absence of double standards; teachers model behaviors they want children to exhibit.

Reflection

Refer to the information in this chapter to answer the following questions:

1. In what ways did your own experiences as a student reflect the values, skills, and relationships of the industrial age?

2. In what ways did your own experiences as a student reflect the values, skills, and relationships of the information age?

3. In what ways have your experiences affected your values and priorities as a teacher?

4. How do your teaching behaviors reflect your values and priorities?

5. What do you want out of teaching? Which needs does teaching fulfill for you? Which needs do you believe teaching *can* fulfill for you?

NOTES

1. John Naisbitt, *Megatrends: Ten New Directions for Transforming Our Lives* (New York: Warner Books, 1982), 12.

2. Alvin Toffler, *The Third Wave* (New York: William Morrow, 1980), 26; James D. Pulliam and James Van Patten, *History of Education in America,* 6th ed. (Englewood Cliffs, NJ: Prentice-Hall, 1995); Stanley I. Greenspan with Beryl Lieff Benderly, *The Growth of the Mind* (Reading, MA: Addison-Wesley, 1997), 218; Naisbitt, 12–14.

3. Reported in Jane Bluestein, *Creating Emotionally Safe Schools* (Deerfield Beach, FL: Health Communications, 2001), 84.

4. See sidebar, "The Push Beyond Factory-Era Skills."

5. Kenneth G. Wilson and Bennett Daviss, *Redesigning Education* (New York: Henry Holt, 1994), 11.

6. Nathan Thornburgh, "Dropout Nation," *Time* (April 17, 2006): 40.

7. Peter Kline, *Why America's Children Can't Think: Creating Independent Minds for the 21st Century* (Makawao, Maui, HI: Inner Ocean Publishing, 2002), xii.

8. This is also why it's often so difficult to switch to new behaviors, particularly within the generally negative context of a power-based, win-lose model. As Wilson and Daviss note: Our struggle to reform schools suffers from the fact that "we've been attempting to repair a building while its underlying foundation is shifting and crumbling." *Redesigning Education*, 15. Also see Alice Miller's *For Your Own Good: Hidden Cruelty in Child-Rearing and the Roots of Violence* (New York: Farrar, Straus & Giroux, 1990); Ann Wilson Schaef's *When Society Becomes an Addict* (San Francisco: Harper & Row, 1987); or Bluestein, "Snags in the Tapestry" and "Brave New World: The Changing Role of the School," in *Creating Emotionally Safe Schools.*

7

Keeping the Big Picture in Mind

When I first started teaching, I remember a great deal of conversation among the veteran teachers about the "good old days" when teachers were respected just for being teachers, when kids were easy to control, and when often the threat of a bad grade or a phone call to the home could usually keep the worst of the lot in line. Clearly, this is a relative concept, because decades later, I visit schools and I'm still hearing the same conversations. Now, maybe because my experience was with challenging kids right from the start, but sometimes I can't help resenting the fact that I seem to have missed these so-called good old days.

For better or worse, the world is changing, and this change is accelerating all the time. When I first started writing about teacher-student relationships, I noted that they weren't the same as they had been even a generation before. That statement has certainly stood the test of time and may be even more true now, twenty-some years later. The world continues to become more connected, competitive, and complex. With so many changes in technology alone, children have greater mobility and access to more information, resources, and temptations than ever before, while many of the social factors that once nurtured character are in decline. Their free time is used differently. Often, they have more responsibility and independence at earlier ages. Though more connected than ever before, many young people are also more isolated, which has led, for some, to a decreased ability to interact positively with others. Increasingly common issues such as cyber-bullying or vulnerability to cyber predators simply did not exist until relatively recently.[1]

> Many teachers contend with young people who have an enormous sense of entitlement and a stunning indifference to authority.

While our students' basic needs are the same as those of any other group of children in times past, the means for satisfying these needs have changed, and motivators, cautions, and deterrents that were effective in the past may not work with many students in today's classroom. Many teachers contend with young people who have an enormous sense of entitlement and a stunning indifference to authority. As authors Gordon Neufeld and Gabor Maté observe, "Children are not quite the same as we remember them being. They are less likely to take their cues from adults, less afraid of getting into trouble." They also describe a generation of kids who "seem inappropriately sophisticated, even jaded" and who "appear to be easily bored when away from each other or when not engaged with technology."[2]

Our jobs as educators (and as parents, for that matter) require more creativity and flexibility than ever before. Understandably, the autocratic strategies of factory-era management can appear attractive, especially to someone struggling with challenging kids. They are, after all, familiar and well supported by tradition. They seem effective and promise results. And they don't challenge us to think beyond what we already know, much less change our behavior. But the outcomes of these strategies are inconsistent with the priorities and demands of our information-oriented society, and the cost of using outdated strategies, in terms of skill development and classroom climate, can be quite high.

As teachers, there are so many things over which we have little or no control, any one of which can have an enormous impact on how our students will learn and behave in school. Overfocusing on specific student behaviors (and what to do about them) puts us in danger of losing our sense of context, much less our ability to maintain our commitment to process. As Margaret Wheatley suggests, "The challenge for us is to see beyond the innumerable fragments to the whole, stepping back far enough to appreciate how things move and change as a coherent entity."[3]

To a large degree, the choices we make as educators come down to intention. What, in the long run, are we trying to accomplish? If, for example, we are committed to getting through the curriculum, we will behave very differently than we will if our commitment is focused on meeting academic and cognitive needs to appropriately challenge each individual student. Similarly, if our goal is controlling students, we will choose vastly different behaviors and policies than we will if our goal is teaching students to control themselves.

So many factors can influence students' behavior in school, including a lack of effective alternatives to handling anger or frustration or the fact that the student's control needs are not being met in more positive ways. Students who refuse to do assignments may be prompted by previous school failures, a genuine sense of *I can't*, a desire to self-protect (minimizing the teacher's expectations or demands), or a need for attention, albeit negative. Weak social skills can have a tremendous impact on class climate and interactions and can also account for a number of problems that arise. Focusing in on one specific aspect of student behavior ignores the context in which these behaviors occur and often allows us to ignore places in our students' lives (much less our school policies and practices) where we could make a significant and positive difference.

As you read through this book, I would like to invite you to keep your eye on the big picture, and consider the strategies suggested in terms of your long-term goals, such as the behaviors in the wish list in Chapter 3. There are loads of suggestions, tips, techniques, and strategies in this book that can help you minimize negative and disruptive behaviors and create a more positive, engaging learning environment. Choose ideas that feel like a good match with the way you teach and the kids you have, keeping in mind that certain ideas will work better with some students (or in some classes) than with others.

Although the ideas themselves are simple, very few will represent a superficial solution or a quick fix for a specific problem. Like a good diet or fitness program, no worthwhile changes happen overnight. I've had students for whom nothing seemed to work until some desperate, often serendipitous, last-ditch idea popped into my head. Don't immediately abandon an idea that doesn't work the first time. We're talking about changing the culture, the power dynamics, and the overall energy of a classroom community. This can take time. Hang in there. Believe that persistence, faith, and flexibility can erode even the most practiced and hardened defenses.

> Don't immediately abandon an idea that doesn't work the first time.

Be willing to get out of your comfort zone and try things you may have never considered. Make the ideas in this book fit your style, your students, and your situation. Just because an example describes something I saw in a high school class doesn't mean it won't work with your fourth graders. If I share an idea I got from a first-grade teacher, try it in your middle-school classroom (or even at home with your own kids). The processes are the same.

I have a friend who continually reminds me that our job is not to teach the students we used to have, the students we wish we had, or the students we should have. Our job is to teach the students we do have. The good old days are happening right now. There is no going back. As crazy as things may seem at times, we have never known so much about how people learn or how relationships can work successfully, and there will always be things, even within the most repressive systems, that we can indeed control and change. Commit to the process, and the time that good, solid processes can take, and you will begin to create the kind of environment that will not only reduce stress, conflict, and opposition, but will also encourage initiative, responsibility, and the kinds of behaviors that will allow you to enjoy the work you came to this profession to do.

NOTES

1. Nancy Gibbs, "Being 13," *Time* (August 8, 2005): 42–44; Michele Borba, *Building Moral Intelligence: A Parent's Guide to Teaching the Seven Essential Virtues* (San Francisco: Jossey-Bass, 2001), 4; Claudia Wallis, "The Multitasking Generation," *Time* (March 27, 2006): 48–55; conversations with Jo Ann Freiberg, educator and bully-prevention specialist.

2. Gordon Neufeld and Gabor Maté, *Hold Onto Your Kids* (New York: Ballantine Books, 2005), 4.

3. Margaret J. Wheatley, *Leadership and the New Science: Learning About Organization From an Orderly Universe* (San Francisco: Berrett-Koehler Publishers, 1994), 41.

PART III

Restructuring Power Dynamics

8

Connecting With Kids

Up until the moment we face our first class, the bulk of our attention and training is focused on what and how we're going to teach. Chances are, we've learned the how-to's of explaining fractions, introducing new reading vocabulary, or demonstrating condensation. We've learned to sequence instruction, prepare presentation materials, and assemble a unit test.

With all this concentration on content, it's easy to become consumed with getting through the books. It's understandable when new teachers get nervous if students aren't in reading groups by the second week of school or if the other history teacher gets a few pages ahead. In departmentalized and secondary classes, limited contact with large numbers of students adds to the pressure. As academic demands mount, it can be easy to forget that we're teaching kids, not content.

The point of this book is to create a classroom culture in which the teaching and learning of content can occur with little or no interference from disruptive student behavior. At the heart of this approach is a teacher-student relationship that fosters student commitment and cooperation. All student behavior, including learning, occurs in this context. Any strategy we use to accomplish our instructional and behavior management goals will have an impact on the classroom climate and can enhance or impair the quality of our relationships with the kids we teach. But there's a circular effect at work here: While any strategy can change the climate (or energy) in a classroom, no strategy works in a vacuum, and the effectiveness of any change we attempt in our classrooms is affected by the relationships we establish with our students.

> . . . no strategy works in a vacuum, and the effectiveness of any change . . . is affected by the relationships we establish with our students.

I've seen teachers who reject one classroom-tested strategy after another, predicting chaos and commotion from even the simplest, most benign idea. Unfortunately, in an antagonistic environment, this may well be the case. If students are competing with us for power, if they have no stake in cooperating or little faith in their ability to be successful, pretty much any accommodation can be used as a weapon of mass disruption. Equating flexibility with permissiveness leaves us afraid to let our guard down for fear that giving that inch will indeed invite them to take the mile. However, rigidity and fear can create additional stress and make a positive, mutually respectful relationship even more difficult to achieve.

Our traditional emphasis on content and control can make it difficult to even see what relationships have to do with education. I've often heard teachers complain, "I've got so much to cover this year and my kids are already behind. Who has time for relationships?"

> Our traditional emphasis on content and control can make it difficult to even see what relationships have to do with education.

(This is especially common among secondary teachers, who may face 140 students or more every day.) And yet, the teacher-student relationship forms the basis for the context in which learning—and, indeed, catching up—can occur. In fact, this relationship may be the single most important ingredient in ensuring a student's academic success in school.[1] Psychologist Thomas Lickona affirms the link between the teacher-student relationship and its effect on behavior. He urges teachers to "use bonding to improve behavior," claiming that "when teachers bond with their students, they increase academic learning and their moral influence on students."[2]

We can have the latest technology, the most appropriate furnishings and supplies, and even be exceptionally skilled in presenting information, but it is our ability to connect with our kids that makes these ingredients work best. (Indeed, if our relationships with our students are encumbered by hostility, resentment, or antagonism, it's not likely that the best teaching skills or supplies will do us much good. If time is indeed an issue, consider how much time is wasted on disruptions and behaviors.)

The success of our instruction and the amount of behavioral interference we will or will not encounter depends, to a large degree, on the quality of the relationships and climate we develop. Working to create these elements of a positive classroom culture—even if temporarily at the expense of the curriculum—can help us avoid being sabotaged by negative attitudes, power struggles, weak learning behaviors, and unrealistic self-expectations as well. And finally, because teaching is an interactive experience, a positive teacher-student relationship increases the likelihood that the time students and teachers spend together will be more effective and enjoyable for all concerned.

Reflection

1. Describe the characteristics of an ideal teacher-student relationship.

2. How can these characteristics contribute to a positive classroom climate?

3. How can these characteristics contribute to the students' growth and learning?

4. How can they encourage responsible, cooperative student behavior (as opposed to fear-based compliance)?

5. How will establishing a positive classroom climate help you achieve the goals you identified as important in the survey in Chapter 3?

6. If you are currently teaching, what are you doing to build a positive classroom climate?

7. What else can you do to improve or enhance the climate as it currently exists?

8. If you are not yet teaching, what do you plan to do to build a positive classroom climate?

NOTES

1. According to Robert Reasoner, retired superintendent and president of the International Council for Self-Esteem, the factor most likely to positively affect a child's potential for success in school—regardless of age, gender, socioeconomic status, quality of home life, ability, or any other factors—is the child's perception that "my teacher likes me." Reasoner cites a study conducted in New Zealand titled "Project Resiliency." He believes the data to have been presented in a workshop in British Columbia by Debbie Kokay.

2. Thomas Lickona, *Character Matters* (New York: Touchstone, 2004), 116.

9

Who's Got the Power?

Back in my early educational psychology classes, when I was introduced to Abraham Maslow and his hierarchy of basic needs, I remember optimistically envisioning my classes filled with all sorts of self-actualizing kids. Unfortunately, I failed to appreciate the fact that this list requires the fulfillment of the more basic needs before we can attain fulfillment of higher level needs (like self-actualizing), and I underestimated the number of students whose needs for things like food, shelter, and clothing were barely being met.

I was also astonished at the creativity and persistence they exhibited in their attempts to satisfy their needs, especially their need for power, control, or autonomy. I honestly believed that if I were creative, clever, and dedicated enough, they'd be too busy to even notice that this need existed! Nonetheless, there were days when my kids seemed determined to fight me on even the most reasonable requests, refusing to do things I would have thought easy and fun. They quickly became immune to my yelling or disappointment and seemed to be so conditioned to the types of punishments available that I actually think they took comfort in their familiarity. (Even getting the teacher to give you detention or send you to the office can give you a sense of control.) The harder I tried to control them, the harder they fought back. So much of my time and energy was consumed by my efforts to manage student behavior, that there were days I felt as if I'd never actually get to teach!

Few things are as frustrating as power struggles between adults and kids.[1] These unpleasant encounters can occur any time our needs conflict with the needs of the young people with whom we are trying to work. How we handle these conflicts and respond to these needs can have a significant impact on our relationships and the emotional climate of our classrooms. Clearly, we need to establish some kind of structure and authority in which our students can function effectively—with us and one another. And it falls to us to create the kind of dynamics in which this functionality can emerge.

If we rely on the traditions of our upbringing, we generally have to choose between two win-lose options in which either we are in control (at the expense of the students' autonomy) or they are in control (at the expense of our effectiveness, sanity, or even our jobs). The truth is, we all need to feel a sense of control in our lives, although our classrooms are not always set up to accommodate this reality. At the same time, each of us needs a certain degree of structure in order to exercise control in a constructive manner.[2] Helping students develop responsibility and self-management skills requires that we offer students both. Win-lose options make this impossible: Powering (teacher wins, students lose) restricts the students' sense of control; permissiveness (teacher loses, students win) denies them adequate structure. We need a third option, a way to run down the middle, with a cooperative approach that establishes our authority while allowing kids a sense of autonomy within the confines of some structure or limits that we create.

Historically, we have had few models for a power dynamic that attempts to accommodate the needs of everyone involved, one that asks the critical question, "How can we both (or all) get what we want?" In what may be the most common sources of stress in any type of relationship, the need to win generally presumes that someone must lose. Creating a win-win classroom invites us to expand our thinking beyond these all-or-nothing options. A more cooperative approach to discipline and motivation asks that we establish our authority without relying on authoritarian, disempowering techniques. It also requires us to examine the congruence between our goals and priorities and the behavior patterns we use in our attempts to achieve these outcomes, because the techniques we know best can have some unexpected and negative side effects—and can even make it harder for us to get what we say we want!

TEACHER CONTROL OR SELF-CONTROL

Most teachers agree on the importance of students developing a variety of self-management characteristics and skills. And yet, how many teacher behaviors inadvertently bind kids to adult control instead, either as a dependence on the teacher's approval or as a need to avoid the teacher's anger, disapproval, or punishment? This is very different from student self-control. While many adults assume that simply teaching students to listen and obey will somehow eventually translate to these same kids being able to think for themselves and make constructive decisions in the absence of adult supervision, such is rarely the case. In fact, compliant student behaviors and cooperative student behaviors, while they may look similar, are generally mutually exclusive, much like the teacher behaviors that encourage these two very different outcomes.

I've known some teachers who had extraordinary control and exceptionally well-behaved students—as long as the teachers didn't turn their backs or leave the room. I'm sure these teachers were simply living up to the old saying that suggests that a good teacher is one whose students listen and do as they're told—the more compliant the children, the better the reflection on the teacher. While few would argue that part of the school's function is to socialize kids to work within a framework of certain conventions and consideration for others, simply training children to do as they're told is absolutely not the same thing as teaching children to develop the kind of self-management skills they'll need when no one is there to tell them what to do (or when someone tells them to do something that is not in their best interests). In fact, there can be great danger in

> Simply training children to do as they're told is absolutely not the same thing as teaching. . . .

teaching children to simply do what they're told, especially without questioning or evaluating what's being asked of them.

When we rely on conditional approval to generate or maintain positive student behavior, we teach kids that their worth and safety depend on their ability to please others. This tendency may be hard to avoid. Let's face it—we love it when students do what we want. And we certainly want our students to be caring and considerate of other people's feelings and needs. But we want to make sure that we don't train kids to self-abandon in the process, inadvertently teaching them to think of the needs of others to the exclusion of their own. A win-win middle ground allows kids to be considerate of other people without losing sight of what's good and necessary for themselves.

As long as we are the ones telling them what to do, there may be no problem—after all, we have our students' safety and well-being at heart. But this isn't always the case, and kids with good self-management skills are typically better at expressing and maintaining boundaries and better able to indeed "just say no" than kids who are more motivated by the approval of others. When students' emotional safety feels threatened, their ability to achieve higher levels of functioning (such as satisfying a desire to learn something new or working to fulfill their potential) will always be undermined by the need to adapt in order to feel safe. Throughout the years, I've seen kids of all ages make some pretty dumb decisions. True, their choices were sometimes motivated by curiosity or lack of foresight, but all too often their decisions were swayed by the anticipated reaction of someone they valued or feared. They could justify breaking rules, stealing, getting high, skipping school, being mean to someone, resisting authority, accepting a dare, or even becoming sexually active, with explanations like "I didn't want her to be mad at me," "I didn't want them to make fun of me," or "I didn't want him to leave me." Nowhere was there consideration for other, more serious, personal consequences. Always, someone's reaction—particularly the possibility of rejection, humiliation, or abandonment—took precedence; always children looked outside themselves before they made their choices.

If we truly want our students to be able to stand up for themselves, to make constructive choices, to effectively resist peer pressure, and to feel safe enough in our classrooms to take risks necessary for learning new things, then it's essential that we do not use motivation techniques that suggest "You are safe and lovable only when you are doing what I want (or when I don't catch you)." Yes, some kids know you really mean it when the veins stick out in your neck, and the thought of you being hurt or disappointed will keep others on track. But for how long? And at what cost? Besides, at some point, avoiding your anger or punishments (or your disapproval or disappointment) may become less important than maintaining power, dignity, and status with peers. Despite its apparent effectiveness with some students, using teacher responses as a primary motivator simply reinforces compliance and teacher dependence and will actually impede the development of self-management skills.

Perhaps the most benign consequences of power dynamics that rely on teacher control[3] are evident from common complaints from teachers who actually have compliant, teacher-directed students: "Sure they do what I tell them, but that's *all* they do!" These children may be great order takers but tend to falter in the absence of directions—and then take the instructions they do receive more literally than they were intended: A kindergarten teacher discovered three bewildered students wandering around the room with their hands full of scraps because she had told them to pick them up without elaborating about throwing them in the trash can afterward. When a number of fifth-grade students forgot to use capital letters on a punctuation review, the teacher, they claimed, was to blame: "You didn't remind us." Wouldn't we prefer kids a bit more skilled in independent thinking and initiative?

Children raised with "Do as you're told!" do not have many opportunities to make decisions, and they often have difficulty solving problems and anticipating the probable outcomes of the choices they make. They can have difficulty seeing the connection between what they do and what happens as a result of their behavior. They are likely to shift responsibility for their choices, blaming people or forces outside themselves for anything that goes on in their lives. (How often do you hear "It wasn't my fault," "He started it," or "She made me do it"? One high school teacher related a conversation in which a student expelled for arson claimed, "Hey, I just lit the match. I didn't know the building would burn down.")

> Children raised with "Do as you're told!" can have difficulty seeing the connection between what they do and what happens as a result of their behavior.

Discipline and classroom management that depend on teacher control tend to eat up a lot of our time and energy and also deprive kids of opportunities to develop a sense of responsibility, decision-making capabilities, self-confidence, and important self-management characteristics and skills. This approach can reinforce victim behavior, disempowerment, and limitations, and may provoke passivity, paralysis, passive-aggressiveness, or even rebelliousness under the strain of conflicting demands from different people. I have had students who came from extremely well-controlled classes freeze when asked to choose between two activities. How well would they fare in the absence of authority when faced, as many frequently were, with opportunities to use drugs or alcohol, for example? I was very nervous about how little practice (and confidence) my kids had when it came to making decisions constructively.

A more cooperative, or win-win, approach will build responsibility and independence instead of deterring it. We are in an excellent position to help students acquire tools for thinking and deciding; to encourage personal empowerment with regard to boundaries, limits, and the needs of others; and to inspire a positive self-concept, based not on the opinions of others but on self-knowledge and confidence. However, we're not likely to accomplish these goals using traditional authoritarian or permissive power dynamics. Fortunately, there is a better way (see Tables 9.1 and 9.2).

Table 9.1 Student Behaviors and Control

Student Behaviors with Teacher Control	Student Behaviors with Student Self-Control
• Motivated by the need to please authority and experience extrinsic approval or the desire to avoid adult anger or punishment.	• Motivated by factors such as the need to experience positive consequences unrelated to others' reactions (including personal power or autonomy).
• May lack confidence in ability to function in absence of authority, lacks initiative, waits for orders or instructions.	• More confident in ability to function in absence of authority, takes initiative.
• Creates safety by keeping others happy (regardless of cost to self).	• Creates safety by identifying and expressing needs, taking care of self.
• Self-concept is defined externally (worthwhile when getting approval).	• Self-concept is defined internally (worthwhile with or without approval, or even with disapproval).
• Self-abandoning, focuses on needs of others.	• Self-caring, focuses on personal needs, respects needs of others as well.
• Difficulty seeing connection between behavior and consequence.	• Better able to see the connection between behavior and consequence.
• Difficulty seeing options or choices available, difficulty making decisions.	• Better able to see options or choices available, able to make decisions.
• Helplessness and teacher dependence common, disempowered, sees self as having few choices.	• Personal empowerment and independence common, sees self as having choices and power of choice.
• Lacks confidence in personal instincts and ability to act in own self-interest.	• Confidence in personal instincts and ability to act in own self-interest.
• Difficulty predicting outcomes or consequences.	• Better able to predict outcomes or consequences.
• Difficulty recognizing or expressing personal needs.	• Better able to recognize and express personal needs.
• Limited ability to get needs met without hurting self or others.	• Better able to get own needs met without hurting self or others.
• Limited negotiation skills, orientation is "You win, I lose" (or "I win by giving you what you want"), gives power away.	• Better-developed negotiation skills, orientation is "You win, I win"; shares power.
• Compliant.	• Cooperative.
• Commitment to avoid conflict or punishment, "keeping teacher off my back."	• Commitment to task, experiencing personal outcome of cooperation.
• May experience conflict between internal and external needs (what student wants vs. what the other person wants); stress may manifest as guilt or rebelliousness.	• Better able to resolve conflict between internal and external needs (what student wants vs. what the other person wants); less inclined toward guilt or rebelliousness.
• May make risky choices to avoid disapproval, ridicule, or abandonment ("so my friends will like me more").	• May make risky choices to satisfy curiosity or from poor judgment or lack of experience.

SOURCE: Adapted from Jane Bluestein and Lynn Collins, *Parents in a Pressure Cooker* (Rosemont, NJ: Modern Learning Press, 1989).

Table 9.2   Student Behaviors and Control

Teacher Behaviors, Beliefs, and Attitudes That Encourage Compliance and Dependence	*Teacher Behaviors, Beliefs, and Attitudes That Encourage Self-control and Responsibility*
• Criteria for requests based on teacher power or pleasure: "Because I told you!" or "I'm so happy you got your work done."	• Criteria for requests based on consequences or outcomes: "Put the lid on the paste so it won't dry out."
• Teacher reaction (anger or approval, for example) a large component of motivation.	• Teacher reaction (anger or approval, for example) is not used to motivate.
• Orders, tells; few choices offered.	• Requests, asks; choices are task oriented.
• May offer choices between "good" and "bad" options, creating pressure on student to make the "right" choice (choose a particular option) to please teacher.	• All options offered are equal (no "good" and "bad" choices); no pressure for students to choose particular option to stay in teacher's good graces.
• Contingencies focus on negative outcomes, states contingencies negatively (threats).	• Contingencies focus on positive outcomes, states contingencies positively (promises).
• Makes decisions for students: "I know what's best for you," likely to mistrust students' ability to make decisions, may fear losing control if choices are offered.	• Avoids making decisions for students, will give students information and encourage decision making based on that information; guides, helps.
• Discourages independence and initiative, may restrict autonomy to feel needed or in control.	• Encourages independence and initiative (does not need to disempower or keep students dependent to feel powerful).
• Warnings and threats.	• Immediate follow-through.
• Inappropriate second chances, inflexible or arbitrarily flexible.	• Flexibility built into contingencies offered so no excuses or warnings are necessary.
• Believes that teacher's needs are more important than student's needs, may disregard or undervalue student's needs or preferences.	• Believes that teacher's needs are as important as student's needs, respects student's needs and often attempts to accommodate preferences.
• Judgmental, authoritative, critical.	• More positive orientation to student, accepting.
• Often inconsistent; likely to have a double standard for adult and student behaviors.	• Tries to be consistent, commitment to modeling behaviors requested of students.
• Outcome oriented.	• Process oriented.

Reflection

Look at the descriptions of the teacher-controlled student and the self-controlled student.

1. In what ways are the characteristics of the teacher-controlled student consistent with the behaviors you would like to encounter or encourage in your own students?

2. Are there any characteristics that concern you? For what reason?

3. In what ways are the characteristics of the self-controlled student consistent with the behaviors you would like to encounter or encourage in your own students?

4. Are there any characteristics that concern you? For what reason?

5. From a personal standpoint, to which characteristics do you best relate?

6. What have been the positive outcomes of these characteristics for you as a student (or child) and as a teacher (or adult)?

7. In what ways have these characteristics created obstacles in your interactions, particularly as an adult?

Now look at the lists of teacher behaviors that encourage teacher-controlled and student self-controlled behavior.

1. As a student, which characteristics did you encounter or observe most frequently in your teachers or other adults in your life?

2. What was the impact of these behaviors on your own attitudes, behavior, motivation, and self-concept as a student (or child) or as a teacher (or adult)?

3. Which characteristics best describe your own teaching behaviors and attitudes?

4. Choose any three characteristics you'd like to adopt or improve. What are they?

5. Why have you chosen those characteristics?

6. What do you plan to do to make improvements in these areas?

Table 9.3   Student Behavior Models

	Options Available With All-or-Nothing Thinking		*A Win-Win Alternative*
Behavior	Rebellious, oppositional.	Compliant, obedient.	Cooperative.
Descriptor	Self-centered.	Self-abandoning.	Self-caring.
Focus	My needs.	Your needs.	My needs and your needs.
Goal	Having my own way, no matter what; power; being left alone.	Avoiding conflict and abandonment.	Getting what I want with a minimum of conflict and inconvenience for others.
Responsibility	Someone else's fault, sees little connection between behavior and outcomes.	"Just following orders," disempowered, sees self as having few choices.	Responsible for own behavior, sees self as having choices and power.
Power play	Uses power to disempower others, win-lose.	Gives power away, lose-win.	Shares power, win-win.
Power tools	Anger, violence; passive-aggressiveness; secrecy, isolation.	Being "nice," being perfect, doing what everyone expects; achievement, recognition; tears, guilt; passive-aggressiveness.	Negotiating, compromise; ability to identify personal needs; awareness and respect for others' needs; self-expression; ability to make a deal one can't refuse.
Feelings	Difficulty expressing feelings in constructive, nonviolating ways.	Feelings are often "stuffed" or denied; vulnerable to tolerance breaks, can be explosive.	Not necessary to use feelings to manipulate, hurt, or control; can express feelings in nonhurtful ways.
Costs	Relationships	Sense of self, self-worth.	May create conflict with authoritarian or manipulative people; can threaten, upset, or alienate people with weak or no boundaries.
Stays safe by	Not needing you, not caring.	Keeping you happy (so you won't criticize, disapprove, or abandon).	Identifying and expressing needs, taking care of self (probably feels pretty safe to begin with)
Boundaries	Few, as far as others are concerned.	Few, as far as self is concerned.	Has personal boundaries, respects others' boundaries.

SOURCE: Adapted from Jane Bluestein, *Parents, Teens & Boundaries: How to Draw the Line* (Deerfield Beach, FL: Health Communications, 1993). Reprinted with the permission of Health Communications, Inc., www.hcibooks.com.

NOTES

1. This is also true in our relationships with other adults. Rest assured that the strategies for creating win-win interactions with students are equally effective in adult relationships.

2. Structure also provides a key component of emotional safety, another basic need.

3. By *teacher control*, I am referring to what might be called *other control* or *outside control* (neither of which sound quite right for my purposes) or any dynamic in which a student's behavior choices are determined in reference to another person. This could be another adult, a stranger, or even a peer. Self-control does not, for a moment, suggest any degree of indifference to other people's wishes or needs (see Table 9.3, the "Student Behavior Models" chart); however, it does allow a greater likelihood that a student will be able to resist inappropriate advances or suggestions, including peer pressure.

10

Win-Win Authority Relationships

I'm visiting an English class in a large, diverse high school. The students come in the room, many of them greeting or joking with the teacher, who stands at the door. The interactions are friendly and good-natured yet polite and respectful. Inside, there is a great deal of rustling and chatter despite the fact that the school bell has just rung, and I wonder how the teacher will ever get the class to settle down. As if in answer to my unasked question, he steps up to his desk and presses a button. A doorbell chimes a surprising long series of notes. However, those fifteen seconds or so appear to be just the right amount of time the students need to stop talking, get out their papers and books, and turn around in their seats. The activities that follow offer students opportunities to interact and make certain choices about their work. The atmosphere is pleasant, the students cooperative and engaged.

How different this class was from the ones I had visited at a different school in a different state, just the day before. In that environment, I found the majority of the teachers to be rigid and authoritarian. If adults spoke to the students, it was nearly always with an order or a criticism. I heard many teachers yelling at kids, in the hallways and classrooms. Few adults or young people were smiling. Students were apparently under control, but any time I saw a teacher leave the room or turn his or her back, the kids went wild. I had the sense that little progress was happening here, either in academic areas or student self-control.

We know that students who cannot satisfy their need for power in constructive ways will undoubtedly find other ways to have this need met. Young children may throw tantrums or simply counter requests or demands with the word *no!* As they get older, they may rebel, shut down, fight back, refuse to listen, swear, threaten, or act sarcastic, rude, or contemptuous. They may become aggressive or abusive or act bossy, controlling, mean, or hurtful, especially with younger or smaller children. They may physically hurt others or themselves, break things, or destroy property. They may drop out, get high, become sexually active, or make other dangerous or destructive choices simply to prove that they aren't controlled by some adult. As therapist and reviewer Jared Scherz notes, "Kids want something to rebel against and we inadvertently provide this" when we try to control them. And author James Marshall attributes much of the hostility that occurs in schools to the "autocratic, undemocratic nature" of schools, from the classroom to the top administration. When students are deprived of their power, rebellious behavior is likely: "The greater the frustration, the greater will be the aggression against the source of the frustration."[1] Strangely, even abdicating personal responsibility can be a way of creating a sense of control. By acting helpless, procrastinating, deliberately underperforming, quitting before they finish, or forgetting something they had agreed to do, kids can often get an adult's attention or minimize expectations or demands adults place on them. Students may also relinquish responsibility for their choices to limit the amount of responsibility they will have to take for their behaviors. (If someone else is calling all the shots and can be blamed for everything, a student has to assume very little responsibility.) There's an odd sense of power in the suffering and self-righteousness of individuals who believe that the things that don't work out for them aren't their fault; after all, they will claim, they didn't have a choice in the matter. In some cases, allowing others to control them allows some children the illusion of controlling the way the controller treats them: "If I do what they want, they won't make fun of me or stop being my friends."

These are the kinds of beliefs and behaviors that can get in the way of our teaching—and their learning. Clearly, the issue is not *whether* to empower students, but *how!* Fortunately, not only is it possible to allow kids in our classrooms to experience control in their lives without having them interfere with the safety and welfare of anyone else—including us—but it's also possible to accommodate their need for structure without preventing them from learning to think. In this way everyone wins.

> Clearly, the issue is not *whether* to empower students, but *how!*

A win-win[2] classroom is characterized by clear and specific limits with opportunities to make choices and experience power within those limits. Everyone is offered a stake in the success of the classroom and everyone has a chance to succeed. Each student is encouraged to be responsible for his or her own behavior, and outcomes are tied to the choices each individual makes.

In a win-win classroom, the teacher is on the same side as the students, and the students know it. Everyone's needs and feelings are valued, and although it may frequently be impossible for everyone to win, there is usually room for flexibility, negotiation, and compromise without undermining the teacher's authority. No one needs to win at the expense of anyone else. As a cooperative climate develops, opposition and defiance become increasingly pointless. Attention shifts from teacher control to student self-control and from discipline to instruction.

> As a cooperative climate develops, opposition and defiance become increasingly pointless.

The notion of win-win classroom management can be a bit disconcerting at first, especially to power-oriented teachers or those struggling to get beyond the all-or-nothing thinking that makes a third option hard to envision. And considering the tradition of an autocratic teaching role, the expectations of administrators, pressures from parents, needs of students, and demands of curriculum and content, how does this model fit?

As long as teachers are held accountable for what goes on in their classrooms, authority relationships will exist between teachers and students. Both win-win and win-lose approaches demand an element of power (authority) on the part of the teacher. Teachers need to have the authority to set goals, limits, and contingencies, and, when necessary, to have the final word on what works in the best interests of the group. But in the win-win classroom, the power of the teacher does not connote the authoritarianism that characterized the win-lose dynamics of previous eras, and it does not rely on our ability to *disempower* our students in order to be effective. Instead, it translates to strategies for empowering students within rules and limits that likewise accommodate the needs of the teacher: "We function within a certain set of boundaries, not because I'm bigger or more powerful, not because I'll like you more, but because we all benefit when these boundaries are respected."

Unfortunately, the win-lose models familiar to most of us simply cannot strike this balance. We cannot establish win-win authority relationships in an environment steeped in reactive, punitive, or "gotcha" policies. We need a new way of working with students to achieve that middle ground between powering and permissiveness. Yet even with a firm commitment to win-win, it is annoyingly easy to revert back to the other models without even thinking. As with any change, we need a new set of behaviors, the willingness to make a conscious effort, and the patience and faith to practice what we want to set in motion.

The approach we choose in our interactions with our students is the product of a number of factors, including our values and attitudes, previous experiences with authority figures, the behaviors of other teachers in the school, and the way we think we should respond. In examining our responses to situations in which our needs are in conflict with others', we may find that we are not actually using the approach we prefer or intended or even the one we think we are using! For this reason, each approach is worth a second look. Table 10.1 clarifies each of the three. Each approach has pluses and minuses, as well as fairly predictable outcomes. Each varies also in its ability to reinforce cooperation over compliance, build responsible learning behaviors, and increase commitment and time on task.

Table 10.1   Authority Relationships: Models of Classroom Power Dynamics

Interaction dynamic	*Powering Approach (Win-Lose)*	*Permissive Approach (Lose-Win)*	*Cooperative Approach (Win-Win)*
	Teacher Needs → Overshadow → Student Needs	Teacher Needs ← Overshadow ← Student Needs	Teacher Needs ⇄ Consider ⇄ Student Needs
Description	Power based; authoritarian, inflexible. Probably the most familiar model of interaction between adults and children (although the teacher may hold a powering attitude and not realize it).	Frequently (and incorrectly) seen as the only alternative to powering; may be employed by teachers who do not perceive themselves as having power, who find the powering model distasteful, or who are afraid of alienating students by expressing limits and needs.	Teacher takes responsibility for own needs while considering needs of students.
	Payoff to student for cooperating includes avoidance of punishment, criticism, and negative involvement with teacher.	Basic belief: If they care enough, they'll do it (for me).	Characterized by direct, honest communication; teacher requests specific behavior or input.
	Little or no distinction between student behavior and student worth, equates student's uncooperative choosing with character flaws (bad choice, bad person).	Does not respect or accommodate student's needs for limits and structure.	Teacher considers students' input in final decision (or gives students specific guidelines or limits for making the decision themselves), respects and attempts to accommodate students' needs for power within limits.
	Does not respect or accommodate student's needs for power and autonomy.	Indirect communications, specific needs of teacher unclear or rarely expressed, lack of clarity or inconsistency may require mind reading from student.	Cooperative goal structure, possible for all students to succeed.
	Basic belief: Students won't do anything right without the threat of a negative, uncomfortable, or painful outcome.	Dishonest and unpredictable; teacher frequently minimizes personal needs, then later expresses criticism or disappointment for student's lack of cooperation.	Teacher focuses on positive, building on what students can do; recognizes positive behavior by connecting cooperative choice to benefit to student (positive outcome not related to teacher).
	Competitive goal structure (nearly always, some students fail).	Teacher rarely willing to take responsibility for own needs; may offer freedoms with little structure and few limits, expecting student to self-monitor in appreciation.	Payoff for student cooperation: may include access to specific activities, materials, structured free time, or greater range of choices, freedoms, and responsibilities; payoff is not related to reaction of teacher.
	General focus is negative (on what student has done wrong or cannot do), may offer conditional approval as long as students are doing what teacher wants, pushes for perfection.	Teacher may offer choices to test student's loyalty or ability to guess correct choice.	Teacher leaves consequences of choosing (positive and negative) with students, students retain responsibility for personal choices and behavior.

58

	Powering Approach (Win-Lose)	Permissive Approach (Lose-Win)	Cooperative Approach (Win-Win)
	Outcome oriented, usually at expense of process, geared to getting immediate results. Teacher makes decisions, student rarely has opportunity to offer input or make decisions (besides do it or else).	Teacher may make decisions and not stand by them; inconsistent in limits, boundaries, tolerances, rewards, consequences, and follow-through. Little or no distinction between student behavior and student worth (or self-worth), apt to take student behavior (positive or negative) personally, disappointment and hopelessness common. Offers conditional approval (as long as student is doing what teacher wants); praise, when offered, is given for pleasing teacher.	Non-life-threatening consequences to undesirable choices allowed as learning experience, teacher resists temptation to rescue but remains available to provide information and help students rethink goals and strategies and try again. Greater consistency in teacher behavior and beliefs than in other two models. Process oriented, allows students to learn from consequences of their choices. Teacher differentiates between student's worth and behavior and is better able to accept student as a person, even if his or her behavior is unacceptable. Basic belief: Even if I can't always accommodate them, the students' needs are as valuable and important as my own. Limits exist in the context of the group (not the teacher's power).
Strategies	Threatening emotional safety: humiliating, expressing contempt, condemning or attacking student's behavior, attitude, and values; depriving dignity, violating self-worth; criticizing, shaming; verbal or emotional violence, yelling, intimidating, threatening, sarcasm; controlling, manipulating, punishing; conditional approval or love; threat of emotional abandonment.	Allowing students to behave in ways that can create problems for the teacher or others. Letting students have their way to avoid outbursts, tantrums, resentment, contempt, or other conflicts. Letting kids do something they want to obligate them to cooperate, attempting to motivate cooperation through guilt or pleasantness.	Identifying, communicating, and maintaining boundaries, having consistent and predictable follow-through, allowing rewards and privileges only when student has done what teacher requests. Offering meaningful positive outcomes: activities, choices, grades, academic progress, recognition, or other privileges important or valuable to the student.

(Continued)

Table 10.1 (Continued)

	Powering Approach (Win-Lose)	Permissive Approach (Lose-Win)	Cooperative Approach (Win-Win)
	Threat to physical safety, physical violence. Punitive or reactive deprivation of meaningful privilege or activity (for example, recess, eligibility, graduation). Withholding credit or grades, allowing student behavior to influence grading, placement, or promotion.[a]	Manipulating cooperation with conditional approval, disappointment, withdrawal, disengaging; with victim behavior, self-pity, martyrdom, or by appealing to students' sense of guilt; or with potential for resentment behaviors such as blaming, condemning, sarcasm, indirect (or implied) attack on student behavior, attitudes, and values; blowing up. Resistance to holding kids accountable, enabling, rescuing, giving warnings, asking for excuses, solving problems for the student. Giving up, perception of having less influence or control than is true.	Identifying, communicating, and maintaining boundaries, having consistent and predictable follow-through, allowing rewards and privileges only when student has done what teacher requests. Offering meaningful positive outcomes: activities, choices, grades, academic progress, recognition, or other privileges important or valuable to the student. Respecting rights, needs, and dignity of others. Willingness to listen, support, guide, inform, and accept. Using promises instead of threats. Making success possible for all. Encouraging self-correction.
Communicates to students	I'm the boss here! What I say goes! I know what's best for you. My needs are more important than yours. I do not respect what is important to you. I can get what I want because I am bigger (or more powerful or more important) than you.	Your needs are more important than mine. My needs are important, but so what? My needs to avoid conflict or your negative reaction are more important than my teaching objectives. External approval is more important than self-care. I'm not very good at this.	Both our needs are important. How can we both get what we want? Win-win is possible. You are valuable (and safe), even if you mess up. It's possible to get what you want without hurting anyone (or misbehaving or using unpleasant or annoying behaviors).
Sounds like:	"Because I said so." "Get in your seat this minute." "You keep your locker like a pigsty." "I told you to get to work."	"I'm so sick of picking up after you kids." "Oh, forget it." (Or "It just doesn't matter," or "It's easier to do it myself.")	"I will continue reading you this story as soon as it gets quiet." "Please work independently so that I can finish with this group."

	Powering Approach (Win-Lose)	Permissive Approach (Lose-Win)	Cooperative Approach (Win-Win)
	"If you don't do what I want, I will punish (hurt, deprive) you."	"I like the way Susie is sitting quietly." "What's your excuse?" "Well, okay. Just this once. . . ."	"I see you forgot your book. How are you going to do your work this period?" "You got your work done early. Now you have the rest of the period free (for a specific activity or privilege)." "You can choose any ten problems on this page." "You can have the jump rope back as soon as you both decide how you intend to share it."
Boundary issues	Does not respect students' boundaries or their need for power or autonomy; violates students' boundaries.	General lack of boundaries, unclear boundaries based on differences between teacher's understanding and students' understanding (Be good. Write neatly.), ambiguous boundaries, or boundaries with built-in loopholes (using warnings, asking for excuses); teacher tolerates violation of his or her boundaries by students.	None. Boundaries are clearly communicated and upheld. Teacher boundaries are maintained (follow-through) and student boundaries are respected.
Overall effectiveness	Can be effective in getting short-term cooperation from compliant students. Cost to emotional environment and quality of relationship between teacher and student is high.	Minimal; usually kids know that they don't have to listen until the teacher starts screaming, for example. Lack of limits and predictability make cost to the emotional environment and quality of teacher-student relationship high.	Best possibility for success of all configurations of authority relationships, especially if your goals include encouraging responsibility, independence, accountability, mutual consideration and respect, and self-management. Actually builds and supports the development of positive classroom relationships and protects emotional safety of all concerned.

(Continued)

61

Table 10.1 (Continued)

	Powering Approach (Win-Lose)	Permissive Approach (Lose-Win)	Cooperative Approach (Win-Win)
Outcomes (advantages)	The model is familiar and well supported by tradition.	May get you what you want (satisfy your needs).	Preventive, proactive; uses clearly communicated contingencies, boundaries, limits, or guidelines before students have a chance to misbehave.
	May get you what you want (satisfy your needs).	Supports desire to feel self-righteous; validates attachment to victimization, disempowerment, and chaos.	Reduces conflict and stress, minimizes power struggles, need, or occasion for teacher reactivity.
	Most effective with students who respond to authority, fear of punishment or deprivation, or need for teacher approval.	Most effective with students who respond to guilt, fear of abandonment, or need for teacher approval.	Discourages resentment and rebelliousness, students recognize that their needs are heard and considered.
			Reinforces responsible, cooperative behavior without depending on teacher's reaction, fear of teacher's power, or need for approval; allows teacher to maintain authority without disempowering students.
			Can accommodate students' need for control and structure without interfering with the needs of the teacher or other students.
			Does not compromise or threaten emotional safety.
			Discourages teacher dependence, helplessness, and need for external validation.
			Helps students make connection between what they do and what happens to them as a result of what they do at an internal level.
			Consequences of students' choices related to intrinsic benefit to student (positive outcome not externally based or referenced in someone else's behavior or reaction).

	Powering Approach (Win-Lose)	Permissive Approach (Lose-Win)	Cooperative Approach (Win-Win)
			Builds personal empowerment, enhances student self-concept, and reinforces responsibility for personal choices and behavior.
			Generates commitment; students have a stake in choosing cooperatively and in the success of the classroom.
			Encourages students to focus on personal needs within set limits, considering the needs of the teacher and other students.
			Results tend to be long term and self-sustaining; does not require constant monitoring from teacher, although reinforcement helps.
			Teaches decision making and responsible, self-managing behavior.
			Models compromise, negotiating, cooperation, and mutual respect.
			Teaches students that it is possible and desirable to get what you want in life without hurting or depriving anyone else.
Outcomes (disadvantages)	Reinforces obedience, teacher dependence, and need for external validation (dependent on doing what teacher wants). May generate superficial compliance, not commitment; passive learning. Encourages students to focus on keeping teacher happy or keeping teacher off their backs.	Least effective means of motivating cooperation from students, although it may get results from students who require teacher approval, respond to guilt, or need to please teacher. Reinforces compliance, teacher dependence, and need for external validation.	Because this method is process oriented, it may take longer. Building student self-management may require teaching students specific learning (noncontent) skills and allowing them to practice. Less familiar than the other two models; often requires learning new interaction, self-care, and

(Continued)

Table 10.1 (Continued)

Powering Approach (Win-Lose)	Permissive Approach (Lose-Win)	Cooperative Approach (Win-Win)
Seemingly positive results tend to be temporary and not self-sustaining (requires monitoring, policing to continue).	Generates compliance (if anything), not commitment.	self-expression skills; may require restructuring perception of authority relationships.
May generate resentment or rebellion, does not accommodate students' need for personal control.	Often chaotic; lack of structure and consistency can be overwhelming, even for self-managing students; may cause resentment and insecurity.	May be perceived as permissive by people who favor powering model (or do not know anything else); may not receive support or acceptance from administration or other teachers—until they see the results.
Does not teach decision making or responsible, self-managing behavior.	Consequences of students' choices related to teacher reaction rather than to intrinsic benefit to student (other than protecting personal safety).	
Discourages personal empowerment (actually disempowers, inhibits initiative).	Does not teach decision making or responsibility, can interfere with development of student self-managing behavior, disempowers through lack of structure.	
Consequences of students' choices related to teacher reaction rather than to intrinsic benefit to student (other than protecting personal safety).	Encourages kids to push the limits.	
Teaches students to use power (bullying, hurting, depriving, threatening, disempowering) to get what they want in life; does not model compromise, negotiation, cooperation, or mutual respect.	Teaches students to use victim behavior (helplessness, manipulation) to get what they want in life (win by losing); does not model compromise, negotiation, cooperation, or mutual respect.	
Depends on students' fear of teacher's power, anger, or reaction, which may be limited or undermined by indifference, overconfidence, or competition for power (the need to win or save face); can inspire rebelliousness, power struggles.	Apt to take student behavior (positive or negative) personally; disappointment and hopelessness common.	
Control-oriented relationships with students can be exhausting, stressful, and unfulfilling; frustration and burnout possible.	Failure of this approach frequently reverts to powering approach when teacher reaches personal limit; frustration, unpredictable blowups likely; may also lead to quick burnout and desire to leave profession.	

SOURCE: Adapted from Jane Bluestein and Lynn Collins, *Parents in a Pressure Cooker* (Rosemont, NJ: Modern Learning Press, 1989).

a. The National Education Association Code of Ethics (http://www.nea.org/aboutnea/code.html) prohibits these strategies. Nonetheless, many are so common that we may believe in their necessity and may not question their use. (Referenced by Jo Ann Freiberg, contributor.)

Activity

Relate the activities that follow to actual personal experiences. If your teaching experience is limited, you can complete this exercise by substituting the word *child, sibling, coworker, employer, parent, roommate, spouse,* or *partner,* for example, in place of the word *student.* You will find the dynamics to be remarkably similar. If possible, try to keep the same reference group for all three activities.

1. Think of a time you used a powering approach in an interaction with a student (or group of students).

   a. Describe the situation:

   b. Your needs:

   c. Your students' needs:

   d. Your reaction (behavior, language):

   e. Short-term (immediate) outcome:

   f. Long-term outcome:

   g. What you learned:

   h. Alternate reaction (behavior, language):

   i. How could this alternative accommodate both sets of needs more effectively?

2. Think of a time you used a permissive approach in an interaction with a student (or group of students).

   a. Describe the situation:

   b. Your needs:

   c. Your students' needs:

   d. Your reaction (behavior, language):

   e. Short-term (immediate) outcome:

   f. Long-term outcome:

   g. What you learned:

   h. Alternate reaction (behavior, language):

   i. How could this alternative accommodate both sets of needs more effectively?

3. Think of a time you used a cooperative approach in an interaction with a student (or group of students).

   a. Describe the situation:

   b. Your needs:

   c. Your students' needs:

   d. Your reaction (behavior, language):

   e. Short-term (immediate) outcome:

   f. Long-term outcome:

   g. What you learned:

   h. How did this alternative accommodate both sets of needs?

NOTES

1. James Marshall, *The Devil in the Classroom: Hostility in American Education* (New York: Schocken Books, 1985), 11.

2. The concept of win-win power dynamics dates back to the 1920s, when educator Mary Parker Follett presented this alternative as a way for business managers to deal with conflicts in a way that attempts to accommodate the underlying needs of everyone involved. From Linda Lantieri and Janet Patti, *Waging Peace in Our Schools* (Boston: Beacon Press, 1996), 19.

PART IV

Establishing Authority in a Win-Win Classroom

11

Mastering Motivation

One year, a new student named Billy came to my fourth-grade class during the second week of school. He was shy and polite and could entertain himself for hours without bothering a soul. Billy also refused to do any work; he neither participated in discussions nor touched any paper-and-pencil activities. He was a very pleasant kid to have around, but I was not willing to accept his presence as merely ornamental.

Reminders, threats, and negative consequences were unproductive, and the call home did not generate the sort of support that might have shaken Billy loose from his resistance to schoolwork. Talking to Billy revealed that he was aware that he could not be promoted from a class in which he didn't do anything, as well as the fact that he was quite content to while away the year counting the holes in the ceiling tile.

I told him that I would continue to give him the day's assignments and be available for help. I would not, however, continue to nag or threaten—these efforts had not only been frustrating and ineffective, but they were also taking away time I could spend with other students. I was not happy with the choice Billy had made, nor was I happy with my inability to turn him around, but clearly his success in fourth grade was far more important to me than it seemed to be to him. For the moment, I could only offer him opportunities to change his mind.

About two days later, the office called my room, asking me to send certain forms down by lunchtime. I had just finished collecting the materials they wanted and looked around for a messenger. Everyone seemed to be busy with something—everyone, of course, except Billy, who was at that moment having a staring contest with a box of chalk. He was certainly available. Still, privilege had its price: I invited Billy to take the

> I had stumbled upon magic: Billy would do anything to get out of my room!

papers to the office if he'd like, as soon as his work was finished. Soon afterward, to my amazement and delight, Billy came to me with work in hand. Everything looked fine. It was the first time I had ever seen his writing. Without even thinking about it, I had stumbled upon magic: Billy would do anything to get out of my room!

MOTIVATION IS CHOICE

It's easy to motivate people to do things that are fun, exciting, and pleasurable to them, especially when it's something they can do successfully. These choices are inherently need fulfilling or satisfying in some way. But what about those tasks that are perceived as uninteresting, irrelevant, unenjoyable, or impossible?

Let's make this personal: Think of a chore you really detest doing but do anyhow, at least some of the time. What's in it for you to do something you really dislike? Doing the chore must have some significant payoff or you would completely blow it off. In other words, you wash the dishes, run the vacuum, or even clean the bathroom because you know that at some point, neglecting these will ultimately have consequences that are more unpleasant than doing the task. Now if you happen to love cleaning bathrooms, you won't need any more motivation than the simple privilege of doing the task. But for the rest of us, the bathroom gets cleaned because we're afraid of the stuff that grows on the shower tile, because our housemates nag us if we don't pitch in, or because company is coming. And if the tile still looks clean enough, if we live alone, or if company cancels the day before, we may not be quite as motivated as we would under different circumstances. The task becomes easier to avoid, and chances are, we're likely to put off this chore until one of those options or another becomes more pressing.

> If you happen to love cleaning bathrooms, you won't need any more motivation than the simple privilege of doing the task.

There is no such thing as unmotivated behavior. There has to be something in it for us—whether the outcome is personal satisfaction; the desire to please; a commitment to certain values or priorities; the pursuit of a larger goal; satisfaction of curiosity, fun, or pleasure; avoidance of punishment or deprivation; access to a more desirable outcome; or some other type of fulfillment—otherwise we simply choose not to do it.

In any situation, we always have choices. Even if the choices are made unconsciously or automatically, we select the options that we believe will offer the most beneficial—or the least painful—result. (Undesirable or unacceptable options are still options!) The belief or perception that "I didn't have a choice" may make it easier to avoid questioning our habits, evaluating our options, or tempting conflict or criticism by doing something other than what is expected or demanded, but we still have options. Whether we eat the brownies or pass them up will depend on whether it's more important to us, at that moment, to stick to our diet, indulge our sweet tooth, please the person who made them, satisfy our hunger, or avoid feeling overstuffed. Even the specter of guilt, remorse, or yet another beach-free summer will, for some of us, all but disappear in the presence of warm, chocolate temptation.

What appears to be the "best choice" for one person or one situation may not be the best choice for others. Clearly, many of the choices students make will hardly appear need fulfilling or beneficial from a teacher's perspective. For example, it's hard to imagine that most students aren't aware of the risks and dangers of smoking, using drugs, or engaging in unprotected sex, or at least that these activities can hurt them. However, if, at the moment they have to decide, the students' priority is to escape, to experience pleasure, or to avoid rejection, ridicule, or abandonment, they will make whichever choice will work best to accommodate that particular need.

When people cooperate with us, they do what we want because doing so serves their purposes in some way. Perhaps they are trying to make us happy, gain our approval, get us off their backs, or obligate us for some later time. Or perhaps the motivation has nothing to do with us. They may cooperate because they like doing what we're asking them to do, because they wish to make themselves feel worthwhile, or simply because cooperating feels good to them. Even if they do what we ask to validate their suffering or confirm a perception of powerlessness, there is always some payoff, some need fulfilling positive consequence, behind their cooperation. Being skilled at motivating others means paying close attention to that very issue: What can they gain by cooperating? What's in it for them to do what we want?

The principles and dynamics of motivation are the same in the classroom and out. Motivating students means first looking for positive consequences that are more attractive than avoiding or resisting what we're asking them to do. Second, it means using this information to create a contingency or boundary that offers them access to what they want when they do what we want. Anything that is meaningful to our students can be used as a motivator, which gives us a lot of positive options, even if we only have them for 45 minutes at a time (and even if much of what is meaningful to our kids would be inappropriate or illegal in a classroom).

MOTIVATING KIDS IN A WIN-WIN CLASSROOM

The choices we make about which types of motivators to use reflect and also establish our orientation to power dynamics—win-win or win-lose. Our motivational strategies strongly influence the quality and type of relationships we create with our students and the degree of emotional safety that exists in our classrooms as well. These factors are critical to the processes our students use in making choices about their own behavior.

If we want to build student self-management and reduce stress in the classroom (both of which will enhance the likelihood of learning and cooperation occurring), we want to be sure that "what's in it for them" to cooperate does not involve the threat of our anger, conditional approval, or punishment. This is where we can see the real benefits of creating a win-win learning environment where motivators will be far more positive, probably coming in the form of some privilege or pleasurable activity instead. This means that we don't need to rely on our reactions to get what we want.

Teachers who use contingencies that connect the things they want with something that is meaningful to their students—something other than the teachers' feelings or power—tend to avoid the kind of stress and conditionality that compromises emotional safety. They can keep the focus on positive outcomes, not negative reactions. Their students get quiet so that the teacher will read the story, not because the teacher will get angry if they don't. They finish assignments and turn in work to get credit or a chance to go on to a new unit, not to avoid a lecture, detention, or being held back. They return their library books so they can take new ones home, not because the teacher feels hurt, angry, or disappointed when they forget.

Such contingencies have been around for a long time. Grandma had this one down when she said we could have our dessert after we finished our vegetables. However things turned out, it was always our choice. If we really hated the vegetable, it didn't matter what the dessert was. And if we really loved dessert, we might have eaten anything to get it. Regardless of the choice we made, the only thing at stake was dessert—not Grandma's love, approval, or temper.[1]

Is this a bribe? Absolutely! It may seem strange that many teachers strongly opposed to the idea of positive bribes are much less uncomfortable with the idea of negative bribes (threats). Perhaps it's the familiarity of punitive structures and strategies, but make no mistake about it: A statement that expresses "When you finish your outline, you can do the coloring puzzle" is no more a bribe than "If you don't do your work, I'm calling your mother." Both offer a payoff to the students for doing what you want, but in the case of the threat, the payoff is always about avoiding a negative response or staying safe in some way. You'll get the same message across with a positively stated boundary—that the desirable outcome is contingent on some form of cooperation or some level of work completion—but with much less stress and much less chance of engaging oppositional, resentful, or passive-aggressive behavior.

LEARNING FOR LEARNING'S SAKE

The echo from the industrial-era authority relationships will question why we need to offer a pleasurable outcome to students for doing what they simply should do. We need to for one reason: It works, and it works better and with much less risk than using the threat of negative outcomes. Further, seeing the positive results of their cooperative behavior helps reinforce the students' responsibility for their choices and increases accountability for their behavior. Experiencing a connection between positive choices and the outcomes they allow strengthens the students' recognition of the cause-and-effect relationship between the behaviors they choose and what happens to them as a result of their choices. Positive consequences also reinforce the students' belief in their ability to positively affect their own lives—personal empowerment in the best sense of the word.

> Positive consequences also reinforce the students' believe in their ability to positively affect their own lives. . . .

It's usually at this point in my workshops that someone challenges this idea: "What about 'learning for learning's sake'? Don't we all want students to work for the love of learning?" Of course we do. Is there anyone easier to motivate than the student who comes to our classroom with a burning desire for knowledge? But surely our aspirations are not simply for our own benefits. Such students are also functioning at some of the highest levels of need fulfillment.

Here again we see the importance of creating an emotionally safe classroom environment. If we look at the range of needs that motivate people, we find a hierarchy in which the more basic needs must be satisfied before higher level needs are accommodated. A hungry student, for example, may not be too concerned with whether her handwriting is improving until she gets some food in her stomach. A student who is worried about being attacked on the way to study hall will have his brain far more focused on this threat than on his ability to conjugate French verbs.

In a win-lose classroom, the frequent existence of arbitrary power and absence of trust are likely to keep kids striving to meet their needs for safety. These students rarely take risks or go beyond the bare minimum to avoid confrontation or to keep from drawing attention to themselves. Even those vying for positions of power and acceptance among their peers or the ones trying to be teacher's pet place these goals above learning simply to assure their safety in some way. Satisfying higher level needs, including the desire for knowledge and personal growth, requires an environment in which students feel safe enough to pursue these objectives. (Self-actualization is a long way off for students focused on self-protection.) Once the basic needs are satisfied, students are free to seek fulfillment of higher level needs. A success-oriented classroom not only allows safety needs to be met, but also acknowledges the students' higher level needs for acceptance and belonging, input and control, and ultimately, success and achievement. The possibility of learning for learning's sake stands a much better chance of transpiring in a win-win classroom than in any other environment.

And yet, doing anything for its own sake must be perceived as pleasurable and rewarding in some way. Even in the ideal environment, many students have a long way to go before they can love learning or a particular subject area if the possibility of success seems to be beyond their immediate reach. Therefore, an activity that is perceived as unfulfilling may, at least at first, have to be connected to something meaningful and immediate to build positive behavior patterns or internalized commitment, let alone a passion for the task or subject itself. The simple promise of long-term results or possible satisfaction might not do it.

Billy's love of running errands and visiting other classrooms (what he wanted) gave him a reason for doing his classwork (what I wanted). For this student, who was initially unwilling to take even the slightest risk, the availability of something more need fulfilling than avoiding the task was absolutely essential. Access to a positive outcome that Billy perceived as valuable gave him the drive that all the threats, lectures, and nagging were unable to elicit. It was a start and one that created a positive association with the entire experience of being—and working—in fourth grade. As that connection became more firmly established, the need for the continual, unrelated reward diminished. After a couple of weeks, Billy had become self-managing and confident enough to do his work without needing to run errands after he was finished (although I still looked for opportunities to send him out of the room once in a while because I knew he enjoyed this privilege, handled it responsibly, and maintained a high level of commitment in class).

Likewise, simply hearing that they would need basic math skills to balance a checkbook and plan a budget had little motivational value to my eighth graders, who had neither checkbook nor budget. The only way to break the inertia was to connect their initial attempts to some immediate, positive outcomes. That might mean working a math puzzle for reinforcement, creating a new bulletin board, grading one's own assignment, getting to help another student, choosing an enrichment activity, working with a partner, or moving on to the next skill at the completion of a task.

> Each time students experienced the positive outcomes of their own cooperative choosing, the connection was reinforced.

Each time students experienced the positive outcomes of their own cooperative choosing, the connection was reinforced. As this association grew stronger, the behavior became increasingly internalized and habitual.

This strategy can work in even the most seemingly hopeless situations. A high school teacher was assigned late in the year to a large group of high-risk and extremely hostile seniors after the original teacher and numerous replacements had quit. The new teacher could barely get their attention, and when she handed out an assignment, every student in the room tore it up. "We never pass anything, anyhow," one declared.

Only somewhat discouraged, she returned the next day with the same assignment and announced, "If you turn it in with your name on it, you get a C." Most of the students simply shook their heads and tore the papers up again, although six or seven defiantly scrawled their names across the papers and turned them in. The next day she came back with their papers graded, as promised, with a C for having turned something in, and another stack of work. Although the students were still suspicious, she suddenly had their attention: "If you can get a C for writing your name, imagine what you can get for doing some work!"

Again, it was a start. And eventually, between making success possible and providing other need fulfilling options for cooperation, she hooked every kid in the class. As the trust relationship grew, students were willing to take greater risks. The hurdles also got higher, and in a day or two, it took far more than writing one's name on the paper to get a passing grade.

As with Billy and the kids in my math class, staying on task, attempting new content, and progressing through the curriculum eventually became their own rewards. Sure, there were students who gained competence and still didn't love the subject area. Let's face it—there are certain activities and chores that may never be rewarding in their own right, no matter how well we can do them. (How many adults whose math skills are adequate to function responsibly in society do not actually love math?) But as achievement eroded resistance, students were becoming learners. If they didn't all find a love of learning in that class, at least it was an invitation to find it elsewhere.

I've met too many teachers who were nearly crippled by frustration, guilt, or inadequacy when they bought into the idea that any positive motivation is harmful and that truly effective teachers have students for whom simply being in their teacher's classroom is reward enough. This is a setup of the worst and most destructive kind. Yes, ideally we'd like kids to do their math assignments for the joy and privilege of working with fractions, and certainly some will. But what about the students who find fractions somewhat less enticing, not to mention too difficult for them to do with the skills they currently have developed? (Even if you absolutely love math, would you clean your bathroom for a chance to do some long division problems in your free time afterward?) Is the point of our interaction and instruction improving our students' understanding and ability, or is it to guarantee that they never need a push, inspiration, motivation, or outside incentive to learn the skill or do the work? If we get too attached to our kids falling in love with our subject area, we may be doomed to a great deal of frustration and disappointment.

There is no such thing as unmotivated behavior. Even the most dedicated among us expect something for the work we do, whether it be our enjoyment of teaching, the satisfaction of knowing we're shaping young lives, the paycheck we get at the end of the month, or the fact that our job gets us out of the house once in a while. Why shouldn't kids want some meaningful payoff for the things they choose to do? We can save ourselves a great deal of heartache when we quit analyzing and making judgments about the reasons our kids are doing what we assign. So long as we aren't motivating with conditional safety or approval, whatever individual, personal forces compel cooperative and on-task behavior are none of our business.

> There is no such thing as unmotivated behavior.

We can certainly improve the odds of getting what we want when we ask students to do something they can do successfully, when the task has some personal relevance to them, or when doing the task gives them access to something they like doing even more. And we can establish a foundation in which learning, success, safety, and achievement can develop into a passion or a much greater commitment than some of our students initially display. However, it's equally true that few people are likely to fall in love with something that represents failure, poor progress, criticism, impatience, or other negative feedback for them.

The point is, a big part of our job as educators involves encouraging—that is, motivating—kids to do certain things, whether they like the tasks or not. If our students know how to construct an outline, write a cohesive paragraph, or determine the area of a rectangle, does it matter that some never look forward to the opportunity to do these tasks? The real test of responsibility is the willingness to do the things we need to do, not just the things we like to do.

MEANINGFUL MOTIVATORS

We promise students an A if they do their work but there are always a few students who are not motivated by grades. We allow students who finish their work to go out to recess but there are always a few who would just as soon stay inside. On the other hand, there is always someone who would do anything for the privilege of straightening the teacher's desk, working on a challenging enrichment activity, or, as in Billy's case, running a stack of papers downstairs. But what about those students who don't seem to be motivated by anything?

> The real test of responsibility is the willingness to do the things we need to do, not just the things we like to do.

Moving away from factory-era thinking means we try to become more aware and appreciative of individual students' preferences and increasingly creative about the types of incentives we offer. Because many rewards and outcomes that are valuable to students would probably not be terribly attractive to us, it's easy to overlook some great motivators. Offer your kids a chance to make a handout for other kids to use, clean the board, work at the computer, change the bulletin board, listen to music, or engage in any number of clean-up chores, and you're bound to see at least a few eyes light up.

Other options may not be so obvious. I once asked a fifth grader to get a box of science equipment out of my car. When she returned, she put the box on my desk and shook her head. "Your car's a mess," she said.

So okay, keeping my car free of papers, plans, materials, textbooks, and at least a few fast food wrappers wasn't much of a priority. "Would you like to clean it out when you finish your work?" I asked.

"Ooo! Can I?"

("Hmm," I wondered. "Do you clean bathrooms?")

Now, I doubt I would have thought of car cleaning as a reward but the task was obviously more attractive to her than it was to me. It's also hard to see "more work" as motivating, yet enrichment and content-related activities can be very appealing to students, especially if there are choices available or if "more work" clearly indicates advancement. (Ever notice how students in basal readers tend to really perk up through the last unit so they can get into the next, more difficult book?)

We can learn a great deal about our students from formal assessment instruments, informal surveys, or even simple conversations. On discovering that the majority of my students preferred working with a partner, greater mobility, and sound in the environment,[2] I could offer one or more of those options during certain activities as long as the students stayed on task and didn't create problems for anyone else. Student engagement, time on task, and productivity increased significantly. This same inventory also revealed that my most difficult reading group comprised students who preferred afternoons and evenings to mornings. Our reading periods were scheduled early in the day when these students were not at their best. It took some juggling, but switching that group to the afternoon made a tremendous difference in the students' attention, participation, retention, performance, and achievement. In each case, attempting to meet students' learning style preferences paid off for me as well. Win-win!

Sometimes a positive consequence can itself be as valuable a learning experience as any classroom activity. One year, our kindergarten teacher was feeling a bit overwhelmed by some of the management and housekeeping responsibilities involved in managing a large, full-day group. I offered to ask some of my upper grade students to help. My kids required little coaxing and began helping out, as always, when their seatwork was done.

> Sometimes a positive consequence can itself be as valuable a learning experience as any classroom activity.

At first, the tasks were fairly mechanical or routine—mixing paint or covering tables for art activities; helping the younger students open their milk cartons, zip their jackets, or get in line; or helping the teacher with organization and clean-up chores. However, these students quickly began offering to help out in centers, play games, put on puppet shows, or review colors, numbers, letters, and various other concepts. Some of my weakest and most resistant readers volunteered to read stories to the kindergarten children. This was a real "I can" experience that was ultimately reflected in their performance in their own classroom.

We were able to get every upper grade student involved as a helper. Students who had never done homework before were asking to do their independent work at home so they could spend more time as a helper. Amazingly, some even asked to give up recess to work in the kindergarten.

My students were suddenly doing larger amounts of increasingly difficult work. Because the privilege demanded that the helpers stay caught up and out of trouble in all their classes, overall discipline was greatly improved. At the same time, their successes in the kindergarten and opportunities to model were beginning to show in their interactions and behaviors with their peers, with other teachers, and even at home. Self-concepts and general attitudes improved. Attendance was up, detentions were down. Students who had rarely, if ever, demonstrated anything in the way of self-management were beginning to behave more responsibly and with greater self-control. One student even walked away from a fight, took the hall pass and stood outside the door until he had a chance to cool down. This was unheard of. I didn't even have to open my mouth! School had become more enjoyable and rewarding for everyone, and I was amazed at the amount of time I had for instruction when I wasn't distracted by student misbehavior.[3]

I offer one caution in looking for meaningful motivators: When we attempt to determine "what's in it for them," we need to differentiate between the assumed or projected benefits (which usually reflect *our* value system) and the actual benefits (what the students perceive as a positive outcome). If Grandma said, "Eat your vegetables and you can have some liver!," how many children would be motivated by this promise, regardless of liver's nutritional value? Adults can often appreciate the long-range benefits of the things we ask our students to do far better than they can. But even a firm grasp of these benefits may not be enough. (Would our efforts at dieting, for example, be more successful if we could actually *see* a difference each time we turned down a doughnut?) For the most part, the more immediate and personally meaningful the positive outcome, the more likely the cooperation.

In some settings, choices and incentives are easy to structure and provide; others require a bit of creativity. Teachers working in departmentalized systems feel a greater degree of time pressure, as they are literally working from one bell to the next. One middle school teacher complained, "I'm barely getting 20 minutes of instruction into a 45-minute class. How can I take the time to provide options and rewards?" Yet her efforts at creating a win-win classroom and particularly her attention to her students' needs and interests paid off. She found that by allowing choices about in-class projects and assignments, offering a variety of related activities or free time at the end of the lesson, or allowing the students to listen to music while they were doing seatwork, she actually increased instructional time by ten to fifteen minutes a day. It may seem counterintuitive (if not a bit crazy) to give up time when we're already far behind, but as one teacher explained, when he would "slow down to speed up," he found that he could gain 15 or 20 minutes of instructional time by giving up five. Another teacher had a similar experience when she gave an otherwise recalcitrant group of tenth graders the incentive to get to her chemistry class by serializing a story and reading for the first five minutes of class to anyone who arrived on time. She offered to read at the end of class, too, if they got through their work ahead of schedule—which they often did—and was delighted when the majority of her students went out and got their own copies of the book to read along.

GETTING BEYOND TRADITIONAL THINKING

When I first started thinking about motivation, I had a great deal of factory-era conditioning to overcome. Although I knew that I wanted to experience meaningful payoff for the work I did, there were times I resented having to motivate kids. This double standard did not serve me at all.

I was worried that motivating kids with positive outcomes would teach them to expect a reward every time they did something, a concern I've heard echoed time and again by educators and parents in my training sessions. Over the years, it's become quite clear to me that no one, grownup or child, does something unless he or she sees some immediate or long-term benefit. It's basic human nature to expect a positive outcome for the choices we make. (Why are you reading this book? Whether to fulfill a requirement for a class you're taking, an interest in the topic, or a need for information, you anticipate some payoff or you would certainly be doing something else with your time.) Motivation doesn't teach kids to expect a payoff, it simply accommodates their need for one.

> Motivation doesn't teach kids to expect a payoff, it simply accommodates their need for one.

I feared that motivating students would encourage selfishness and manipulation until I understood that it's not the desire for the payoff that is selfish or manipulative but the behaviors that follow when we don't have healthier ways of getting what we want that can be selfish and manipulative. Good motivation actually *discourages* selfishness and manipulation. Even accommodating kids who like to negotiate and make counterproposals builds valuable life skills, and, in the long run, can create incredible levels of commitment and cooperation.

In the true spirit of scarcity thinking, industrial-era programming sounds another concern: "If you let Billy take a message to the office, don't you have to let everybody take stuff down when they finish their work?" Of course not. In that particular class, some kids would work for the grades, some would work to get on to the next assignment, others would work for some structured free time, and a few did the assignment because they really liked that particular subject and usually did well in it. Sending them on an errand as motivation would have been silly and redundant. Likewise, I had students who found no fascination with running around the school on missions for me. Attempting to motivate them with messenger privileges would have been pointless. Students do not have similar personalities, tastes, and work habits, and most genuinely appreciate having their individuality recognized.

Regardless of these differences, when it comes to motivation, we all have our price and we always have choices and so do our students. It's well worth our while to offer them something they can't refuse. And as long as everyone's dignity and safety are protected, that doesn't have to cost us a thing.

Hot Tips for Motivating Your Students

- Offer outcomes (positive consequences or incentives) that are meaningful and important to students to elicit otherwise nonexistent behaviors you desire—that is, to motivate them to do something they are currently *not* doing.
- Keep in mind that the process of motivating is different from strategies used for *reinforcing* existing cooperation or *intervening* when a misbehavior occurs.
- Remember that offering a variety of acceptable choices can successfully accommodate students' desire for autonomy and control. Very often, simply having choices will be motivation enough.
- Offer positive outcomes for completion of specific tasks. For example, "If you finish this worksheet by the time the show starts. . . " or "As long as your report is turned in by Friday at 3:00. . . " is preferable to offering a reward for "being good." Be clear about what you want the student to do as well as what the student will get to do in return.
- State contingencies in a positive manner: "If you do . . . ," "When you finish . . . ," or "As soon as . . . ," for example. Avoid using threats and negative consequences or communicating the contingency as a threat of punishment or deprivation: "If you don't. . . ." Typically, the implicit conditionality of the availability of the positive outcome is the only hint of negative consequence necessary.
- Keep initial demands small, short, and simple and keep positive consequences small, frequent, and immediate. Raise the hurdles gradually and decrease the reward over time. (For a student like Billy, you might start with an errand after each assignment he completes, working toward finishing the morning's work and then the full day. Eventually, verbal reinforcement with sporadic opportunities to run an errand will probably be sufficient to maintain the desired behavior.)
- Identify student preferences and what your students perceive as meaningful through dialogue, observation, or assessments (interest inventories, learning styles surveys, sociometric questionnaires, time-on-task assessments). Use this information to plan and select positive outcomes.
- Select only win-win outcomes (those that will not hurt, deprive, or inconvenience anyone else).
- Make rewards available on a noncompetitive basis. Rather than offering copies of the dinosaur word search puzzle to the first row that's finished, make the puzzle available to every student as soon as he or she is done. (Students who do not finish in class can take the puzzle home to complete it there.)
- If the positive outcome can be available to only one or two students at a time (such as cleaning the board or emptying the trash), make sure the other students have access to those privileges at some other times and that they have other incentives available to them in the meantime.
- Although it would be silly, if not impossible, to hide the fact that we're pleased when our students do what we ask, try to avoid using conditional approval or acceptance as a motivator (for example, routinely asking students to do something because it would make you happy or because you "really like students who. . . .").

- Tokens and stickers can be effective, even with older students, if they are limited to very specific tasks, available to everyone, and used infrequently. However, think about activities you can offer instead, as these tend to be more effective than tokens.
- Use outcomes that help build responsible behavior, and, if possible, reinforce content: enrichment activities, structured free time, grading one's own papers, peer helping or tutoring, access to a DVD, an extra trip to the library, filing, research time on the computer, or housekeeping chores, for example.
- Activities that involve cooking or food preparation can be valuable motivators and great learning experiences but avoid offering food, especially sweets, to counter resistance, reward cooperation, or cheer or pacify a student who is upset.
- If possible, state the contingency once. Avoid nagging and reminding. If the student fails to cooperate, lack of access to the positive outcome is a far more effective consequence than a lecture. Continue to offer the contingency on subsequent days so students can learn to be more self-managing, even if they don't get it right the first time.
- If a student does not complete the task or does not seem to be motivated by the reward you've offered, consider the following:
  - Can the student do what I've asked him or her to do?
  - Is the student overwhelmed by the amount of work required in the time I've allowed? Do I need to change the requirements or back up a bit?
  - Is the outcome meaningful to the student? What else might work?
- If the student does not complete the task because he or she is just having an off day, hold the incentive, if possible, for another time: "Let's try again this afternoon (or tomorrow)."

Use Chart 11.1 or create a similar chart on a separate piece of paper.

Chart 11.1   Motivation Exercise

Desirable Student Behaviors	What's in It for You	Long-Term Payoffs (Benefit to Students)	Immediate Payoffs (Benefit to Students)

In Column 1, list some of the behaviors you ask of your students.

In Column 2, tell what's in it for you if the students perform the behaviors you have listed in Column 1.

In Column 3, identify the long-term objectives for the students (what *you* feel the students will get out of performing each behavior in the long run).

In Column 4, identify the immediate payoffs for *them* (what the students get or perceive as a meaningful outcome when they perform each behavior).

Now go back and look at Column 4. Of the responses you marked, how many (or which) . . .

- were related to teacher approval or avoidance of punishment?

- offered tokens, tickets, stickers, or food?

- offered higher-interest activities on completion of the task?

- offered choices related to the task itself?

- were left blank?

In what ways are your motivational strategies successful . . .

- in getting your students to do what you want?

- in building responsibility, initiative, and self-management?

- in protecting the emotional climate in your classroom?

In what ways have you investigated your students' needs and preferences?

What Do They Like?

It's easy to make assumptions about what kids like or need to learn; however, it's also easy to miss opportunities to engage kids because we don't have a clear enough picture of their preferences. If you feel you need more information, take some time out to collect some data before going on with these exercises. If you've got more than one class, choose the one you find most challenging. You might try the following:

- Develop a fill-in-type inventory, with questions such as "After school I like to _____." "The best thing about school is _____" or "I wish I could take a class in _____." Students can write in answers, dictate answers, or interview one another.
- Develop a checklist-type inventory, with a number of hobbies, sports, types of music or TV shows, types of stories, afterschool activities, and so on. Ask students to check activities they have tried or use the inventory to evaluate their interest in each item, say, on a scale of 1 to 5.
- Administer a commercial learning styles or interest inventory.
- Discuss the students' interests in a formal discussion or values activity.
- Have your kids write letters of introduction, telling you who they are, what they like to do, what's important to them, and so forth.
- Explore the students' interests informally, in a casual conversation with the students.
- Consider the students' interests as perceived by their parents or other teachers.
- Ask your colleagues what has worked for them in motivating particular students.

Design a chart similar to Chart 11.2. Plan enough space to devote one line to each student. If you are working with several classes, you may wish to select one class (or group of students) that has been the most difficult to motivate.

Chart 11.2   Student Motivation

Student	Motivators

Write the students' names in the left-hand column, and in the space to the right of their names, keep track of topics or activities that interest each individual. Add to this list as you learn more about each student.

From this information, what other kinds of activity-type motivators might work in your classroom, activities you are willing and able to provide and that your students might find need fulfilling?

What changes would you propose in your motivational strategies?

Try implementing some of the changes you proposed above for at least three or four weeks. Describe the impact of the contingencies you implemented on the following:

- Student cooperation

- Student self-management, responsible behavior

- Student attitude, self-concept, initiative

NOTES

1. I use this example with caution. While we all know that food can be quite effective as a motivator, let's remember that there are many individuals with food issues (including addictive relationships with food) and food allergies. For more information, visit http://ga.efoodaddiction .com/ and http://www.feingold.org.

2. I learned about these students by administering an inventory from Kenneth and Rita Dunn's *The Educator's Self-Teaching Guide to Individualized Instruction* (Englewood Cliffs, NJ: Parker Publishing, 1975).

3. This experience became the basis for my doctoral dissertation, *Building Responsible Learning Behavior Through Peer Interaction* (University of Pittsburgh, 1980). It also proved to be one of the most effective strategies for engaging and motivating my students, including those who seemed impervious to nearly all previous efforts.

12

The Power of Choice

Ms. Cahill, a first-year teacher, was trying to get her eighth-grade math students to warm up with ten subtraction review problems in the first few minutes of class. After two days, the students had used up most of the class period *not* doing the review work! Ms. Cahill collected completed assignments from only a handful of students and never did manage to get to the new material she intended to teach after the planned ten-minute review period.

Frustrated but undaunted, this teacher came in on the following day with a new approach: Instead of ten problems, the students walked in to find *fifteen* on the board. (As the saying goes, nothing changes until something changes. The changes don't have to be complicated, but something has to be different.) Not surprisingly, several students groaned at the increase in work. One boy walked in, outright defiant, refusing to do the problems on the board. "That's too much work," he insisted.

> Nothing changes until something changes.

Now to me, an observer in this class, this seemed like the perfect opportunity for Ms. Cahill to put her foot down and let this kid know exactly who was the boss in that class. And in fact, that's exactly what the teacher did, although she did it with a rather nontraditional, back-door approach. Rather than get into an argument, she did something that, I've since realized, is one of the most effective ways for defusing conflict with anyone, including other adults: She agreed with him!

Ms. Cahill turned and looked at the board, looked back at him, and laughed. "I was having a lot of fun putting those problems on the board. I guess I got carried away." Then turning to the class, she simply suggested that they choose any ten out of the fifteen that they wanted to do. Guess what? Before the class let out, every student had completed at least ten problems; amazingly, over half had done all fifteen.

As Ms. Cahill's supervisor, I was delighted to see this approach work, but to be honest, it worried me a bit. At that time, I was struggling with the concept of a win-win authority relationship, and frankly, still stuck in a bit of all-or-nothing thinking. I didn't say anything that day, thinking I'd wait to see where she was going with this approach. And although the class became far more productive and cooperative over the next few days, that same young man came in with that same defiant attitude: "I'm sick of doing the problems on the board," he said. Once again, the teacher agreed with him. Unperturbed, she encouraged any student who was tired of the problems on the board to either make up ten of their own or do ten of the problems on Page 36 in their book. Even the defiant student had a hard time passing that up.

I sat there and watched every child in the room get down to work, finishing in time for the teacher to introduce some new material. Clearly her approach was working. Still, I couldn't let it go. At the end of class, I confronted the teacher with what had been bothering me: "Aren't you teaching him that it's okay to be disrespectful to you?" And in the "light bulb" moment that finally allowed me to grasp the true essence of win-win teaching, Ms. Cahill just smiled and said, "No, I'm not teaching him that it's okay to be disrespectful. I'm teaching him that it's *unnecessary*."

> "I'm not teaching him that it's okay to be disrespectful. I'm teaching him that it's *unnecessary*."

Not only did the teacher not react to the student's apparent affront to her authority, but she also ended up using his defiance as a way to leverage his (and his classmates') cooperation. At no point did she relinquish her authority or compromise academic requirements. The next few days were devoted to improving their time, but most important, a pattern of win-win, cooperation, and on-task behavior had been established. (I suspect that she originally increased the number of problems with the intention of asking everyone to choose ten, but the student provided an opportunity for her to make it seem like it was their idea.) It didn't take long for the students to realize that Ms. Cahill was on their side; to the best of my knowledge, she never had a problem with this student after that, and the degree of cooperation and sense of partnership she developed with the entire class was fairly well cemented by the second or third week of school.

BUILDING COMMITMENT AND COOPERATION

My experience with Ms. Cahill reminded me of an experience I had handled in a similar fashion without even realizing it. I had never been terribly creative about the spelling lessons I assigned and early on had a student named Donald register a complaint about the required practice of writing each word five times: "This is stupid!" he announced.

Okay, so it wasn't my best assignment, but it was the best I had at the moment and besides, the repetition did seem to help some of the kids. Additionally, Donald happened to challenge me on one of those days when I didn't have a lot of energy to argue with the kids. So I put it back on him: "Well, Donald, the whole idea here is to learn these words. If you have a better way to do it, put it in writing. I want it on my desk first thing tomorrow morning," I said.

The next day, Donald came in with all twenty words written into a story. On another paper was a crossword puzzle using fifteen of the words, with definitions he had made up himself. He had also created a word search puzzle with nineteen of the words, which, he informed me, I could duplicate for the rest of the class to see if they could figure out which word he had left out! Of course by then, he knew these words inside out.

I imagined that if that freedom worked for Donald, it might just spark the rest of the class. So the following week, instead of the traditional no-choice program we had been following, I came in with a list of ten possible activities, including oldies but goodies like "Write each word five times" and the various assignments in the book. (Unlike Donald, some of my students loved these assignments.) I also included the ideas Donald had inspired and left Number 10 as "Design your own activity using at least fifteen of the words." These choices allowed the students to accommodate their personal learning needs. Some preferred the security of the sequence we'd always used; others favored the challenge of the newer choices. Others skipped around, trying one set of activities one week, another the next. And Number 10 inspired some projects that were far more complex and creative than anything I would have dreamed up for them to do.

To get full credit for the seatwork portion of this class, each student was to choose any three of the ten activities and have them in by the end of the day on Thursday. It quickly became clear that the brain does indeed crave novelty when the majority of the kids were turning in six and seven assignments for the first few weeks. Productivity was up, not just from the kids who had always done well in spelling and had become bored but also from students who had never done much in this subject. The students were taking more responsibility and initiative for their own learning, and everyone was practicing decision making. The simple addition of choice accommodated power needs and made the tasks more attractive, bringing us one step closer to that precious goal of learning for learning's sake. (When my top spelling group picked words from the science unit, I was delighted, if a bit surprised, when they went for—and learned—words like *meteorology* and *brontosaurus* instead of *wind* or *dirt*.) Perhaps even more important, however, was the opportunity for me to model a bit of flexibility and cultivate a win-win classroom dynamic: "Your needs (freedom and creativity) are important and so are mine (your performance and learning). Here's how we can both get what we want."

BUILDING DECISION-MAKING SKILLS

The importance of offering choices initially became apparent to me for an entirely different reason. After unsuccessfully attempting to get my fifth graders to participate in learning centers that required far more independence and self-management than my students actually had developed, I decided to try something simpler. The next morning, I came in armed with two stacks of worksheets, one for math, the other for spelling.[1] I distributed each at the same time and told the students that both needed to be done before recess, which was an hour away. Immediately, one of the students asked which one they had to do first.

"It doesn't matter," I answered. "Just get them both done."

The class sat there, stupefied. They looked uneasily at one another and back to me. I was amazed at the difficulty the students were having. Faced with a choice between math and spelling, they were lost. I could understand how asking them to design their own projects could have overwhelmed them. But how could they possibly be confounded by two worksheets? These kids were in fifth grade—more than a few for the second or third time. How much more simple could I make this?

I waited as a few students began to eye their papers. One or two actually started working on one sheet or the other. A few, however, appeared stricken. One student was on the verge of tears. I couldn't stand it anymore: I asked her if she wanted me to help her choose (which, incidentally, is a choice in itself). She sniffed and nodded.

"Why don't you do the math assignment?" I suggested.

She hesitated. Almost imperceptibly, she answered, "I'd rather do the spelling." (This was another one of those moments when I wondered why I had ever gone into teaching.[2])

Later that day, I realized that this trauma was simply a part of her process in learning the skill of decision making. And I also thought about the number of truly consequential decisions these kids currently faced or would be facing in the not-too-distant future: How could we expect them to make intelligent decisions about taking drugs, finishing school, or participating in gang-related activities if they were paralyzed by something as simple as choosing which assignment to do first?

> How could we expect them to make intelligent decisions about taking drugs, finishing school, or participating in gang-related activities if they were paralyzed by something as simple as choosing which assignment to do first?

As if I didn't have enough to cover that year, now I had to teach decision making, too! I was just beginning to appreciate the fact that learning to choose was a skill as much as any other I would have to teach, one that needed to be taught from the ground up and practiced and refined along the way. Well, it seemed as good a place as any to begin, and I knew that unless I helped them develop and practice these skills, I'd never see the kind of independent learning behaviors my plans would require.

The practice of offering choices to our students serves several purposes, including reinforcing decision-making skills, addressing the students' needs for input and control in their lives, and motivating cooperation through empowerment. This process is quite different from simply telling students what to do. The authority behind a command (and its disregard for the students' need for autonomy) is in itself likely to provoke resistance. We defuse that resistance and put the responsibility back on the student when we switch from demanding to giving choices.

Choices also generate commitment from students. Had I simply handed those two papers to the students, insisting that they do math first, I would have probably seen some students comply, although there would have been a few who would have argued for spelling just to be difficult. Either way, the only person committed to the activity would have been me. Having a choice, they made a commitment the second they put their pencils to one of the two papers.

When They Don't Like Your Choices

You offer a choice to a student. He can't make up his mind. You offer to help him decide. He agrees. (That's a choice, too.)

At this point, you will often find that the child wants to do the exact opposite of whatever you suggest. I can assure you that every cell in your body will want to yell! But what if you just agree instead? Think of the difference in the energy you create by expressing your well-deserved frustration versus the energy you create by simply agreeing: "Great choice!"

There's no stress to bring up the student's defenses, and it doesn't make much sense for a student in this situation to become resistant or defiant.

OFFERING CHOICES IN A WIN-WIN CLASSROOM

I'm convinced that the longer kids are in school, the worse they get at making decisions. Between our making their decisions for them, limiting the number of choices we offer, and then stacking the deck by offering "good" and "bad" choices (and responding negatively when they don't pick the right one), it's not surprising that middle and high school teachers report that their kids will either choose impulsively when offered options or stare like deer caught in their headlights, freezing at the prospect of having to decide.

Unfortunately, this simple strategy—offering choices—is rarely used to its best effect. I was in a classroom where the teacher asked his kids to choose between two assignments: After listening to music for about ten minutes, they could either draw a picture of what the music brought to mind or they could write a three-page analysis. The teacher was furious when they all chose to draw. It doesn't take long for children to learn that they are not well- served by independent thinking, deciding, or initiating in a school setting when these efforts attract criticism, reprimands, or punishment. (Have you noticed how kindergarteners will automatically go for a mop or a rag to clean up a spill, but by second or third grade, many of these same students will freeze after knocking something over and wait for the teacher to yell at them?)

And then there are classrooms with too many choices and demands for independent learning behaviors that students have either lost or not adequately developed. Many of us, especially when we're first starting out, are so excited about teaching that we want to try every exciting plan and idea we've seen, heard about, or concocted the moment we're in front of a group of children. This was certainly true in my case, where I was also hoping to curtail resistance, indifference, and a variety of disruptive behaviors by inundating my students with activities that were creative and interesting enough to hold their attention. But even students who are pretty adept at making choices can be overwhelmed by too many options (or too few limits).

Experienced or intuitive teachers know the value of starting small in a rather structured environment and then relaxing the structure gradually as students develop and demonstrate independent learning and decision-making skills. A little initial restraint can go a long way; we'll have plenty of chances to offer greater challenges to their self-management as they build up to them. As students develop confidence in their decision-making capabilities, we can ease up on the limits, offering more and increasingly complex options. And as the limits expand and options increase in number and complexity, students gain a stake, not only in the overall climate of the classroom but also in their own learning and personal growth as well.

> As students develop confidence in their decision-making capabilities, we can ease up on the limits, offering more and increasingly complex options.

But even Ms. Cahill had some concerns about this strategy, successful as it was. "Does the practice of offering choices cause children to expect a choice about everything?" she wondered. "Am I putting them in charge?"

In a way, we are putting children in charge because we know that autonomy encourages commitment and that the greater the buy-in, the more cooperation we can typically anticipate. But of what are the students actually in charge? They're not controlling the classroom, and they're certainly not in charge of us. They're simply in charge of which ten problems they're going to do on a particular page or how they're going to demonstrate their understanding of a particular concept. Kids generally do not need to control much, but they do need to control some things in their lives in order to develop the kinds of skills, if not mental health, we wish to encourage.[3]

Offering choices can engage kids and assert our authority in a very positive way. It does not, in fact, teach kids to expect a choice about everything. There will always be assignments, requirements, tests, or deadlines that are nonnegotiable, and teachers in win-win classrooms report that their kids tend to be far more accepting and understanding when even reasonable options are simply not available. And of all the potential benefits for offering choices, this increase in respect may serve us all best.

Why Build Decision-Making Skills?

- Responsible behavior includes the ability to connect "what I've done" to "what happens or happened as a result of what I've done." Likewise, self-concept and self-motivation are influenced by an individual's belief that "I have the power and ability to impact my environment and change what isn't working in my life."
- Offering choices not only builds valuable lifelong skills, it is also a way to create win-win power dynamics in your classroom. Additionally, a sense of empowerment is reinforced every time an individual has the opportunity to experience the outcomes of his or her own choosing.
- Offering choices (within clearly defined limits) has numerous advantages, including the following:
  ○ Modeling flexibility and respect for student preferences.
  ○ Providing ways for the student to meet various learning needs.
  ○ Generating commitment from students.
  ○ Empowering students, increasing the likelihood of student cooperation.
  ○ Building mutual respect and increasing respect for authority.
  ○ Teaching self-management and building decision-making skills.
  ○ Helping students connect their choices to the outcomes of their choices.
  ○ Offering students opportunities to develop and practice valuable skills such as exploring available options and weighing alternatives, identifying personal preferences, making independent choices, and developing a sense of multiple options or solutions in problem-solving situations.
  ○ Increasing opportunities for students to take responsibility and initiative in their own learning.
  ○ Decreasing resistance, defiance, and other oppositional behaviors that often accompany commands (no choices offered).

Options, Options…

Here are some choices you can offer to your students:

- Deciding which of two activities to do first.
- Choosing from a list of five topics to research.
- Selecting any three crayons to use in a drawing.
- Deciding which two of three language puzzles to complete.
- Picking ten of the math problems on a certain page.
- Determining where to sit for independent work.
- Choosing a work space where you will not be tempted to talk.
- Deciding, in a group, how to share two cookies between three people so that all three are satisfied with the decision.

- Designing a science experiment that will demonstrate an understanding of photosynthesis.
- Deciding how to arrange certain materials in a display.
- Determining, as a group, the order in which the class will discuss certain nonsequential topics.
- Choosing a sports figure or entertainer to contact in a letter-writing activity.
- Deciding, as a group, whether to take a one-minute break now or a three-minute break in ten minutes.
- Deciding which center to visit during self-selection.
- Choosing whether to display your drawing or take it home.
- Deciding whether you still need more practice on a particular skill.
- Choosing three out of the five activities suggested in the history contract.
- Determining the supplies and equipment you (or your group) will need to construct a biosphere.
- Deciding whether to practice a math skill by doing a page in the book, a cross-number puzzle, or a skill card in a commercial kit.
- Choosing how to arrange certain materials in a display.
- Selecting a topic and design for a new bulletin board.
- Choosing among various activities or centers during independent work time.
- Deciding whether to present a report in written, drawn, constructed, performed, or video format.

Hot Tips for Using Choices to Build Cooperation and Decision-Making Skills

- Choices encourage cooperation through input and empowerment. Offer choices in the absence of desirable student behavior to engage the students, motivating them to perform a particular behavior they are not currently demonstrating.
- Choices can help *prevent* disruptive behaviors; however, other strategies are more effective for *responding* to negative behavior.
- Present available options in a positive manner. Be careful the choice doesn't sound like "do it or else" (which, by the way, is also a choice).
- Make sure that all options you offer are acceptable. Avoid suggesting conditional approval if they choose the "right" option. Make sure there are no wrong choices. If you don't want the students to choose something, don't make it an option. (For example, if you want them to do the outline first, offer sequence options about the other activities, after the outline is finished.)
- Make sure the choices you offer are clear and specific. Asking a child to "select a meaningful learning activity" leaves you open for some pretty broad interpretations. Instead, define choices with clearly stated limits: "Select one activity from the five on the board" is much easier for the student to understand, and perform successfully.
- Start simple. If a student is having difficulty making decisions, it may be that there are too many options or that the limits are too broad or unclear.
- If a student is having difficulty with even a simple choice, add a time limit (after which you choose). Be patient. Some young students and well-conditioned order takers need time and practice to develop confidence in their ability to choose.
- Increase options as the students can handle them, either by widening the range of choices you offer or by making the options more complex or open ended.
- Depending on your goals, schedule, and resources, you might leave room for students to change their minds if they are disappointed with a choice they've made. If time and management require students to make a choice and stick with it, make that clear when you present the available options. Reassure the students that they can "try again later (or tomorrow or next week)."

- As they become more capable, encourage the students to participate in setting up choices (or negotiate an alternative assignment, for example) whenever possible. Clear limits are especially important in such cases; you might also want to suggest that they present their ideas to you for a final okay before they act.
- If students suggest a choice that you think is inappropriate, tell them your concerns and ask if they can come up with another idea. Reiterate your criteria if necessary. If something is just plain nonnegotiable, say so and help the students look for more acceptable options.

Use Chart 12.1 or create a similar chart on a separate piece of paper to list the kinds of choices that are available to students in your classroom. Clarify the options you offer by describing the choices in the left-hand column and the limits on the right. (If you aren't offering many choices in your learning environment, use this space to describe some choices you could offer.) Take a few weeks to try out some of the choices before coming back to complete the following questions.

Chart 12.1   Available Student Choices

Choices	Limits

How many of the choices you offer relate to . . .

___ time or sequence (order of activities, when the students can do the work)?
___ location (where in the school or classroom the students can work on the activity)?
___ social preferences (choosing to work with someone, selecting a partner, working alone)?
___ content (choosing their own topics, selecting activities or topics from a given list, designing their own projects)?
___ medium of presentation (oral, written, drawn, or using computers or audio or video equipment)?
___ other?

In what ways have your students had difficulty making decisions?

What have you done or what are you doing to remedy those difficulties?

In what ways are the choices helping . . .

• to establish a win-win classroom environment (and teacher-student relationship)?

• to generate cooperation and productivity?

• to build responsibility, self-management, empowerment, and independence?

• to develop decision-making and problem-solving skills?

• to encourage win-win behaviors such as flexibility and negotiation?

• to encourage learning for learning's sake?

What other choices could you offer your students?

NOTES

1. Let me assure you, I'm not a big fan of drill-and-kill-type worksheets, and I've yet to meet successful adults who attribute their accomplishments to stacks of handouts done in school, but at this point my intention was behavioral rather than instructional. I figured I could worry about more creative and challenging assignments once the kids learned how to function independently and with a bit more self-control.

2. See the "When They Don't Like Your Choices" sidebar for a practical approach to dealing with this situation effectively.

3. Researcher Michael S. Gazzaniga, in *Mind Matters* (Boston: Houghton Mifflin, 1988, p. 205), suggests that problems can arise from our efforts to undermine people's need for power and control in their lives. "All modern experimental work points to how important for good health is the perception that an individual is in charge of his own destiny," he asserts. If we lack this sense of power—or even if we just believe that we lack this sense of power—we become susceptible to increased levels of stress and all the compensating behaviors that go with it. (From Bluestein, *Creating Emotionally Safe Schools*.)

13

The Beauty of Boundaries

One of the few concrete suggestions offered in my teacher training program encouraged us to involve the students in making the class rules. This strategy seemed to relieve any reservations I may have had about being completely in charge and responsible for creating a structure for my class and also appeared to acknowledge and accommodate the students' needs for input and control. I also believed, or at least hoped, that their contributions would magically inspire a commitment to the rules they were creating. I was wrong. Aside from killing the entire morning, this exercise did little beside producing hundreds of "don'ts," nearly a quarter of which had to do with a range of objects the students felt they should not throw in the classroom. I quickly realized that the brunt of enforcement would ultimately rest on my shoulders, and with all those rules, their list would have certainly kept me hopping, putting me more in the role of policing these children than teaching them.

Clearly, no class can succeed without some kind of structure and authority, and when we think about the ways in which we can create this kind of structure and authority, the concept of rules is likely to be the first thing to come to mind. Rules certainly are familiar, and when I started teaching, there wasn't much else available. But there was always something one-sided and authoritarian about rules and too many places where the methods and dynamics of rule making and enforcing just didn't fit in with the climate I had hoped to create. But what else was there? Was there a way for teachers to truly get what they wanted from their students without creating additional conflicts, resorting to powering, or somehow compromising the emotional climate of the classroom?

> No class can succeed without some kind of structure and authority.

Over time, I have found that rules themselves aren't the problem as much as the structure and process of *using* rules can be, especially when the rules aren't followed. When I became a teacher, I was drawn to a popular (and, at the time, fairly new) trend that referred to "punishments" as "consequences" when referring to a response to a student's misbehavior or uncooperative attitude. Although consequences were still negative, the attempt to focus on the more predictable, more related, and supposedly less hurtful or arbitrary qualities of consequences was admirable. I valued the intention to get away from using criticism, derision, humiliation, deprivation, isolation, or physical pain to manage behavior, and I appreciated the fact that the child's feelings, self-concept, and self-motivation were deliberately being considered. I also applauded the dedication to finding strategies that were less concerned with the morality of an act and less likely to dramatize the wrongness of a student.

But I still found too many similarities between the way most teachers, myself included, used negative consequences—logical though they may have been—and the way we used punishment. In most cases, the only real reframing in shifting from punishment to consequences was linguistic; in terms of energy and process, they were identical. Both options relied on negative reactions to negative behavior and most of the so-called consequences I saw teachers use had all the characteristics of the punitive behaviors we were supposedly trying to avoid.

The next shift on this conceptual journey provided the breakthrough I'd been looking for, suggesting that we start thinking in terms of *positive* outcomes, or what some might call reward orientation, where consequences became the good things that happen as a result of cooperation. I had noticed that promises (as opposed to threats)[1] were more positive, more effective, and less power oriented than rules, and that the most successful teachers were those able to ask for what they wanted with clarity, assertiveness, and great respect for the needs, preferences, and dignity of their students. Additionally, research and work in fields that included business management, child development, counseling, and addiction (family systems as well as chemical dependency) gave me a few more critical ingredients to throw in this stew. The result involved reframing rules as boundaries, and suddenly the whole process fell into place.

> I had noticed that the most successful teachers were those able to ask for what they wanted with clarity, assertiveness, and great respect for the needs, preferences, and dignity of their students.

Now I'm hardly the first person to write about boundary setting (although not all definitions include the characteristics I believe to be essential),[2] and quite frankly, the idea is, in many ways, not all that different from more common terms like limits, contingencies, or, in some ways, rules. But the energy and interaction patterns involved in this technique are quite different from those used with rules, and they're still pretty uncommon in most educational settings.

Among the hundreds of schools I've visited throughout the world, there always seemed to be the inevitable lists of Class Rules (or School Rules). In some settings, the rules were displayed in every classroom; in others, in just a handful. Some schools had imposing lists to greet students, staff, and visitors as they entered the building; others had more covert documents with formidable titles like "School Discipline Code."

Regardless of format or conveyance, these lists were invariably negative. Often the rule itself was stated negatively: "No hitting," "Don't call out," or "Eating in class is prohibited," for example. However, even when the rule was stated positively ("Turn in work on time," "Speak respectfully," or "Raise your hand to speak"), the result of an infraction was always negative. In some instances, the punishments—usually called consequences although they were generally punitive—were listed right along with the rules. Frequently, to my amusement, the list included consequences for the first infraction, the fifth infraction, the thirtieth infraction, and so forth. Okay, so maybe they didn't go up quite that high, but think about it: If you've got plans (and expectations) for second, third, fourth, or whatever occasions to catch kids doing something wrong, clearly something is not working. In many cases, the negative consequences of the first several transgressions were so inconsequential that the message to the students was clear: "You can break this rule so many times before anything serious happens to you. You don't need to change your behavior until right before then." There has to be a better way.

Characteristics of a Good Boundary

Clarity: Communicates clearly what students are being asked to do and what they get or get to do as a result of cooperating: "I'll know that you're ready for dismissal when your desks are clear." "You can receive credit for your work as long as it's on my desk by the 3:00 bell." "'Done' means complete and legible."

Win-Win: Attempts to provide some specific, meaningful, and positive outcome to students. Can accommodate students' need for power within teacher-defined limits while also accommodating the teacher's request for specific student behaviors. Communicates how students can get what they want by doing what the teacher wants: "You can sit anywhere you'd like as long as you don't block the fire exits or interfere with anyone else's learning." "You can do any ten problems on Page 83." "Do the morning activities in any order you choose." "If you need extra credit, you can create a one-minute demonstration of one of the simple machines described in Chapter 6."

Proactivity: Focuses on prevention—*before* there is a problem or before the problem gets worse. Tells students how to make their lives work for them, how to get what they want. Most effective when we can anticipate students' and teacher's needs, specific demands of a particular situation, and any possibilities for misunderstandings or mistakes: "You will be able to take new books home next week as long as you return the ones you borrow today." "You're eligible to play as long as you stay caught up in your classes." "You're welcome to listen to music during your seatwork as long as you take your headphones off when I flick the lights."

Positivity: Offers access to a positive consequence under certain conditions or after students fulfill certain requirements or responsibilities. Stated positively, as a promise emphasizing positive outcomes: "I'll read the story as long as there's no talking." "You can work on the puzzles after you finish your workbook pages." "If we finish early, you'll have time to start on your homework." "Get your report in by Friday afternoon and you can play on Saturday."

Follow-Through: Essential for boundary setting to be effective, this characteristic requires a willingness to insist on students doing what we've asked, within the constraints or requirements previously described, before allowing access to positive consequences (or before allowing access to continue). Requires *immediate* withdrawal of privilege upon any infraction of the boundary or continued withholding of desirable outcome until students change their behavior. See Chapter 14 for more information.

SOURCE: Adapted from Jane Bluestein, *The Parent's Little Book of Lists: Do's and Don'ts of Effective Parenting* (Deerfield Beach, FL: Health Communications, 1997).

A POSITIVE APPROACH

There are subtle differences, in process and focus, between encouraging cooperative behavior and discouraging uncooperative behavior. A child who is doing the work so she can have access to enrichment activities when she's done looks a whole lot like the child who's doing the work so you don't yell at her, give her detention, or call her mother. But there are significant differences in outcomes, particularly with regard to commitment and learning, not to mention stress levels, with the use of each of these approaches.

Rules and penalties depend on the students' fear of the negative consequences. If the children are afraid of bad grades, missing recess, or having their name written on the board (see sidebar), then they may do what you want, at a cost to their stress level and emotional safety. But how many kids aren't fazed by even the most severe negative consequences? (Indifference is a great tool for creating safety in an otherwise unsafe environment.) Either way, if you're committed to win-win priorities, with negatively oriented rules, you lose.

> Indifference is a great tool for creating safety in an otherwise unsafe environment.

Why Not Write Names on the Board?

Writing a child's name on the board as a negative reaction to misbehavior is so counterproductive that its popularity defies logic. When you consider the number of kids who act up for attention, and the fact that writing the name on the board actually gives *more* attention to a misbehavior, it shouldn't be much of a surprise that this technique actually reinforces misbehavior. Every time you write the child's name on the board, unless this child is absolutely desperate for teacher approval (which may decrease in an antagonistic environment), you are pretty much guaranteeing that you are going to continue to see this behavior over and over again. If you have any doubt, look at the names on the board in October. Go back later in the year and it's a fair bet that you'll see the same names. (I've often heard about classes in which students compete to see who can get their name on the board first or who can get the greatest number of checks after their name.) Additionally, many teachers as well as former students have reported that this approach creates a great deal of distractions and stress for the nonmisbehaving students, having little positive effect on the student whose name is on the board. Restructured power dynamics, improved teacher-student relationships, and more positive incentives to behave are far more effective. Please read on for details.

Boundaries do not rely on fear or power, other than the teacher's power to allow a positive consequence to occur when the students have done their part or as long as the students are behaving in positive ways. Where rules and punishments focus on what we *don't* want (negative student behavior), boundaries emphasize the more desirable alternative. This positivity represents an important characteristic of a boundary, as well as an important difference between boundaries and rules. This emphasis also requires a significant—and often difficult—shift in our thinking. Conventional wisdom has always focused on the bad thing that happens when students don't do something we want or when they do something they're not supposed to do. Getting in the habit of thinking about the *positive* outcomes that are conditionally available—that is, depending on a student's cooperation or completion of a task, for example—can present a bit of a challenge. (When the entire staff of a school complained that their students rarely did homework, I discovered that there really was no payoff for kids who did the work, other than avoiding a minus in the teachers' grade books. Although at first resistant, the teachers agreed to a simple change, and almost overnight, they saw a dramatic increase in the amount of homework kids were doing when they could earn a plus instead of avoiding a minus.)

In addition to being positive, boundaries support win-win power dynamics because they are themselves win-win. Even the most reasonable rules are oriented to the power of the adult, with information for the students about what to do to not lose. Rarely do rules communicate how students can win in any other, more positive way. Boundaries, on the other hand, are far more respectful of the desires of the students they attempt to motivate.

Additionally, boundaries are proactive, attempting to prevent problems in positive ways. Where rules typically focus on the negative or punitive reaction of the teacher (or the system) when a student gets caught, boundaries offer kids the information they need to be successful in achieving positive outcomes. The difference in focus and energy between these two processes is enormous. Both rules and boundaries can prevent misbehavior, but because the payoff to students for compliance with rules is simply avoiding a negative consequence, the process of enforcing rules becomes unavoidably reactive. (This is why simply posting a bunch of rules, penalties, or punishments before kids misbehave is proactive only in forewarning of impending reactivity!) With a boundary, a positive outcome simply does not occur until or unless the desired behavior occurs; its absence—pending cooperation—is, in most cases, the only "reaction" necessary.

The subtlety of the differences between boundaries and rules makes it easy to discount the impact each can have on the emotional climate in a classroom and the quality of the relationship between teachers and students. However, teachers who endeavored to shift from the win-lose familiarity of rules to the win-win prospects of boundaries report a significant decrease in conflicts and power struggles in their classes and far greater success in reaching kids previously deemed difficult, unmotivated, or in some instances, even dangerous, than with any strategy previously attempted. (See Chart 13.1 for a clearer picture of how rules and punishments stack up against the process of following through on boundaries.)

HOW BOUNDARIES WORK

To illustrate the way boundaries work, consider how a retail store operates. Let's say that this particular store opens at 8 a.m. and it closes at midnight. Now, these hours act as a boundary: Get to the store between these hours and you can shop; get there after midnight and you'll probably find that the doors are locked. There won't be anyone out front to ask you for your excuse or to lecture you about being more responsible. The store is closed. And it stays closed—even if you have a good excuse—not to teach you a lesson, not to punish you for being late, but simply because it's after midnight. There's nothing personal, punitive, or vindictive going on here. It's a safe bet that the next time you want to go to this store, you will probably make different, more constructive choices, and this will happen without anyone ever yelling at you, giving you detention, or calling your mother. This is how good boundaries operate. The process works just as effectively in a school setting as it routinely does in the "real world."

Boundaries can help us meet the child's needs for power and control within limits that protect others. They can also create a sense of safety, structure, and predictability in our classrooms, and they are a terrific way to increase student accountability. Since boundaries convey the conditions under which a positive consequence is available to a student, the lack of this desirable outcome is directly related to the student's misbehavior, lack of cooperation, or failure to meet the conditions specified. The students get credit, advance academically, or have access to a privilege *only* when their behavior warrants these outcomes. Boundaries are not structured either to hurt the student or bring satisfaction or revenge to the teacher. They can minimize power struggles because they come from the desire to protect everyone's needs and safety—not from the teacher's power. And boundaries are far less likely than punishments or negative consequences to create resentment, hostility, and resistance, or fuel power struggles or further disruptions.

Chart 13.1 Options for Following Through

Rules and Punishment	Boundaries and Follow-Through
Win-lose.	Win-win.
Power-oriented.	Interaction-oriented.
Goal: Punish negative behavior; apply negative consequences to shame student, teach student a lesson, make student lose.	Goal: Encourage positive behavior; give incentives for cooperation; also to stop destructive or disruptive behavior and reestablish positive behavior, encourage student self-correction; build commitment to cooperation.
Operates by exacting payment or penalty which, once served, does not obligate student to change behavior (instead, encourages to avoid further punishment).	Operates by allowing positive consequences (meaningful outcomes) for cooperation, work completion.
Result of teacher's power, getting caught.	Result of students' choices and uncooperative behavior.
Rarely related to the problem behavior.	Directly, specifically related to negative behavior (and loss of previously established privilege).
Equates student with behavior; attacks person.	Separates student from behavior, deals with behavior.
Related to worth of student; both behavior and student are wrong or unacceptable.	Unrelated to student's worth, only behavior is a problem (student is still acceptable).
Judgmental, focus on morality of behavior.	Objective focus on outcome or effect of behavior.
Arbitrary, often comes as a surprise; often no limits (or unclear or ambiguous limits) are set beforehand	Logical, predictable; limits, requirements, and outcomes established beforehand.
Teacher is responsible for correcting negative student behavior.	Student is responsible for correcting negative behavior.
Teacher role: Setting and expressing rules; policing, catching, blaming, disempowering; exacting penalties for misbehavior (application of negative consequences).	Teacher role: Setting and communicating limits, intervention, facilitating student processing; removing or withholding positive consequences until desired behavior appears.
Lesson: avoid power, invites students to get sneakier.	Lesson: personal responsibility; invites students to change behavior.
Conflict resolution model: force, hurt, deprive, threaten.	Conflict resolution model: negotiation, compromise; mutual respect.
Outcome oriented.	Process oriented.

Rules and Punishment	Boundaries and Follow-Through
High cost to students' feelings, dignity, sense of control.	Protects students' feelings, dignity, sense of control.
High cost to teacher-student relationship.	Does not violate teacher-student relationship.
Students may respond with hostility, aggressiveness, rebelliousness; can create additional conflict.	Students more likely to respond with cooperation; can avoid additional conflict.
Teacher may experience anger, disappointment, resentment, vengeance.	Teacher can remain neutral, calm, and accepting of student; may get angry but generally the experience is less stressful to all involved.
Need fulfilling to teacher, focus on teacher's need.	Need fulfilling to student and teacher.
Message to student: How can you avoid what you don't want?	Message to student: How can we both get what we want?
Focus: What do I do when a student misbehaves?	Focus: What do I do to encourage cooperation and commitment?
Punishment often maintained even after negative behavior stops.	Negative consequences (absence of positive consequences) usually discontinue once student chooses more positive behavior.

SOURCE: Adapted from Jane Bluestein and Lynn Collins, *Parents in a Pressure Cooker* (Rosemont, NJ: Modern Learning Press, 1989).

If I haven't sold you yet on the benefit of using boundaries (that is, offering positive outcomes instead of negative or punitive ones), consider the following: Boundaries allow teachers to achieve the same immediate objective as the threat of a negative outcome, but they also provide students with access to processing and problem-solving steps that are generally not available in a penalty-based system. Therefore, boundaries reinforce for the student the relationship between his or her behavior

> Boundaries allow teachers to achieve the same immediate objective as the threat of a negative outcome. . . .

choices and their consequences—good and bad. As is often the case with process-oriented strategies, boundaries may take a little longer to achieve long-term goals like building accountability, decision-making skills, and a commitment to more constructive or cooperative student behavior.

Additionally, boundaries focus exclusively on the behavior, not the worth of the student. The students are still acceptable, valued, and welcome in class, even if their behavior is not. Neither previous behavior nor personality traits are factors, nor are the teacher's feelings about a student. While the positive consequences promised by a boundary are conditional, the teacher's caring and acceptance are not. Boundaries allow us to respond constructively to student misconduct (withdrawing or withholding the positive outcome) and still maintain our win-win intentions.[3]

But there's more to boundary setting than simply communicating in positive ways the connection between what the teacher wants and what the student wants. The key to making boundaries work—indeed the only way they *will* work—is with good follow-through. Follow-through is the part of the process that puts the authority in win-win authority relationships, establishes our credibility, creates the sense of safety and predictability students need, and most effectively gets us the commitment and cooperation we want. Let's see how the process works.

MAKING BOUNDARIES WORK FOR YOU (AND YOUR STUDENTS)

The more positive choices and consequences that are available in a classroom, the more the students have to lose when they do not cooperate. Teachers who use boundaries in a reward-oriented environment typically confront far fewer problems and see less resistance, negativity, or irresponsibility than teachers who rely on more traditional punitive approaches. Because the conditional availability of a desirable activity or privilege rests on cooperative choices, boundaries offer us a tool not just for motivating kids but also for reinforcing cooperation (as well as the connection between positive student choices and the resulting positive outcomes). Further, when conflicts, disruptions, or off-task behaviors occur, boundaries also offer a powerful tool for intervening without creating additional stress, simply by withholding or withdrawing the positive outcome until the kids demonstrate the desired behavior.

In the classroom, as in real life, any time we have a negative consequence available, a positive consequence is surely lurking nearby. If a child can't take out another library book until he brings back the one he has at home, it is equally true that he *can* take another book out *as soon as* he brings the other book back. Now I know this may sound like splitting hairs, but changing our emphasis from the negative to the positive outcome represents a major shift in the energy dynamics in an authority relationship. Not only does it invite cooperation and reduce resistance and opposition, but also—and this is the best part—focusing on the positive outcome puts all the responsibility back on the student!

For example, let's say we want our students to remember to put all the game pieces back in the box before they leave the work area. We can state this boundary by threatening, "If you don't put everything in the box, I'm taking it out of the center." Although this response may be perfectly reasonable and logical, we can restate the exact same contingency with a promise instead: "If you put all the game pieces back in the box, I will leave it in the center." In both cases, we give the same basic message, connecting the consequence of their cooperation to the privilege of the game's continual availability. Although the threat of having the game removed is clearly implied in the promise to leave the box in the center, by shifting our emphasis to the positive consequences of the students putting all the game pieces away properly, the implication of teacher control and responsibility is sharply reduced. In the first example, the game's presence in the center is a function of the teacher's power; in the second, it becomes a positive consequence of the student's cooperation.

The difference is subtle, but this shift gives teachers a powerful tool for making students accountable for their behavior. For example, one middle school teacher reported that her students were disturbed when she changed her boundary from "If you're not quiet in the next ten seconds, you're not watching the video," to "You can watch the show as soon as you get quiet. This offer is good for ten seconds." Although the tone and presentation were far more respectful, one student explained her classmates' dismay at the change: "Now if we miss the video, we can't blame *you*."

In a reward-oriented classroom, a negative consequence typically refers to the lack or removal of a positive consequence. Whether we ask students to split up and sit elsewhere when their talking becomes disruptive, withhold credit for work that isn't completed or turned in on time, or turn off the movie when students start talking, we make it clear that the good stuff is available only on those terms previously announced. (This is the proactive part of the boundary. If we haven't set up the contingency beforehand and simply react to misbehavior, the "gotcha" response becomes punitive.)[4]

> In a reward-oriented classroom, a negative consequence typically refers to the lack or removal of a positive consequence.

Feedback from hundreds of teachers (as well as my own observations) strongly suggests that schools that have the greatest number of rules often have the greatest number of misbehaviors. It seems that the more behaviors we try to control, the more kids have to rebel against. And regardless of the rationalizations for insisting that students not talk in the lunchroom, leave their Ninja stars at home, or "walk on the blue line with their hands at their sides, eyes forward, and mouths shut,"[5] the more we try to micromanage kids' lives and behaviors, the fewer opportunities they have to learn to manage themselves. (I've worked with teachers who are charged with measuring the designs on students' tee shirts to make sure that they fit within a three-inch-square limit. Is this really the best use of our time and professional talents?) I urge educators to examine the rules they have in place and instead of relying on rules and punishments to establish order, to look for ways to create a sense of community that nurtures consideration and self-control.

So yes, we absolutely need structure. But in my search for effective ways to create structure and good management techniques, the effectiveness of boundaries—for generating cooperation, building responsibility and self-management, and encouraging strong, solid relationships between teachers and kids—is consistently far greater than anything I've observed that relied on the use of negative consequences as deterrents.

BUILDING INDEPENDENCE WITH BOUNDARIES

Boundaries can also be enormously effective with needy kids who aren't exactly disruptive but demand a great deal of your time and energy. How often, in the course of your day, do you find a student at your elbow with some problem or another: "What are we supposed to do?" "My dog ate my homework." "Alex is bothering me." "I can't find the paste." Regardless of the age of the student—and, by the way, I have heard various versions of these examples at all grade levels—boundaries are ideal for helping us manage situations like these.

Our students' lives can seem pretty cluttered at times with problems that, they will try to convince us, require our help. These interactions can be rather distracting: They eat up a lot of valuable instructional time although they can usually be resolved without our intervention. Yet there these kids are, wanting our time and attention, maybe just for the sake of sharing and social contact, or perhaps looking for acknowledgement and validation. Some are just killing time or getting attention, although some kids—especially good order takers—honestly feel incapable or powerless in facing even the simplest dilemma.

A student experiencing a crisis does need our help. Traumas involving abuse, neglect, divorce, or death usually require more support than a classroom teacher is able to provide. Clearly, these instances should be referred for outside intervention, although our support and understanding can provide tremendous solace.[6] Fortunately, however, most of the drama affecting our students on a day-to-day basis is more likely to involve complaints such as "She looked at me!" or "Somebody stole my pencil." When students bring problems to the classroom and are unable or unwilling to solve them on their own, their problems can very quickly become *our* problem. At any grade level, teacher dependence and a student's need for attention can become a never-ending distraction, one that will eventually erode even our deepest desire to be needed. For our mental health and the needs of the other students, we need to prevent student problems from interfering with teaching, learning, and the overall operations of the classroom. How do we put the responsibility for students' problems back on their shoulders—without ignoring or abandoning them—when these problems do come up?

As a teacher in a multiage primary classroom, Mr. Marshall was plagued by one first grader he privately dubbed his shadow. No matter where Mr. Marshall went—in or out of the classroom—it seemed that Shadow was never far behind. Shadow didn't need much time, he was just always there. Now, although the student's need for attention is certainly the student's problem, his inability to meet that need without making continual demands on the teacher invites joint ownership of the problem. Had Mr. Marshall been exclusively concerned with his own needs, he might have been able to win by isolating the student in some way. Had his concerns been only for the student's needs, Mr. Marshall could have completely relinquished his own requirements for privacy and time with other students to devote his attention to Shadow. But Mr. Marshall came up with a win-win solution—a boundary that not only acknowledged the student's need for his time, help, and attention, but also set limits that would protect the teacher's own needs as well.[7]

He approached Shadow with five paper clips and a plan: "I understand that you need to talk to me during the day and I really enjoy visiting with you. And you know, sometimes I spend so much time with you that I don't get to talk to the other students and I don't get my work done. What I'd like to do is to give you these five paper clips. Put them on your belt, okay?

Now whenever you want to talk to me, it'll cost you one paper clip. These need to last until recess. I'll give you five more afterward to last until lunch and more for the afternoon. As long as you have a paper clip, I'll be happy to take the time out to talk to you. Once the clips are gone, you'll have to wait until after recess to get some more."

Of course, on the first go-round, it didn't take too long for the paper clips to disappear. Mr. Marshall knew it would be a very long time until recess came and that his follow-through during that stretch would be essential. Being out of paper clips didn't slow Shadow down a bit, but Mr. Marshall's reaction did.

On the first five visits, Mr. Marshall excused himself from the group he was teaching, held out his hand for a paper clip, and then gave his full attention to Shadow. On the sixth visit, Mr. Marshall simply said, "Let's talk at recess." He then turned around and continued with what he had been doing. He did not say another word. If Shadow persisted, so did his teacher, firmly, politely, never once giving Shadow the impression that he was angry or didn't care. This was not a moral victory but simply a matter of everyone's rights being protected.

> This was not a moral victory but simply a matter of everyone's rights being protected.

In a traditional, win-lose classroom, most of us deal with attention-getting behavior somewhat reactively. (How many teachers, unwilling to set a boundary for fear of hurting a child's feelings, will blow up at the child after three or four interruptions?) Mr. Marshall's request had all the characteristics of a well-stated boundary. It was proactive, communicating the limits and payoffs before Shadow had a chance to take up all his time again. It was stated positively, promising five opportunities for Shadow to get the attention he wanted. It was clear, having a tangible and finite number of paper clips on his belt and a specific time limit (until recess). It was win-win, allowing both student and teacher to get what they wanted. And because Mr. Marshall had the courage to kindly and firmly follow through, it worked. The teacher did not need to yell or punish—which, incidentally, would have fed Shadow's desire for attention, negative though it would have been; he simply needed to maintain his boundary.

Suddenly, Shadow had to determine the importance of his questions and decide if Mr. Marshall was the only person who could help him. He was somewhat more selective with his use of the five late-morning paper clips, even more so by the end of the day. By the end of the week, he was down from twenty to ten clips a day; within a few days, he had been weaned from the paper clips—and his need for Mr. Marshall's constant attention—having become more capable of solving real problems on his own (or with the help of a classmate). He became more sensitive to Mr. Marshall's needs, as well as the other students' needs for the teacher's attention, and made genuine attempts to avoid interrupting—not bad for a six-year-old!

In a terrific example of how these processes can be adapted for other age groups, I heard from a high school teacher who employed the paper clip strategy to contain the number of questions she would typically get from kids during a test. She distributed the tests with two designer paper clips attached to each one. She explained that the students could trade in their paper clips for one question each. Even some of her seniors, she reported, spent much of the period heading to her desk, then turning around after scanning their test papers and finding things further down the page that might really need further explanation. What a great way to teach kids to manage their resources—a skill that can serve them throughout their lives.

In each of these examples, the key to the teachers' success was their willingness to follow through. Of all the characteristics of good boundaries, this is the one that most consistently challenges people who work (or live) with children. The following chapter examines where we drop the ball—as well as some practical alternatives, all in the name of making boundaries work.

How Boundaries Work

- Boundaries allow teachers to express limits and to communicate the conditions or availability of certain privileges students desire.
- Boundaries prevent conflict and build win-win power structures. They help teachers assert their authority while attempting to accommodate their students' needs or desires as well.
- Boundaries build a reward-oriented classroom environment. They emphasize positive consequences—desirable outcomes available with cooperation.
- Boundaries create less stress and fewer power struggles than rules and demands, which are typically win-lose and often focus on punishments or negative outcomes for noncompliance.

(Continued)

(Continued)

- Boundaries build mutual consideration and respect and do not threaten or violate students' emotional safety.
- Boundaries do not rely on the fear of teachers' reactions (such as anger or disapproval) to help teachers get what they want.
- Boundaries allow positive and negative consequences to occur in a nonpunitive environment (negative consequences simply being the absence of positive consequences).
- Boundaries build student responsibility and accountability, as long as teachers allow only positive consequences to occur when students have done their part.
- Boundaries invite students to change their behavior in order to get their needs met. While rules or threats emphasize the penalties for misbehavior, boundaries focus on the ability to make more constructive choices.
- Boundaries offer students a model for assertiveness and a tool to help them stick up for themselves in their dealings with their friends and other students.

SOURCE: Adapted from Jane Bluestein, *The Parent's Little Book of Lists: Do's and Don'ts of Effective Parenting* (Deerfield Beach, FL: Health Communications, 1997).

Activity

Following are several scenarios. For each, think through what you want the students to be doing and what your needs are; specify these as your objective. Then identify what the student wants (or wants to avoid) in each situation. Finally, develop a powering response, a permissive response, and a win-win or cooperative response (a boundary, stated as a promise). To construct a boundary, consider the positive outcomes available or possible in your classroom. Write the responses as quotations.

Lamont and David want to sit together during independent work time.

Objective:

Student needs:

Powering response:

Permissive response:

Cooperative response (boundary):

You've assigned three worksheets but your students would prefer to work on the word search puzzle they got in another class earlier today.

Objective:

Student needs:

Powering response:

Permissive response:

Cooperative response (boundary):

Adrian spent the entire library period absorbed in a new adventure book. At the end of class, she pleads with you to allow her to check out the book so she can finish it at home. Adrian has not returned the books she borrowed four weeks ago.

Objective:

Student needs:

Powering response:

Permissive response:

Cooperative response (boundary):

Your sixth period class never seems to get to your room by the time the bell rings. You always have to wait a few minutes for the stragglers to show up.

Objective (what you want, your needs):

Student needs:

Powering response:

Permissive response:

Cooperative response (boundary):

NOTES

1. Please note: I have had some people take this suggestion literally and want to point out that I am not referring to using the word promise *in* a threat: "I promise you, if you don't. . . ." The term *promise* refers to a shift from using the threat of a negative consequence to the promise of a positive outcome for behaving according to certain conditions or on completion of a task. In this sense, I have found promises far more effective and less destructive than threats.

2. See "Characteristics of a Good Boundary" sidebar.

3. See chart titled "Options for Following Through" at the end of this section for a comparison of the benefits of using boundaries with positive consequences (and good follow-through) instead of rules and punishments (or more negatively oriented consequences).

4. The next chapter talks about adding or changing a boundary if unanticipated student behavior becomes a problem.

5. These, by the way, are actual rules as recently shared by teachers and students. I can certainly understand how these and other rules evolved, and by questioning them, do not think for a second that I'm advocating for their exact opposite (chaos in the cafeteria or halls, for example, or any form of weapons in school). That would be some serious all-or-nothing thinking! But I have to wonder how long a list of rules must be if it includes a ban on Ninja stars (or how many kids would have thought to bring one to school had the rules not included them on the list). I also think kids will have more respect for the limits we establish when these limits make sense to them and respect their intelligence.

6. See Chapter 22 for more information on supporting kids in crisis. Additionally, Kendall Johnson's book, *Trauma in the Lives of Children: Crisis and Stress Management for Counselors, Teachers, and Other Professionals*, 2nd ed. (Alameda, CA: Hunter House Publishing, 1998), and William C. Kroen's *Helping Children Cope With the Loss of a Loved One: A Guide for Grownups* (Minneapolis: Free Spirit Publishing, 1996), provide some outstanding guidelines for helping students deal with crisis and traumatic events in their lives.

7. Mr. Marshall also discussed his intentions with his administrator, support staff, and Shadow's parents. Additionally, he devoted some class time to helping his students develop a number of problem-solving skills and social interaction competencies, topics I address in later chapters.

14

Following Through

When it comes to student behavior, "What do I do when. . . ?" may well be the most persistent question I encounter. The difficulty in overcoming a win-lose, reactive orientation to undesirable behavior is evident in the impatience I occasionally encounter: Even teachers intrigued by the idea of preventing discipline problems often can't get past the notion that misbehavior must be countered by a negative adult response. I once spent five intensive days teaching a graduate class that emphasized the proactive principles and strategies of The Win-Win Classroom. On the last day, a man in the class was still not sold: "Yeah, yeah. . . . Relationships. Prevention. Win-win. That sounds nice and all, but what do I do when one of my kids throws a chair at me?"

I thought for a second: "Duck?"

Now I honestly wasn't trying to be glib. I simply didn't know. Put me in a situation where I've got furniture coming at me and I slip into survival mode just like everybody else. But this isn't about what to do when a child throws a chair. The whole point of this process is to develop an environment in which it would never *occur* to children to throw chairs, either because they had other, more constructive outlets for their anger and frustration or because prior needs—for example, for power or attention—had been adequately accommodated beforehand. An extreme outburst can be a rare and isolated incident in even the healthiest environment, but more often than not, this type of behavior is a pretty good indication that the relationships and power dynamics in that classroom need some work.

> An extreme outburst can be a rare and isolated incident in even the healthiest environment, but . . . the relationships and power dynamics in that classroom need some work.

If things have gotten to the point where you have a student-initiated projectile sailing toward your head, you don't have time to determine the most effective win-win strategies; your only recourse is to take whatever action is necessary to avoid injury. Higher level needs will always take a back seat to more basic demands, and there are few things more basic than protecting one's physical safety. Unfortunately, functioning at a survival level takes a tremendous toll on relationships and emotional well-being, not to mention learning.

Teachers who encounter a great deal of resistance, rebellion, or aggression from their students can either devote their energies to containing or suppressing these behaviors (which often includes escalating measures of reactivity and disempowerment) or to improving the quality of our relationships with our students. Now this latter option takes longer, requires more work, and a greater degree of consciousness, deliberateness, awareness, and commitment on the part of the teacher than simply reacting. Restructuring relationships and reconfiguring power dynamics also require a willingness to change—to adopt different behaviors, attitudes, and even language patterns—in the way we interact with kids. Is it any wonder that so many of us are willing to look for a quick fix to bail us out when something disruptive occurs? I can certainly understand why so many discipline programs that promise magic solutions with simplistic formulas and procedures for reacting to misbehaviors are so attractive and popular—and ultimately disappointing. But I'm guessing that if you've made it this far you're looking for something beyond survival and that you're not just searching for reactions and strategies that allow you to win at all costs.[1]

WHEN WE HAVE TO INTERVENE

Unfortunately, we can devote our entire teaching existence to developing positive interactions and win-win dynamics and still, on occasion, have to deal with disruptions from time to time. Negative behavior can occur in any classroom. However, because of the interactive footwork and relationship dynamics previously established, these incidents are handled quite differently in a win-win environment than in the autocratic classroom of past decades. Let's look at a fairly simple example of disruptive behavior and several different ways we can approach the problem.

Imagine that Jamie and Nicholas are fighting over who gets to read a particular book first. Both are pulling on the book and shouting at one another, creating an uproar in the classroom. Students are being distracted from their work, the teacher is unable to continue the lesson, and who knows what's happening to the book.

Now, there are a number of possible teacher responses to this conflict behavior. For example, a teacher might get up and burst out, "What's wrong with you two? Put that book down and get to your seats! You'll both be in after school to write a few pages on how you are supposed to behave in class." Understandable though this may be, other than possibly restoring quiet, the only real benefit of this win-lose technique is that it might protect the book. This is a punitive response that teaches more about the teacher's power than about effective ways to share books or resolve conflicts. The teacher has taken responsibility for the misbehavior; the students have learned nothing about negotiating or problem solving. Chances are the next time they run into a similar conflict, they will attempt the same approach, only a little less publicly so they don't get caught.

> This is a punitive response that teaches more about the teacher's power than about effective ways to share books or resolve conflicts.

As an alternative, the teacher might also go over and take the book from the students, saying, "That's going to damage this book. Here, Jamie, you take it until lunchtime. Nicholas, you can have it for the rest of the afternoon." The fact that the teacher does not personally attack the students will certainly make this response seem a bit more attractive than the previous example, but there is still no opportunity for the students to learn self-management from this conflict. Again, the book is safe and the fight has been broken up, but at what cost?

The teacher has absorbed the responsibility of solving the problem; however, in this example, the solution is arbitrary and seems to punish one child while rewarding the other. The conflict has not been satisfactorily resolved in the students' minds—even for the student who got the book (and has probably lost interest by this point). The teacher's intervention can actually escalate the negative feelings generated in the original argument. There has been no opportunity for negotiation and problem solving; in fact, the teacher's behavior reinforces dependence and helplessness by repeating a pattern in which conflicts are solved by someone else.

> The teacher's behavior reinforces dependence and helplessness by repeating a pattern in which conflicts are solved by someone else.

As another option, the teacher might take the book away and ask, "Okay, what's going on here? Who started this?" Now it might seem logical that if we can just determine how this problem started and why it's happening, we can make the most impartial judgment. But beware of this temptation to jump into disagreements between kids. For one thing, the involvement can be incredibly tedious, time-consuming, and unproductive. For another, asking for background—especially with the intention of collecting data so that we can solve the problem, puts all that responsibility on our shoulders. Most of the time, what's really at the heart of this approach is a desire to assign blame and punishment, which reinforces teacher power and compromises emotional safety.

So how can we protect the book and get the noise to subside? Perhaps a more effective approach might sound like the following: "Stop! Books are not for pulling! Please put that on my desk until you can decide how it will be shared."[2] For an even greater chance of success, we might also remind that resolving the problem means talking—not yelling or hitting—and that neither the process nor the actual solution can create problems for others.

This approach offers quite a few benefits. The teacher has attacked the problem without attacking the students, without dredging up judgments about personalities or past misdeeds, and without lecturing or arguing. In addition, the teacher left responsibility for solving the problem with the ones who had created it. True, absolute silence had not been restored, but then, interpersonal problems don't generally get sorted out in silence.

This approach also does not guarantee immediate quiet and harmony: the teacher allowed the conflict to continue, but by setting limits and using a boundary to explain how the students could have what they wanted (access to the book), the kids also had a chance to engage in a process of resolving a conflict without disturbing anyone else.[3] The only misbehavior addressed was the argument over the book, and the only consequence of the misbehavior was the removal of the object both students desired until a solution could be reached. There is no need for blaming, punishing, or making anyone wrong, so the worth of the students, the value of their feelings, and the importance of their needs have been respected.

WHAT'S WRONG WITH WARNINGS AND REMINDERS?

The rule of thumb for setting boundaries is this: If we aren't willing to follow through, we don't bother setting the boundary in the first place. Yet most teachers admit to having a pretty poor track record when it comes to following through. Obviously, we want to avoid putting our students in the position of having to miss out on desirable outcomes or suffer for accidents, slips, or mistakes in judgment. But we can provide every opportunity for each student to make cooperative choices and there will still be incidents these measures fail to prevent. Then it's time for following through.

Some of the biggest roadblocks we face in our attempts to follow through are built right into the system, or at least heavily supported by tradition. If we state that a privilege is available only under certain conditions, once a student has violated these conditions, the situation must change in order for the negative behavior to stop (or for a more positive behavior to appear). Unfortunately, there is often a great deal of time between the misconduct and the removal of a privilege or positive consequence, as we tend, instead, to fill the gap with inconsequential responses, such as warnings and reminders.

In addition to being colossal time wasters, warnings undermine a teacher's credibility. (Why respect a boundary if you can get away with ignoring it several times?) Warnings also communicate a great deal of inconsistency: We tend to be fairly arbitrary in our use of warnings as well as the number of warnings we're willing to give students before we really let them have it. This response may come at any time (after maybe four or five reminders on a good day, after one or two if we're a bit more irritable) and is nearly always critical and threatening. When we get in the habit of giving reminders after or during a misbehavior, we are, in essence, undermining our authority by devaluing the limits we place on the privileges we offer, inviting the students to not take them seriously.

Additionally, by giving warnings, we're also removing the power from the boundary itself and putting it back in our laps. When the loss of privilege occurs immediately, the first time the misbehavior occurs, it is a function of the student's uncooperative behavior choices; delayed by warnings, it becomes a function of the teacher's power. Additionally, we compromise emotional safety, partly because of the absence of predictability and partly because, when the warnings don't work, we usually blow up, reacting out of anger and frustration.

Not all warnings are verbal. Frowning, finger wagging, or writing a student's name on the board simply delay a meaningful consequence from occurring. As with verbal warnings, these teacher behaviors do little besides drawing attention to the misbehavior—which actually ends up reinforcing what we're trying to stop. In addition, warnings rarely work because they don't prevent or interrupt access to a positive consequence—the students can continue to sit together, watch the movie, or take home another library book anyhow. Where is their incentive to change their behavior? In nearly all instances (except those, perhaps, involving the most diligent teacher pleasers), continuing the negative behavior will always be more need fulfilling than avoiding Teacher's dirty looks.

Warnings seem convenient to us because it's actually easier to tell someone not to do something again and again than it is to actually intervene and withdraw a privilege. Warnings may seem generous and kind, and for a while they do protect children from experiencing the negative outcomes of their own behaviors. But this is exactly the long-range result we're trying to avoid. This interference is called enabling; by protecting students from negative outcomes, we not only fail in our obligation to hold them accountable for their behavior but we also sabotage our authority as well. Giving warnings or reminders by restating a boundary before there is a problem is completely legitimate and will help prevent many problems. However, once a disruption, violation, or instance of forgetfulness occurs, the immediate and unequivocal removal of a privilege makes quite clear our willingness to insist that the terms of our boundaries be respected in the future.

NO MORE EXCUSES!

Other time wasters include lecturing about the importance of cooperation, asking the student to repeat the rules, bringing up previous failures, engaging in discussions or arguments about the fairness of a consequence, or bringing in our own feelings of disappointment or frustration. Closely related is the tendency to ask the student why he doesn't have his homework, why he forgot his pencil, or why Lamont was bothering him. Asking why is a common response that seems harmless, even constructive, but it also engages us in the students' problems. The question invites excuses, implying that if the student is creative or pathetic enough, he's off the hook. Excuses invite the arbitrary use of teacher power and acceptance—"Impress me and maybe I'll let you out of your responsibility." More often than not, the student's response will evoke negative teacher reactions, because the excuse can also provide ammunition for criticisms, lectures, or attacks.

If you have a boundary or a policy about homework, does it really matter whether Alfred doesn't have his because "a tornado took it out of my lunch box" or because he felt like watching TV instead? Does he no longer need to turn it in? Asking why suggests that your limits are limits only if students can't find a loophole. There's no reason to respect a boundary you can talk your way out of. Plus, asking why puts us in a position of having to judge the validity of an excuse, which can be

> When we intend to follow through on our boundaries, "why" doesn't matter, even in the most extreme cases.

very arbitrary. I've also seen teachers become rather resentful when a student comes up with an extremely compelling story, which puts the adult in the position of having to relax boundaries in order to not seem like a completely unreasonable human being. However, when we intend to follow through on our boundaries, "why" doesn't matter, even in the most extreme cases.

A high school teacher once told me a rather dramatic story about one of her third-period English students. A typically reliable senior, he came in early and told her that he didn't have his assignment ready to turn in that period. Instead of asking why, the teacher simply repeated her homework policy: "As long as it's on my desk by the time the three o'clock dismissal bells rings, you can still get full credit for it."

The student countered, "No! You don't understand! I did my homework last night. I did all my assignments. I put everything out in the car before I went to bed so I'd be organized when I got up. Well, my father got drunk again last night and took my car after I went to bed and didn't come home. I don't have any of my stuff with me today."

The teacher responded, "I have three things I want to tell you. First, I want to assure you that you are in no way responsible for your father's drinking.[4] Second, I want to tell you that you are in no way responsible for what your father does when he drinks. And third, I want to tell you that you are responsible for the assignments you get in this class. If you want credit for this one, it needs to be on my desk by the time the three o'clock bell rings."

The student was stunned. "That's not fair," he protested. "I'm not doing it again."

The teacher responded, "I understand. I want you to know that I respect whatever you decide to do about this assignment. You have until three o'clock to change your mind."

This is a superb example of how possible it is to be completely supportive, loving, and unconditionally accepting even while maintaining our boundaries. I applaud the courage this teacher exhibited in not succumbing to a very convincing, reasonable, and, by all accounts, true story. Don't imagine that this experience didn't cause her many hours of soul searching, either. But by the end of the day, she was convinced that she had done the right thing, for at about five minutes before the deadline, the young man came in with his paper done over.

"It's not as good as the first one," he confessed.

"That doesn't matter," the teacher responded. "A hundred years from now, nobody's going to remember this paper. But for the moment, there are bigger things at stake here, not the least of which is the fact that you're living with someone who can make your life pretty complicated, even if it's not on purpose. Have you given any thought to how you can take care of yourself in the future?"

"Yeah," he answered. "I'm gonna keep all my stuff in my room from now on in. He won't mess with it in there."

"Sounds like a plan," she concurred.

There are many times in life when "why" won't matter: The IRS doesn't care why your income taxes are late. The store won't reopen, the movie won't start over, and the restaurant won't serve you a meal after closing time—no matter how good your excuses are for not getting there on time. Look at the learning that took place when this teacher had the courage to maintain her boundaries. Compare the message this student would have received had this teacher arbitrarily decided that her policies didn't apply in this case, to the learning that occurred when she held fast. Here was a wonderful opportunity to see the extent of his accountability and to learn to fulfill his responsibilities rather than fix blame (or be a victim), an opportunity that would have been lost had this teacher not followed through.

FOLLOWING THROUGH

When we have done as much as we reasonably can to make success possible and the student still makes a noncooperative choice, it will take a great deal of courage, commitment, and consistency to allow students to encounter the negative consequences of their behaviors. If a child forgets his permission slip, he misses the outing. If she breaks or spills something in the classroom, she fixes, replaces, cleans up, or works off the damages—whether the damage was done accidentally or in anger. If he can't control his urge to splash in the paint center, he has to play somewhere else for that period (or day).

It may seem cruel to refuse to buy a student a meal the fourth time he forgets to bring in his lunch money (even if you told him last time that he'd reached his credit limit), but for the sake of the child's growth toward responsible adulthood, there is no more loving response. Unless a student's life, health, or safety are threatened, being allowed to regularly experience the connection between her behavior and the outcomes of her behavior encourages alternatives to blaming, helplessness, and irresponsibility, and also assists the student in making more positive choices down the road.

Now, before you accuse me of being completely heartless, let me suggest that there are ways to build flexibility into your boundaries proactively without arbitrarily relaxing limits when your students have a convincing story or happen to catch you on a particu-

> There are ways to build flexibility into your boundaries proactively without arbitrarily relaxing limits. . . .

larly compassionate day. Setting a blanket grace period or offering almost-full credit for work handed in a day late can accommodate students with more serious excuses as well as those who simply didn't bother. Some teachers count only a percentage of the work due, say 32 out of 35 assignments, giving students three assignments they can "forget" for whatever reasons or perhaps do for additional credit, even if those extra assignments are turned in late. Some teachers let students earn a night off when they've turned in homework complete and on time for ten days in a row. Others offer to drop each student's lowest grade. A teacher in a high school with a large gang population was able to boost the number of homework assignments he received when he simply stopped requiring them and offered extra credit for any assignment the kids turned in. "We went from ten percent of the class doing homework to eighty-five percent," he said. Another teacher gave all 160 of his students a "Get Out of Jail Free" card, which could be used once a semester to get out of anything except a test. If children didn't do their homework and turned in the card (or simply said they needed to use the card, in case it had been lost), they got full credit; if the card had already been used, no credit was available, regardless of the excuse.[5]

Following through on a previously announced boundary is a pretty straightforward affair. As always, actions speak louder than words, so keep words to a minimum and let the actions speak for themselves. Announce, "I will continue reading this story as soon as it gets quiet. That offer is good for ten seconds." Then act—waiting, sitting quietly, with a neutral (not angry) facial expression. Fight the urge to repeat the announcement or embellish it with any further discussion. Either one will sound as if you're trying to talk the kids into doing what you want. Your silent and explicit refusal to read over their conversation is far more powerful, and convincing, than anything you might say.

And even *that* may not get them quiet (although I've seen this approach work in all grade levels once the kids have figured out that teacher-staring-at-watch signals something worth their attention). Students will always choose the more need fulfilling option, and in this instance, will cooperate only if their need to hear the story overrides their need to chatter.[6] If the uncooperative behavior persists, it's time to close the book and get on with the day: "Please take your seats and get your spelling folders out. Let's finish this story tomorrow (or later)," using the same neutral tone as that used for expressing the boundary in the first place.

Now look at what you've accomplished. You've asserted your need for quiet attention when you read. You've connected their choices (talking) to a consequence (not getting to hear the rest of the story), one that has nothing to do with your patience, approval, or feelings. You have not expressed anger, nor have you criticized the students. You've kept your blood pressure down. You've reinforced the conditions that allow the privilege of hearing you read without using power or force. You've helped them learn that different choices bring different outcomes without suggesting that anyone is bad, stupid, or even wrong. And you've also left the door open for them to try again at another time.

But what about those situations in which only one or two students are disrupting the reading? Let's say you've gone out of your way to allow them to choose where to sit or have offered to allow them to play with a beanbag or read along with you from their own books or say, a digital presentation.[7] You've selected something they would normally find really interesting. That being said, you can take every precaution and still have children talking or acting up. If we've said that we'll read only while there's no talking, it doesn't matter if there's only one student talking or thirty. We close the book and move on to something else. (Reassure the students: "We'll try again later.") Teachers who are consistent in following through report that even very young students will exert pressure on one another—for the benefit of the group—for everyone to settle down quickly. Once the boundary is expressed, the responsibility for hearing the story in these classrooms is completely out of the teacher's hands.

> Teachers who are consistent in following through report that even very young students will exert pressure on one another. . . .

And what about those situations in which we can't really abandon what we're doing to move onto something else? Stopping in the middle of a special, high-interest activity is one thing, but we certainly can't drop every plan that doesn't sustain our students' attention. Once again we can see the value in proactivity when we infuse our classrooms with attractive options that offer incentives for cooperation.

A former student told me about a strategy his geometry teacher used. The teacher would have a specified amount of material to present in the forty-five-minute class. Once the lesson was finished, the students could stay and start on their homework or leave the class. "It was tremendous motivation for us to pay attention to him and to focus and to not miss a trick of what he was teaching us. The only rules were that when we left his classroom, we couldn't make noise, slam doors, or be disruptive to any of the other classes."[8]

One first-grade teacher made a habit of stopping midsentence as soon as she noticed that the kids had gotten distracted. Most of the time, her silence brought them back immediately. It didn't take the kids long to learn that any wasted time would cut into their self-selection period (a collection of high-interest activities scheduled for later in the day). Saving the valuable, fun enrichment activities for the end of the day and making the amount of time these activities were available dependent on the students' cooperation throughout the day gave her kids the incentive to stay on task. After the first few days, she rarely had to do more than stop talking and look at her watch to get her students' attention.

Sometimes drastic measures are required. I taught a class of fifth graders right before lunch one year. This group seemed to take forever to get ready for dismissal. I found myself giving these students more and more time to get ready to leave until I realized that ten minutes into the lesson, I was starting to feel the pressure to clean up for a lunch period that was still thirty-five minutes away. Giving the students additional time had obviously not resolved the problem.

At the beginning of the next class, I announced, "Listen, we've got a lot to cover today. Getting ready for lunch has been a problem for us, and today we'll have less time than normal. I'll let you know that it's time to clean up. I'll say it once. After that, it's up to you. As soon as you clear your desks and get quiet, you can go down to eat."

Now, I had thought that the potential for missing out on high-priority lunch and playground time would clear up this nonsense once and for all. I was wrong. For some reason, it almost seemed to have invited the kids to test how serious I was. (This may tell you something about the previous consistency of my follow-through.) Students who hadn't been doing much of anything earlier in the period suddenly decided to get busy. Quiet kids started talking.

There was a part of me that wanted to scream. It took every ounce of self-restraint to stay calm. I sent a note down to the lunch service staff, but to the students, I did not say another word. I didn't even glance at the clock. Every student had heard my announcement; every student had heard the lunch bell. Now, it was up to them.

It took them twenty-two minutes to get ready. Evidently, some had seen friends out on the playground and more than a few had started getting hungry. Two minutes later, we got down to the lunchroom, where the students were dismayed to find that their lunches had gotten cold. A few had barely gotten out the door to the playground before the bell rang to return to class.

> My students had finally figured out what was necessary to get to lunch on time.

Of course, the students were upset. I wasn't too thrilled myself about not getting a lunch break that day.[9] But the sacrifice was worth it: The next day, I noticed, at 11:56, that each student was ready to be dismissed. For the most part, that was the end of the lunchtime blues. My students had finally figured out what was necessary to get to lunch on time. Consistent follow-through from that point on allowed cooperation to become increasingly habitual and internalized.

Any form of follow-through will seem drastic or even frightening for teachers who have a tendency to back down on their boundaries, as many of us often do. Following through requires tremendous courage, commitment, and consistency. There will always be ways to rationalize caving in on our boundaries, but the best learning often happens when we can resist the temptation to surrender to a good excuse, pressure from parents or other faculty, or the sheer exhaustion that makes a warning so attractive. The alternative to sloppy follow-through is a well-run class where we can respond to undesirable student behavior without increasing stress in the classroom (or in our nervous systems) and, if we're good at this, without even raising our voices.

NOTES

1. Over the years, I've heard from countless teachers, some in the toughest schools imaginable, who said that their survival (which was a very real issue on a daily basis) depended on their willingness to make significant positive changes to their own behaviors and their approach to students. There will always be an apparently easier way, but quick-fix strategies are not the ones that offer the most profound, long-term changes we seek, and they are not the strategies that will prevent continual recurrence of problems, since they don't actually fix anything.

2. For more examples of the language of acceptance and other valuable communication strategies, see Haim Ginott, *Teacher and Child* (New York: Scribner Books, 1993).

3. See Chapter 23 for more information on problem solving.

4. This, incidentally, is a really nice thing for a child of an alcoholic to hear—and often is the exact opposite of what the child grew up hearing, or at least feeling.

5. You know your kids. What works for you? In some cases, you may use one policy with your second-period class and a different policy, or combination of policies, with fifth period. Whichever policies you select, you might want to run them by the office to get administrators' support (and let them know what you're up to). Also, send a note home, not just to inform the parents of your policy, but also to let them know that they'll never have to write an excuse note for homework ever again. That's a big selling point, especially when they see that your policy protects kids from being punished when they have a bad night, or simply forget, as we all do sometimes.

6. If the behavior continues because they are competing with you for power, then it's critical to reconsider how your authority relationship is structured. Over time, creating win-win power dynamics will eliminate, or at least minimize, the number of incidents that occur when kids feel they have to prove "you can't make me!"

7. Many low auditory learners actually listen better when they have something to play with (tactile anchor) or when they can read along (visual anchor). You'll find more about these topics in Chapter 18.

8. This is from a story by Charles Whitfield in *Mentors, Masters and Mrs. MacGregor: Stories of Teachers Making a Difference,* by Jane Bluestein (Deerfield Beach, FL: Health Communications, 1995).

9. I also suspected that the parents would be upset, so I drafted a letter explaining what had happened to send home with the students at the end of the day. I also made sure to call the parents who might not get my note before they heard a slightly different version of what had happened.

15

Responding Nonreactively

I f ever our ability to withstand our win-lose programming is challenged, it will be when a student misbehaves. Whether failing to cooperate, demonstrating disruptive behavior, or refusing outright to do something we ask or assign, it can be remarkably easy to take negative behavior personally, especially if we've been committed to building a positive learning environment all along. Undesirable student behavior can push all sorts of buttons and bring up every counterproductive relationship pattern we've ever learned. But although it may take a great deal of practice before some of us automatically respond to spilled paint by directing the child to a sponge instead of barraging him about his clumsiness, constructive, nonreactive alternatives clearly exist.

I remember a professor back in my preservice days talking about the value of ignoring certain student behaviors. Prone to thinking in rather black-and-white terms, I dismissed her advice, equating ignoring with condoning. I have since discovered that there are indeed certain behaviors that truly do not warrant teacher attention and those that deserve only the most minimal regard. I believe that this professor was simply admonishing us to pick our battles carefully, attempting to let us off the hook for feeling as if we needed to control or get involved in every single behavioral exchange that occurred in our classes.

IS IT REALLY A PROBLEM?

Not all behaviors require intervention, or even acknowledgement. If a student knocks over a stack of papers and immediately bends down to pick them up, there is absolutely no reason for us to react at all. One teacher complained about a young student who sucked his thumb, asking what she could do to get him to stop. She admitted that the behavior did not keep the student from doing his work and, since he did not talk with his thumb in his mouth, it did not interfere with his ability to communicate clearly. This behavior was not a problem for anyone except the teacher, and it bothered her only because it "looks funny." Surely there are other, more important matters to which we can devote our time and energy.

Similarly, a high school counselor told me about a student who had been sent to her office as punishment for drawing a picture of a dragon instead of listening to a history teacher's lecture (or perhaps, taking notes in a more traditional, linear way). The girl tearfully explained to the counselor that drawing actually helped her listen and proved this fact by pointing to various sections of her drawing and relating, nearly word for word, what the teacher had been saying as she drew this part or that. Here is a perfect example of a teacher creating a discipline problem out of a nondisruptive student behavior which, because of her particular learning styles (low auditory, high kinesthetic), was actually on task and helping her absorb the information he was presenting.

We all have pictures of how student learning should look but these expectations don't always match the way students actually learn. So let's ask ourselves, before we negatively judge a particular behavior, is it really a problem? Is the behavior interfering with our teaching? Is it keeping other students from doing their work? Or is it perhaps helping that child learn and function in the classroom—and if so, are we willing to advocate for this student? Let's also be willing to examine the degree to which we're concerned with how *we* will look if someone observes this child in our classroom because looking at students' behaviors through this filter can become a source of stress for all concerned.[1]

NOT A MORAL ISSUE

In addition to the temptation to take student behavior too personally, there will always be the appeal of righteousness when students aren't doing what we want. The more we can deal with the behavior—and not the wrongness of the behavior—the less power and energy we give to what's bothering us. In fact, many disruptions can be intervened quickly and quietly, with a minimum of involvement. I've seen very chatty children suddenly get down to work simply because the teacher walked over to their table in a friendly, nonthreatening way. Simply getting closer to the disturbance was the only involvement necessary; the teacher didn't need to say a word about the kids breaking any rules or being off task a few moments before. Also, nonthreatening eye contact or humor can be extremely effective in redirecting students' attention and getting them back to doing what we want.

Certainly, any attempts to set up no-fail situations in the first place will help. Success orientation techniques such as expressing our boundaries before there is a problem ("I will read each spelling word only once"), giving special directions ("Here's how you can transfer the solution without spilling it"), or providing instructions verbally and in writing will certainly avert a myriad of misunderstandings. Often, additional information will be all that is necessary. If children create a mess they don't know how (or are afraid) to clean up on their own, simple directions or an offer to help go much further than criticism, a lecture, or an impatient look.

Even catching kids in the act doesn't need to signal an automatic criticism or punishment. I once observed an activity with four- and five-year-olds examining a collection of keys. The teacher asked the students to describe the key each had selected and tell what that key might be able to do. As the children offered their suggestions, she noticed one boy attempting to slip his key into a pocket in his pants. Without skipping a beat, she turned to him and said, "That's right! It can fit in our pockets! Look at the key and tell me where you think it would work?" In an instant, she reengaged the child, had the key back on the table, and interrupted a misbehavior, all without making this child wrong. A middle school teacher told me about a boy who picked and pulled at the fidget toy he had made in class (a balloon filled with flour and rice) until it broke. Rather than attack him for making a mess, she sympathized: "Oh, I'm so sorry! That's one of the problems with these things. Why don't you clean that up and help me think of how we can make them last a little longer." Sparing him the humiliation and punishment he might have earned in some other classroom went a long way to ultimately gaining this child's commitment, cooperation, and devotion. (And he was, from that point on, incredibly protective of the materials and resources in that classroom.)

The key is to keep it low key, nonjudgmental, even impersonal. Not being offended, rattled, or particularly impressed by students' bad attitudes can actually be pretty disarming. Although tradition would have us think otherwise, children really can learn a lesson without being made to feel embarrassed, stupid, or ashamed. It can be hard to resist reacting to hostility and drama, but I've seen and heard of instances in which an adult was able to engage a student by responding to whatever part of the student's behavior was ultimately cooperative. In other words, if you ask the student to sit down and open her book and she curses under her breath, slams the book down on the desk, and then gets to work, it really is okay to acknowledge what she's done right: "Thanks for getting to work. Let's talk about the attitude a little later."[2]

> Not being offended, rattled, or particularly impressed by students' bad attitudes can actually be pretty disarming.

Many teachers quickly eliminate occasional outbursts of offensive language, for example, simply by responding with a raised eyebrow or a simple, nonreactive comment: "Uh-uh" or "Let's not say that word in here." I recently heard from a junior high special education teacher who described an encounter in which her request to a particular student was met with a string of invectives, including a number of rather strong four-letter words. Although the school had its policies (and punishments) for abusive language, this teacher responded by looking the child in the eye, raising her eyebrow, and saying, "I love you, too." This was certainly not the response he was expecting. The level of engagement and participation she eventually achieved with this student accomplished far more than a trip to the office or any penalty the office would have imposed.[3]

Down and Dirty: Language in the Classroom

We all have our level of tolerance for swearing—in or out of the classroom. Dealing with inappropriate language can eat up a lot of time and energy. Regardless of the reason kids swear, we can respond in ways that will contribute to the demise of such language (or to its becoming increasingly pointless) in our classrooms and schools.

1. **Students want to provoke a reaction**—This is more likely to happen in win-lose, antagonistic environments, or in a class in which kids are competing for power.
   - Proactive: Change the relationship and the power dynamics and the incidence of this kind of behavior drops sharply.

(Continued)

(Continued)

- Response: Minimize the offense (even if you really are offended) and refrain from moralizing or even criticizing. Give a minimal response, or simply request different behavior: "Let's not use that word in here" or "Whoa. Please don't use that word around me."

2. **Students are in emotional overload**—When the midbrain takes over, it's not uncommon for strong language to accompany strong emotions.
   - Proactive: Provide appropriate outlets for emotions and strategies to help kids connect with the more rational parts of their brains. Provide a physical space in the room or building for kids to go when they need a minute to collect themselves.
   - Response: Stay calm and use a quiet voice. Respond to feelings, not language. Provide validation (agreement): "Of course you're upset about that" or "I can see that really bothered you." (Make sure you're not provoking, disempowering, or adding fuel to the fire.)

3. **They're not aware that they're swearing**—For many kids, certain words are so common in their world that they may not be aware that the words can be offensive and inappropriate in other circumstances or to other people.
   - Proactive: This is a great teaching opportunity. Without getting too specific, spend some time talking about the difference between "street language" and "classroom language" and where and when certain words are considered inappropriate or offensive. Minimize judgment.
   - Respond: Provide only a minimal reaction, such as raising your eyebrows or saying "uh-uh." Remind and request: "Let's not use that word here." (Make sure you don't have power issues interfering with the relationship.) This includes responses to the occasional slip, especially if it's followed by an acknowledgment or apology: "Oops, I forgot!" or "Sorry!"

I've also known teachers who relied on their good modeling when confronted with certain language or even a tone they did not like: "Wait a minute! Do I use that kind of language (or tone) when I talk with you?" Assuming the student can't honestly say yes, the teacher will follow with a request that the student try again, without the language or attitude.

Here is one other caution: I hear teachers use the word *inappropriate* with their students quite a bit. The problem here is that often, to the student, the language (or the behavior or attitude or whatever) may feel entirely appropriate to the situation or to the student. We have a long history of labeling undesirable behavior. Why not focus instead on helping the child avoid problems, find solutions, and achieve goals? And as far as getting our own needs met, making the student (or the language or behavior or whatever) wrong is generally less effective than asking for what we want instead.

But little things can sometimes become bigger than they really are, even if only in our minds. For way too long, my students knew they could get a rise out of me—and waste all kinds of class time—by telling me they didn't have a pencil. I hear this all the time, especially from teachers working with upper grade students or in departmentalized settings. If a student shows up in our classroom without a pencil or a book, obviously he or she has a problem. But the student's lack of preparation does not automatically have to become our problem as well. And it does not have to bring up issues of power, character, or morality.

> We get to be right, but they're still unprepared. The problem is not only still unsolved but can also often escalate to a point at which the emotional climate of the learning environment is impaired.

Oh sure, the arguments are good ones: "But they *need* a pencil. They *know* they need a pencil. They *should* have a pencil. What's wrong with them?" Sadly, self-righteousness affords scant advantage: We get to be right, but they're still unprepared. The problem is not only still unsolved but can also often escalate to a point at which the emotional climate of the learning environment is impaired. (I honestly think my kids would deliberately come in unprepared at times, just to get a reaction.) Think about how often we blow up, criticize, and deliver a lecture about responsibility and self-sufficiency, after which we either give out a pencil or we don't. In the meantime, we've gotten upset and wasted valuable instructional time, and our students are no more self-managing or responsible as a result.

One of our favorite rationalizations for punishing students' forgetfulness is the claim that in the "real world," they will need to be prepared. Of course this is true, but people borrow tools and supplies all the time without losing their jobs, and there probably isn't a teacher on this planet who hasn't left a stack of papers or materials at home, even when these items were needed in the classroom that day. It is possible to deal with a forgotten pencil in a nonemotional, disengaged, and nonjudgmental frame of mind. We handle similar situations with adults that way. (Imagine being yelled at in a store when you went to sign a check and had to borrow a pen. What would you learn from an encounter like this besides the fact that you didn't want to shop there anymore?)

We do not need to adopt the students' lack of preparedness as our own problem or take it as a personal assault. What are your boundaries? What are your resources? Do you have enough pencils to keep a few on hand? Are you willing to loan them out without making a big deal out of it? If so, when, how, and under what conditions? Can they borrow a pencil from a friend? Many teachers sell or even "rent" pencils to kids, returning the collateral (money, a toy, or a jacket, for example) when the pencil is returned. Make sure the kids know their options ahead of time so they have the information they need to succeed.

The real issue is that the student needs something to write with to do her work, right? Sure, it would be nice if she remembered, but for the moment, she didn't. It usually doesn't cost us much to loan a child a pencil or keep a few in a can for emergencies. It certainly costs us nothing to give a student a minute to find a pencil while we get the class ready or after the other students begin their seatwork. This is the heart of success orientation and win-win teaching. (I eventually found

> I eventually found that the less fuss I made over pencils, the fewer problems my kids had remembering.

that the less fuss I made over pencils, the fewer problems my kids had remembering. If my extras disappeared, they borrowed from one another, and even started restocking the can on their own.) Although tradition would have us believe otherwise, a forgotten pencil does not devalue students or make them bad. Loaning them pencils no more teaches children to be irresponsible than your needing to borrow a pen at the checkout counter ensures future forgetfulness.

ASSERTING, NOT ATTACKING

The smaller our reactions, the less energy we feed a potential conflict. Teachers who are open to students' negotiations for alternate or self-designed activities and assignments, for example, often encounter somewhat outrageous proposals at times, either from students who are naive or unrealistic about what could actually work or those testing the limits of acceptability. Either way, if students propose that you cancel a lesson in favor of using the period for a game or time off, it's not necessary to attack them for trying to take advantage or thinking you're a pushover. Instead of taking offense or exclaiming, "What? Are you crazy?" a simple, straightforward statement like "That won't work for me"[4] conveys your unwillingness to accept their suggestion without criticizing, shaming, or making them wrong. You might even make a counterproposal that will work for you and for them: "How about settling down and doing what I've got planned? We should be able to finish a few minutes early. You can earn some free time at the end of class."

And simple courtesy and respect can work wonders. Students are much more likely to respond cooperatively to "Please put that item[5] away until lunchtime" than "Put that thing away now!" On occasion, however, a student will resist even the most positively stated request. There are a few tricks to avoiding a situation in which we back students into a corner. For example, switching from telling to asking can help: "You need to clear your desk. Where would you like to put that toy until lunchtime?" offers a number of positive choices. Putting the item away is not negotiable but the location is. Much resistance can be avoided when we respect a child's need for dignity and power within these limits.

Offering two or more specific positive choices can also help prevent resistance and opposition: "Would you like to put that in my desk drawer or in your locker?" Adding a reason can also help: "Please put that [item] away so that it can remain in this center [so that no one trips over it or so that you can get back to work now]." Likewise, the word *until* offers hope and a promise of getting one's needs met at a later, specific time: "Please put that in your locker until your work is done [or until the dismissal bell rings]."

Finally, any time we can validate a student's desire to do something that we're not willing to allow, we can also promote cooperation: "This is a really nice toy. I know you wish you could play with it now. We need to get ready for the test and I think it might get in your way. Why not put it on my desk for now? You'll have some time to play with it when we're finished." All of these techniques leave the student with a forward focus and an understanding that his or her needs are being considered and respected.

Our old win-lose patterns can be instantly engaged when we confront an obstinate student.[6] Unfortunately, if the child refuses to give up the toy despite all our positive efforts, our first instinct is to immediately back up into power: "Give it to me now" or "I'll take it and you'll never see it again." Giving in to the urge to overpower a student can undo a great deal of the positive results gained by working toward a win-win environment.

A point-blank refusal can quickly turn into a no-win situation. The first casualty is often our perspective, if not our commitment to maintaining a win-win environment. A

> A point-blank refusal can quickly turn into a no-win situation. The first casualty is often our perspective.

high school teacher approached me in a recent workshop, still clearly rattled over an exchange with a student that had escalated out of control very quickly. The student had forgotten to turn off her cell phone and when it rang in class, the teacher demanded that the student surrender the phone. The teacher kept insisting, "but it's a school policy," although frankly, it sounded like she would have been just as happy if the girl had just turned off her phone. But once the teacher made the demand, she said she got stuck in the loop of referring back to school policy, despite the girl's flat-out refusal to give up the phone. The situation came dangerously close to getting physical, and now the school and the girl's family are in arbitration. I'm also trying to imagine how much this student is learning in this class at this point. This is the ultimate casualty of a no-win situation. The sad irony in all of this was that during this seminar, there was invariably one incoming call or another after every break. Even teachers sometimes forget to turn off their phones. (This has happened in practically every workshop I've ever conducted, with *my* phone ringing on more than one occasion as well.) Once again, common courtesy can go a long way.

Backing off may mean sacrificing a short-term objective (getting him to give up the toy in the earlier example) to a long-term process (becoming responsible for doing his work regardless of temptations and distractions). But only in a win-lose classroom will your unwillingness to overpower or hurt a student make you come out a loser. Is it worth a power struggle that may or may not work (and then, if it does work, will do so for all the wrong reasons)?

Ideally, it's best to avoid power confrontations, but if one does come up, disengage quickly, if at all possible. We can always refuse to argue or try to coerce the student to cooperate: "I'm not about to try to force you to give up this toy. If you can work without being distracted by it, there's no problem. If not, I'll be happy to help you put it away. Keep in mind that your work must be finished for you to participate in this afternoon's activities (go out for recess, go on to the next lesson, get credit for the assignments, or merit whatever meaningful outcome is dependent on the work's completion)." Then walk away.

If students' behavior is causing problems only for themselves, the eventual lack of access to the meaningful consequences will teach them far more than your power or anger. (And if their behavior is not causing a problem for anyone, including themselves, there may not have been a need for your involvement in the first place.) Think, instead, of ways you can avoid similar incidents from occurring in the future. When cool heads once again prevail, announce, "You know, we've never needed limits about toys, but keeping toys at your desk is interfering with your learning. I know these things are important to you. At the same time, your attention is important to me. If you want to bring your toys to school, you'll have to keep them in your locker or my desk during class time. You can have them again during recess (or when the bell rings)."

There is no blaming, scolding, or moralizing. We've gotten around the "I'll show you" mentality of a punitive, win-lose relationship because we don't need to cause someone to lose for us to win. We now have tighter limits and more specific boundaries. If the problem persists, further action—from a letter home requesting support for our limits to a total, if temporary, ban on toys—may be necessary. But remember, they will benefit more from learning where, when, and how to use these items than they will from our insistence on simply outlawing them.

WHAT IF SHADOW DOESN'T SIT DOWN?

Often teachers will stop me and ask, "But what if they *still* refuse?" (We can be relentlessly attached to that reactive context.) No matter how many proactive strategies we discuss, the dialogue always seems to return to "but what if. . . ?" These teachers are usually terribly disappointed—and sometimes actually feel betrayed—when I tell them, "I don't know." But the point is that I don't know, and I am no better equipped for handling win-lose (or no-win) confrontations than anyone else. I will, however, assure these teachers—just as relentlessly—that as a win-win classroom climate evolves, this type of opposition and rebelliousness becomes increasingly rare. Once the students recognize the teacher's investment in their getting their needs met, disruptive or obnoxious behaviors become increasingly pointless.

> As a win-win classroom climate evolves, this type of opposition and rebelliousness becomes increasingly rare.

When I tell the story in my workshops about Shadow and the paper clips, the fact that the child responded positively to the teacher's follow-through, that he actually did sit down when the teacher declined to engage after he had run out of "tickets," nearly always provokes this kind of reaction. I'm sure, for these teachers, the story triggers an anticipation of failed attempts with students they know who would simply refuse to sit down. Of course, in a win-lose environment, kids will revert to what they know best, what's worked for them in the past. It's our job to make different options available and to help them recognize that they really *can* get their needs met when they stop making so many disruptive, annoying, or dumb choices.

> In a win-lose environment, kids will revert to what they know best, what's worked for them in the past.

Nonetheless, I can reassure the doubtful with feedback I've gotten from teachers who insist that regardless of the grade level, they get further with needy students by offering a bit of reassurance—reaching over to squeeze a child's hand or stating when they can talk later, such as at recess or after class—than they ever have with any punishment or negative reaction. So many of our kids have been disappointed by the adults in their lives (if not neglected or worse) that it may take some time for them to trust that we really will be there for them, even if they have to wait for a time that will work better for us.

BACKING OFF IS NOT BACKING DOWN

The process of becoming self-managing is gradual and it often takes time. However, if the positive consequence is meaningful and significant, and we have the courage to follow through when there is a problem, the process usually doesn't take too long. One teacher told me about a time her limits—and her patience—were tested by a group of middle school kids who were working together. As will often happen, the noise level quickly escalated to the point at which she could barely hear the student sitting next to her.

She excused herself from her group and went over to the noisy center. "This isn't working,"[7] she told them. "You guys need to find someplace else to sit this period. We can try again tomorrow."

Nonetheless, as respectful as she was, every student in this group started to protest: "That's not fair." "It wasn't me." "We weren't talking." She told me that it took more restraint than she ever imagined she had to keep herself from completely losing control. Instead of falling into what was quickly beginning to look like a no-win situation, she calmly announced, "I know that you like working with your friends. And I know that you can appreciate that this can happen only when working together doesn't create a problem for anyone else. Well, it's creating a problem for us. I'm going to give you another minute to decide how you're going to handle this situation. I'm sure you can work this out because we all want this privilege to continue." And then she walked away.

The students grumbled for a few seconds and then they all got up and found someplace else to work. At worst, the teacher was willing to revert to individual assignments and assigned seating the next day, perhaps giving the class a chance to try group work again after a few days. Fortunately, her willingness to back off (which is not the same as backing down) and her commitment to the students winning under cooperative circumstances helped avert what could have become a rather nasty incident.

RESPONDING IN A WIN-WIN CLASSROOM

In factory-era authority relationships, student misconduct is an invitation for the teacher to exercise power at the expense of the students' autonomy or dignity. Our immediate response in this situation is, "What can I do to the student who has misbehaved? How can I teach him a lesson?" In a win-win classroom, the lessons to be learned from one's misconduct come from the outcomes of the misconduct, specifically from missing out on privileges and positive consequences—not from the power of the teacher. (This, ironically, is the true source of teacher power.) This also gives us the freedom to allow students to regain access to privileges once they have stopped misbehaving and, if necessary, repair any damage the misbehavior has caused. Students miss lunch, free time, self-selection, or the rest of the story because they failed to behave within the terms or limits that would allow those privileges to continue. They did not miss the activities as a punishment for misbehaving.

With a punitive or reactive response, we're tempted to remove a privilege forever: "You'll *never* be able to sit together again!" What does the student have to gain by cooperating now? Some students take a while to really get how this process works. We always want to continue

> We always want to leave the door open for kids to get it right.

to invite kids to get it right, even if it takes more than one try: "You can try working together again this afternoon." "You're welcome back here when you feel you can work without hitting." "You've got until Friday's last bell to get caught up so you can play on Saturday."

Boundaries allow you to leave the door open for the students to change their behavior and get it right. This means that Andy can return to the group as soon as he feels—and demonstrates—that he can control his urge to hit. Keisha can have another crack at the paint center tomorrow as long as she is willing to confine the paint to the paper. Donia can work on the computer as long as she confines her research to relevant Web sites.

Even students who have refused to do their work—a behavior particularly hard for most teachers to deal with—are more likely to rethink their refusal if we can leave them a way out: "You will need to decide if not doing the work is worth missing out on credit (a grade, recess, graduation, or whatever positive outcome will be available as a result). In the meantime, I will leave your work on your desk in case you change your mind."

When a misbehavior occurs because no previous limits had been set, it is certainly appropriate to back up and insert additional limits or instruction: "Move those CDs, please. I forgot to tell you to be careful not to put them on the heater," or "By the way, you have one minute to find a place to work and get busy." From that point on, student violations require us to act. Once the announcement has been made, we are well within our rights to remove the CDs for today or assign the indecisive student to a seat of our choosing. These are the consequences of the students' inability to function within the previously announced limits: The CDs are removed so that they don't melt; the student is assigned a seat so that the class can go on with its work.

This sounds great, but how can a busy and distracted teacher think so fast? Like all the other skills discussed in this book, learning to react constructively in a negative situation is a process. These responses are difficult to plan, but as you move from blaming and punishing, and as you realign your interactions with win-win values, the rest follows. Start noticing what you say. When you can, take a second to think about what you *want* to say. (One teacher told me that she would often respond to unexpected questions or requests with, "Wait! I need to think about how I want to answer you.") Energy follows intention, and the behaviors and language we would prefer will come more automatically in time.

INTERRUPTING NEGATIVE BEHAVIOR

When a student behaves destructively, hurting or endangering another student, property, or himself, our immediate goal is to intervene before further damage can occur. Very often, one word firmly spoken is enough. I used to ask my students to "Freeze!" when I wanted their attention. They always enjoyed stopping in whatever position they were in—the sillier the better—until I released them with "Unfreeze." The same technique was also effective in preventing various students from dropping crayons in the fish tank, following through on a punch, or continuing to absently carve gouges into the top of a desk. The word "Stop!" can also work, giving students a chance to stop and think before any damage is done, or before they get in any deeper, and back up and correct mistakes whenever possible. The break can also give us the chance to get students' attention for further information, to suspend a privilege, or even to momentarily remove a student from the situation, if necessary.

When a student's behavior becomes extremely distracting or disturbing to others (without posing any actual danger to life or limb), our attention shifts closer to survival—and preventing things from getting worse. These are the instances in which we'll see the greatest value in providing an outlet to reduce emotional stress or strong feelings.[8] It's difficult, if not neurologically impossible, to have a constructive dialogue or make a positive decision if one is near hysterics. (This goes for both teacher and students.) Frequently, a soft word of understanding or a gentle touch on the arm can prevent an incident from escalating, but this is possible for us to do only if we stay calm.

We can also help the child by validating her feelings and offering an alternative to taking it out on the class—or on us: "I can see that you're upset. Why don't you get a drink of water and we can talk when you get back?" Asking the child to leave the environment is not a punishment for the angry student. It is a technique to help us stay calm, to protect the rest of the class, to give the student a chance to disengage and catch her breath, and to alter the negative energy that's built up. Although it's extremely unlikely to happen in a truly win-win classroom, if the student becomes too violent or dangerous to approach, send someone for help.

Students who have consistently been on the losing end of win-lose authority relationships, students who have used explosive behavior successfully to get out of work (or class), and those who have built a habit of solving conflicts by hurting other people, need some concrete alternatives to lashing out. They also need time to develop trust in you and the system. A win-win classroom, with a measure of time and faith, can provide the options, acceptance, and acknowledgement that will enable even the most severely damaged children opportunities to find more constructive means of fulfilling their needs.

> Students who have consistently been on the losing end of win-lose authority relationships . . . need some concrete alternatives to lashing out.

NOTES

1. See Chapter 18 for more information on differences in how children learn. Keep in mind that many people—and not just those outside our profession—are conditioned to judge our competence and effectiveness by factory-era criteria that are anachronistic and inappropriate to contemporary, win-win objectives. We need to educate the community (and many educators as well) to gain support for changing outdated expectations.

2. This strategy was observed in a seminar entitled "Practical Strategies for Working Successfully With Difficult, Noncompliant Students," presented by Spencer Henry for the Bureau of Education and Research.

3. See sidebar: "Down and Dirty: Language in the Classroom."

4. Or try "That won't work this time" or "Hmmm . . . that's not going to meet the objectives for this unit," for example. See Resource B, "Magic Sentences."

5. The item can be anything that is distracting this student, other students, or the teacher. Let's also make a point to let kids know ahead of time the conditions under which they can keep toys, cell phones, computer games, pagers, or whatever, in the room.

6. Keep in mind that in a win-win environment, students learn that this type of oppositional behavior really isn't necessary. It may take a few kids a while to really get this point, especially if their oppositional patterns have been effective or necessary in the past.

7. Listen to how neutral and nonaccusing this sentence is. There are no attacks, no criticism, no lectures about their rudeness or lack of consideration: This isn't working. You need to move. Period. See Resource B for more information on "magic sentences."

8. See Chapter 22 for more information.

PART V

Success Orientation

16

Managing a Win-Win Classroom

A few weeks into my first year, I presented my students with what I believed to be a perfect lesson. I had designed a well-orchestrated environment with elaborate plans, plenty of materials to go around, color-coded direction cards, and enough stimulating activities to keep them all busy until Easter. These kids were in fifth grade, some practically in their teens; certainly they would be able to navigate the work centers under my watchful, nurturing, facilitating care. Right?

Wrong.

For starters, no one at the mural center could agree on a theme. The kids in the media corner were fighting over who would operate the projector. And all the markers for the art activity mysteriously vanished within the first minute of class. Evidently no one had ever worked with a ruler or used an encyclopedia before, and although I had explained everything inside and out, I had a steady stream of kids tugging on my sleeve asking me what they were supposed to do. I stood in amazement, watching weeks of planning and work go straight down the tubes. In the midst of the chaos, all I could think was, "But I laminated everything!"

I received two shocks that day. I had expected my creativity to carry far more weight than it actually did; instead, it was unappreciated and overwhelming. Second, I had expected the students, who seemed so mature and streetwise, to have already acquired cer-

It seemed as if my expectations were actually creating problems. Now what?

tain responsible learning behaviors. Yet they were unable to work independently in small groups, care for materials, or make decisions about their learning. It seemed as if my expectations were actually *creating* problems. Now what?

WHAT'S WRONG WITH EXPECTATIONS?

Most of us enter the teaching profession with all sorts of expectations—conscious and unconscious. Depending on what we believe our students can (or should) do, what we hear from other teachers, and our values and sense of our own capabilities, we construct a mental picture of a classroom that may or may not reflect the reality we encounter.

To make things more interesting, how often have we heard that children perform to the level of expectations and that teachers with high expectations end up with students who perform better than teachers with low expectations? Given this admonition, I introduced myself to my first class with a long list of my expectations: "I expect you to take care of materials" "I expect you to behave respectfully," "I expect you to put your names on your papers," "I expect you to love learning," and so on. Imagine my consternation when the students countered my pronouncements with bored looks, eyes rolled to the ceiling, and an exasperated chorus, after a few seconds' silence: "So?" This is where I first discovered that all too often, "high expectations" is a metaphor for wishful thinking. Clearly, the only person committed to my expectations was me!

> Clearly, the only person committed to my expectations was me!

Maybe teachers with high expectations do get better results, but this experience led me to suspect that these individuals have more going for them than their expectations, and I strongly doubt that it is the expectations themselves that generate high performance. I imagine that the students' performance is more likely to be a reflection of intention, inspired by the teacher's beliefs and behaviors, than by his or her expectations. True, we won't get much out of kids we don't ultimately believe in, but believing that students can learn, achieve, or cooperate—and teaching to their capabilities and potential—is quite different from simply expecting them to perform.

One of the problems with having expectations is the lack of commitment from the person or people on whom we project our expectations. Simply expecting does not secure agreement or generate commitment to learning or cooperation, certainly not as effectively as win-win power dynamics, interactions, and relationships or opportunities to experience fun, success, belonging, discovery, or power, for example. Additionally, our expressed expectations are often at odds with our faith in our students; kids can have a pretty sharp instinct for adults who don't believe in them.

It's also easier to have an expectation than it is to actually ask for what we want—a behavior that is often discouraged in our culture despite the fact that in the absence of this skill, we often resort to far more toxic alternatives like powering, manipulation, passive-aggressiveness, or constantly being disappointed by not getting our needs met. Perhaps we can use our expectations as a means of identifying our intentions and what we would like from others. In this sense, expectations are simply starting points, great places from which to anticipate what we want to accomplish and what we'll need (or need to do) to achieve our goals. Nonetheless, I'm betting we'll get a lot farther with things like clear limits, positive incentives, encouragement, direct requests, and a belief in our students' ability to learn and grow, than with even the most reasonable and well-stated expectations.

TURNING EXPECTATIONS INTO INSTRUCTIONS

While I was wrestling with this issue of expectations, my students were visiting Mr. Grey for art twice a week. When they came back from his class, I would ask them what they had done. Each report detailed monotonous exercises such as getting the scissors out of a box, putting the lid back on the box, putting the box back in the cabinet, sitting down with the scissors, then putting the scissors back again, and so on, over and over. For the first few days of school, the kids did nothing besides practice getting, holding, passing, using, and returning the things they'd need for art class. Period.

I asked Mr. Grey what he was up to. "Don't you have a curriculum to get through this year?"

"I sure do, and it's massive," he replied. "But if we don't do this first, we'll never get through any of it."

"You mean to tell me that these kids don't know how to get paint jars out of a storage closet?"

"Some do, sure. But most don't. Or at least they don't think about it on their own. This way, there are no questions later about where things go or how I expect them to be used."

There was that word again. "Don't you expect them to know this stuff?"

"It doesn't matter. I can expect all day long and never get what I want. Expecting kids to clean calligraphy pens and put them back in the boxes doesn't teach them how to do it. I still have to show them."

It was true. Few teachers placed higher demands on the kids than Mr. Grey. But it was neither these demands nor Mr. Grey's expectations that turned his classroom into an exciting and productive place. While he may have started with a mental picture of busy, capable, independent, and responsible students—and a great deal of faith in their ability to rise to the challenges he'd present to them—he did not leave their behavior to chance or forge ahead on a set of assumptions about what these kids should know. If Mr. Grey expected success from his students, he certainly gave them the training necessary to fulfill his objectives.[1]

YOU WANT ME TO DO *WHAT?*

Sometimes, little misunderstandings can turn into bigger problems. When success is elusive, whether because of unclear directions, lack of prerequisite skills, or absence of self-management capabilities, chaos and discipline problems are sure to follow. I was observing a new teacher during the first day of school as she announced to her kindergarten class that it was time to get in line. A few students stopped and stared; the others started running around the room. In the mayhem, I wondered if "Get in Line" was some strange new game until one five year-old came up and asked the teacher, "What's a line?"

We know that our students need clear instructions to succeed at the tasks we set before them, but what could be more clear than "Get in line"? As that new teacher quickly found out, instructions are clear only if the students understand them. The request to "Get in line" assumes that they know what a line is, where it starts and ends, which way to face, whether it is single- or double-file, and all other conditions regarding talking, touching,

> Instructions are clear only if the students understand them.

and what, if anything, they need to take with them when they get in line. She may as well have given the directions in another language. Imagine the confusion possible with more complex assignments.

Lack of clarity is a common problem in giving directions. For the student, not knowing what to do becomes a source of confusion, helplessness, frustration, and feelings of inadequacy. (I once saw an entire class of first graders break down in tears when the teacher innocently announced that they could go home as soon as they "pick up the floor." Another teacher told me that she could barely get her kids to come in out of the rain and mud after telling them they had to "scrape off their feet" first.) Poorly communicated instructions also build teacher dependence, waste time, and often result in reactive or negative feedback from teachers. We can avoid these pitfalls by getting very clear, in our own minds, about what we want, and then breaking down the directions step by step and using language the students are not likely to misconstrue, especially the first time we ask them to do something. It can also help to walk the students through each step of the directions, particularly those involved with routines, the use of equipment or materials, or movement, to increase the likelihood of their success. Remember, if it's important to us, it's worth the time to think through our goals, state our instructions in ways that reduce ambiguity and vagueness, and increase the odds of our kids' success with however much practice they need.

INCREASING SUCCESS

When one of my eighth graders interpreted my instructions to "behave yourself in the media center" to mean that he shouldn't smoke in there, it dawned on me that sometimes our kids create very different pictures in their minds from the directions they receive than the images we try to convey with our instructions or requests. To promote clarity, let's be careful about the adjectives we use. We know what we mean by *good* handwriting, *exciting* characters, *thorough* research, and *clear* presentation. Do they? Do we let them know, before their work ends up on our desks, the particular skills we will evaluate? Telling them what we're looking for, or grading for, helps focus students' efforts and promote success.

> To promote clarity, let's be careful about the adjectives we use.

Students are bombarded with verbal instructions from teachers and other adults, as well as written instructions from books, the board, and assignments. It's no wonder that they often tune us out. But even when they are focused and engaged, we don't always give directions in a way that makes sense to their nervous systems. We will almost always have a wide variety of learning styles among the students in our classes or groups, and providing instructions in more than one way can help ensure wider success, even with the simplest instructions. This is especially true when introducing more complex tasks or new routines.

For example, instructing a group to do "the first ten problems on Page 86 and any five problems on Page 93" might be fine for our auditory learners (if they are really listening), but other students will have greater success with some additional cues. Writing the directions on the board, in a folder, or on a task card can serve as a reminder and a learning aid for these students. Written instructions also free us to move on to other tasks. Once we've given our instructions in oral and written form, the students have recourse to something besides bothering the teacher with questions about "what page?" or "which problems?" When possible, using codes (like colors or symbols), cues, or illustrations with written directions encourages independence, even among poor readers or very young students. If sequence is important, listing the steps in a specific order is essential, particularly with projects that involve a number of steps; writing and numbering the directions also helps.

We can also make success-oriented decisions about when to give instructions. I've seen far too many lessons fail—and far too much time wasted when teachers have to repeat directions over and over—because the teacher did not have the students' attention when directions were given.[2] Sometimes waiting a few seconds until they finish putting things away or get settled in their seats or the work area will save time and prevent confusion down the road. If we give information to students without first asking for their attention, we shouldn't be too surprised when the majority get it wrong.

Say It Once!

Here are tips to ensure that you never have to repeat your instructions:

- Be sure you have the students' attention first. Wait until they have finished talking, writing, or cleaning up, for example, before you begin speaking. Use an auditory signal (e.g., bell, chime, a phrase or word like "Look at me" or "Freeze") to help shift their attention.
- Give the instructions verbally, as simply and clearly as possible.
- Make sure the instructions are available in written form as well, on the board or on their papers (or on a task card, for example).
- Make it okay for kids to ask one another for clarification. (If you have many kids asking each other for help, you may want to back up and reexplain what you want to the entire class or group.)
- Let the parents know your policy for giving directions before you implement it and the options their children will have, just in case a story gets home that claims "the teacher wouldn't tell me what to do."

If you need to interrupt their work, a signal from a bell or chimes, flashing lights, or clapping hands, for example, creates a shift in the auditory or visual field and can be very effective at getting your students' attention. Giving directions to inattentive students communicates a lack of self-respect (you are worth listening to, aren't you?), and it sets them up to fail as well. Likewise, hold off, if possible, on presenting new or important instructions as kids are getting ready for lunch or dismissal if the information can wait; unless those instructions have fairly immediate relevance, they'll probably be remembered better at another time.

> Good instructions offer structure.

In addition to clarity, good instructions offer structure. "Choices within limits"—the anthem of the win-win classroom—applies quite clearly to the directions we give. But if the limits are too broad, students can be overwhelmed. Although some kids can turn the vaguest instructions into creative and meaningful learning experiences, others, regardless of age, need a starting point—something concrete from which to depart. These students will find a certain amount of security, for example, in writing from a story starter or turning a simple design into a drawing. This initial structure makes it easier for

> Although some kids can turn the vaguest instructions into creative and meaningful learning experiences, others, regardless of age, need a starting point—something concrete from which to depart.

them to eventually face a blank piece of paper than starting from scratch. We can also provide structure by limiting length (one side of a paper), media (a picture made on the computer), expression (written in the present tense, drawn with only one color of ink), content (using all twenty spelling words, people involved in the women's movement during the 1970s), or any number of criteria.

Our ultimate objectives for any assignment will help us determine which choices we can offer and the amount of structure necessary. Many teachers now use rubrics with levels of completion or competence according to a list of the important components and criteria of the work assigned. This information gives a clear description of what the students need to do to attain the score at each level.[3]

Educator Jo Ann Freiberg insists that "learning should not have to be a secret! Helping students be successful means providing them with helpful and structured guidance." She notes, for example, that students study harder for an exam when they have a study guide than when they are just told to "study everything we've been over so far." Regardless of how the information is presented, identifying details about tasks to be done or specifying the criteria for a particular assignment can save a great amount of time in reexplaining and help avoid student confusion and mistakes as well.[4]

GIVE THEM A GOOD REASON

As we saw in the value of stating our boundaries positively, the language we choose in giving directions can help us encourage cooperation, build responsibility, avoid reinforcing teacher dependence, and discourage rebelliousness. Since our language and attitude are so closely linked, changing one will invariably change the other. As we commit to a positive, win-win focus, we will become increasingly aware of negative tendencies in our words and the tone of our voice. Likewise, as we shift from threats and warnings to promises and positively stated contingencies, our attitude mirrors that change.

Similarly, the reasons we give for asking for certain behaviors can either work for or against us. Our instructions and boundaries are most effective when they appear to make sense to our students. In power-based, authority relationships, the reason for doing something, whether stated or not, is connected to the power of the authority and the punitive consequences of noncompliance. Asking students to "do it for me" may not sound particularly authoritarian, but the implication of conditional approval actually works in the same manner as "do it or else."

In a win-win classroom, teachers give kids credit for being able to make positive choices even when the outcomes do not involve the threat of deprivation or punitive consequences. "Please put the lids back on the paint jars so the paint doesn't dry out" communicates much more respect for students than "Put the lids back on these paint jars or you'll never see them again." There is a clear and sensible reason for putting the lids on the jars; the request has nothing to do with the teacher's power and in no way threatens to compromise the emotional climate in the classroom.

When we ask our students to do something, we usually have a better reason for asking them than "because I said so." The actual, logical, and intrinsic reason for a boundary—so the markers don't dry out, so that we don't disturb anyone on our way down the hall, so that no one trips and falls, so that we'll have time to hear the entire story—can help build commitment and cooperation, and engage otherwise defensive or defiant students in ways that simple commands never will. These criteria are stated for the benefit of the student and the class as a whole. The request has nothing to do with the teacher's needs—although, as part of the group, these needs will be served as well. The fact that this approach clearly focuses on what's in it for the students, individually or as a group, can account for an increase in cooperation. It may take a few extra seconds, but the extra information we provide in giving the students a practical reason for doing what we ask fosters respect for the value of the task and for our request as well.

All of these techniques will work best when we can overcome the resistance to having to explain our requests, especially when it comes to things we believe students should already know in the first place. For a long time, I honestly resented having to take time to show fifth graders how to correctly use the pencil sharp-

> It was certainly easier to get irritated and blame parents or previous teachers who either never had bothered to teach these skills to my students, or whose instructions, for whatever reason, just didn't seem to transfer to my room.

ener, to show eighth grade gang members how to put books back on a shelf, or to end each of seven classes with a daily reminder to push the chairs under the desks. It was certainly easier to get irritated and blame parents or previous teachers who either never had bothered to teach these skills to my students, or whose instructions, for whatever reason, just didn't seem to transfer to my room.

And yet, when I finally surrendered to these necessities, a few things happened, not the least of which was that my life in school got easier and my relationships—with my students and my job—improved. The few minutes I devoted to these seemingly redundant instructions and my eventual willingness to repeat them ad nauseam significantly increased the likelihood that I would get what I wanted. Better still, after a few weeks, the end-of-class bell would consistently elicit a chorus of kids, mockingly reminding everyone to "push in your chairs."

To be honest, I'm not sure I even had a logical reason for wanting the chairs pushed in. If I were really reaching, I suppose I could argue for safety's sake—a common justification despite the fact that the chairs didn't really pose much of a threat. I think I was just after whatever reduction in chaos a room full of pushed-in chairs might represent. Maybe it was just a "thing" I had, but the fact that the kids were willing to humor my fixation and accept my priorities and quirks was ultimately far more valuable to me than anything they might have done with the furniture.

USING EXPECTATIONS CONSTRUCTIVELY

It can be disappointing to discover that entering an inspiring classroom environment does not trigger some magic that enables children to use a pencil sharpener, recap the paste, alphabetize resource books, or move around the room nondisruptively. Even if the lessons are well planned and our mood is positive and enthusiastic, without information, instruction, and guided practice, we actually doom our students—and ourselves—to failure.

There are hidden assumptions and expectations in every lesson we plan. We will do well to take nothing for granted. Even if we firmly believe that they should know how to handle science equipment, use a dictionary, work with a partner, move to various parts of the room, staple papers together, or put their assignments in a particular place, it's possible that at least a few will not. Certain routines and procedures may be so basic or obvious that they're easy to overlook, especially for teachers new to the profession or those working with a grade level in which they haven't had much experience. Obviously, we cannot predict every single need that will arise, but the better we can account for the skills and behaviors our activities demand, the better we can plan for success, and the less likely we are to be undermined by students' confusion, frustration, or ineptness.

We will often need to invest time in filling the gap between where the students are and where we would like them to be. I once had a group of high-risk eighth graders spend a few minutes practicing putting the caps on felt-tipped markers they enjoyed using but routinely forgot to recap. I could not afford to keep replacing the markers when they dried out, so I did a half-humorous lesson on recapping the pens, making sure that we listened for the click that indicated they were on tight (a trick entirely unfamiliar to most of my students). From that point on, the markers seemed to last forever, and the students became remarkably committed to their care.

Building independence and self-management requires more than expectations. We need to encourage initiative and allow kids to behave in ways that they can actually self-manage. This may mean allowing them to get supplies, move about the room, interact with a classmate, or use a certain piece of equipment at specific times without asking permission first. (Having those options can also accommodate the kids' mobility needs as well as their need for autonomy, eliminating a lot of those annoying and attention-getting behaviors we might otherwise see.) Instruction, guidelines, and practice make student responsibility and self-management a reality. Combined with meaningful, positive consequences for cooperation and opportunities to succeed, this type of preparation encourages the positive behaviors that high expectations can indeed inspire.

> Instruction, guidelines, and practice make student responsibility and self-management a reality.

Hot Tips for Increasing Success

- Create a clear mental picture of what you want. Think about any special details or conditions that will be important to you: Do you require a certain heading on the papers they turn in? Will it bother you if someone starts to sharpen a pencil while you're addressing the whole group? Where do you want the materials put when the students are finished with them?
- Identify behaviors and skills your students will need to complete a particular task or function independently and responsibly in your class. Tell your students what you want, preferably before they have a chance to mess up. Let them know how it will benefit them to head their papers a certain way or put materials away properly, for example.
- Assess the levels of ability and self-management your students have already developed. Watch them work—or not work. What happens when you ask them to do routine things in the classroom? Are they able to solve problems on their own? Are they allowed to ask a classmate for assistance when you're not available? Are they bewildered by choices or directions? What does your room look like at the end of the day?
- Assume nothing other than the fact that your students may not be sure what you want—and start from there. Even if they know how to take care of the books in the classroom library, they may not know how *you* want them to do it.
- Have your kids rehearse daily routines. Have them practice moving from their seats to the reading table before you start teaching reading in groups. Have them practice getting equipment and putting these items away before you ask them to do so as part of an activity.
- Have one small group at a time learn to play a game or operate a piece of equipment before they need to use it in a center, a small group activity, or on their own. You often need to train only a handful of kids yourself. Students can learn quickly and well when they know that they will get to train their classmates in turn.
- Unless you intend to spend your entire year guarding, dispensing, and retrieving classroom materials, teach your students how to get, use, and return things when they are finished.
- Whenever possible, make your verbal directions also available in written form.
- Accommodate kinesthetic learners by literally walking them through routines.
- Give instructions in logical sequence. Write complex instructions out, when you can, numbering the steps for clarity.
- In giving verbal directions to young students, low auditory students, or students who have not had much practice developing their listening skills, go slowly, giving directions a step at a time. If possible, wait until the students are ready for the next step before giving them additional information.
- In determining how much information to give out at one time, consider the age and maturity of the students, their experience with your directions, and the complexity of the instructions you have to offer.
- Let your kids know that you're giving them information, even if it's really basic and obvious, only because you want to increase the odds of them being successful, not because you think they're dumb.
- Let the kids monitor the materials. I once decided the best person to keep track of the cards in our individualized handwriting program was the one student who seemed to lose track of them most often. She took her job quite seriously: Not only did she never lose a card after that, but she also once kept the entire class from going to lunch until the "Capital R" card turned up!
- Have the students practice working independently. Assign some seatwork and put yourself off limits while you work at your desk. Make sure the kids have enough to keep them busy, preferably something they can do easily, such as review work, practice drills, or a puzzle. Remember, the emphasis here, for the moment at least, is on building independence—not academic competence.
- Encourage students to help one another or go on to a different task until you are available to help. You'll be amazed at how much progress you can make when your time isn't tied up dealing with behaviors your students can learn to manage on their own.

Activity

Use the Activity Checklist to plan or evaluate the directions you assign for various activities.

Activity Checklist

Product and/or Behavior

    Objective:

    Criteria for successful completion:

Clarity

    Skills or behaviors (cognitive, social, motor) required by this activity that may be new to the students:

    Materials or equipment used to complete this activity that may be unfamiliar to the students:

    Other considerations (for example, movement within or outside the classroom, need for other facilities or resources):

Presentation of Instructions

    Verbal:

    Written:

    Illustrated:

    Other (taped, signed, other language):

    Samples of finished products available:

Structure

    Limits, starting point, or focus:

    Choices available:

Other Success-Oriented Features

    Getting students' attention:

    Time-related (that is, *not* when they're wound up about something else or too far in advance for them to remember):

    Small steps:

    Logical sequence:

Evaluation Summary

    In what ways were these directions success oriented?

    In what ways did the students have difficulty with the directions?

    In what ways might these directions have been even more success oriented?

    Note to self: Next time, remember to . . .

Directions are more meaningful and more likely to engage student cooperation and success when there is a logical reason and benefit to them. Complete Chart 16.1, using the instructions provided.

1. In the first column (or on the left-hand side of a separate piece of paper folded into three columns), list specific behaviors you would like to request from your students.

2. Column 2, identify the primary reason you want them to do what you're asking. Think in terms of logical outcomes ("…so the paste doesn't dry out," " "…so the cables don't get tangles," etc.) or benefits to the students, rather than how this would please you, make your life easier, or help the kids avoid an angry or punitive reaction..

3. Column 3, create a request or set of instructions connecting the two: "Let's keep quiet in the hall so we don't bother the other classes." "Please pick the blocks up off the rug so no one trips on them." "Put the CDs back in the case so they don't get scratched." "Get your note in by Tuesday so you can go on the field trip."

Chart 16.1 Developing Clear and Logical Instructions

Desired Behaviors Requested	Reason for Request	Instructions to Student

NOTES

1. How often do we refuse to teach or demonstrate a skill because it's not on our grade level curriculum? As long as I resisted having to teach things they "should have learned by now," I doomed my class, and myself, to needless misunderstanding and misbehavior.

2. See sidebar, "Say It Once!"

3. Adapted from the definition of rubrics on the Ozarka College Web site: http://www .ozarka.edu/assessment/glossary.cfm.

4. Jo Ann Freiberg, e-mail message to author, February 7, 2006.

17

Planning for Success

If you've ever had an otherwise well-planned lesson bomb because you didn't have enough handouts, underestimated the complexity of a necessary piece of equipment, or assumed that your kids were better able to work independently in groups, you can appreciate the value of success-oriented planning. Many otherwise well-planned lessons have been doomed by the simplest omissions, timing mistakes, or errors in judgment. One first-grade teacher watched a terrific art activity fall apart when she realized she hadn't borrowed enough staplers. Another saw her plans to have her kids make their own bingo cards falter from her students' inexperience with rulers.

Good planning is mostly common sense, and a bit of anticipation and forethought can prevent monstrous headaches—and the discipline problems that go with them. Sure, there will be emergencies, and many things can affect our plans that are simply beyond our control. Consider the seventh-grade science teacher who planned an entire week's worth of lessons around a shipment of fruit flies that had died in transit. Another teacher discovered, at the last minute, that the media

> No matter how much I tried to overplan, there were always days when we'd get through a lesson in much less time than I'd anticipated.

center had shipped the wrong DVD. I've seen an essential piece of equipment break right before a teacher's demonstration, and watched as another teacher had to switch gears when the server was down during the period his kids needed to do some online research. And no matter how much I tried to overplan, there were always days when we'd get through a lesson in much less time than I'd anticipated. (This is when a good set of emergency backup plans can save the day.)

With good planning, we can minimize confusion, additional movement, off-task time, and interruptions, and our attention to these details can curtail opportunities for discipline problems to develop. But the greatest challenges in planning go beyond logistical considerations; they actually involve what we teach, where we generally have far less discretion and control.

FACING THE CONTENT GAP

It always amuses me to talk about my work with noneducators who have very strong opinions about the "terrible state of education." When they start in on the tired-but-typical speech about how their businesses would go straight down the tubes if they were run like the schools, I'm always amazed at how recklessly they impose the context of their world on a culture that operates with very different goals, structures, and constraints. Having run a business for much of my adult life, I can clearly see the places where their logic is flawed: If merchandise arrives in bad condition, I send it back; I am not obligated to accept or pay for damaged books. However, when I was in the classroom, I wasn't even offered choices of grade levels or subject areas, much less kids. My principal handed me a list and, trust me, there were kids on that list who were in pretty bad condition. (Even as a teacher educator, I often have people in my audiences who do not want to be there, who have been sent to my seminars as "punishment," or who just aren't open to hearing what I have to say.) When it comes to our students, we don't get to return "defective merchandise"; we get what we get, and we do the best we can to connect with them all.

Now if that weren't enough, when we walk into our classrooms, we also get a second list, this one with a set of curricular mandates, the stuff we're supposed to teach. And this is where it gets tricky, because I've met very few teachers who did not have a bit of a gap between the two lists, with kids on List 1 who simply weren't cognitively or academically prepared for the stuff demanded by List 2. At some point, every teacher will have to make an excruciating decision about which list he or she will honor. Unfortunately—for the teachers, the kids, and, sadly, the profession—many teachers are under tremendous pressure to get through the curriculum.

> Unfortunately—for the teachers, the kids, and, sadly, the profession—many teachers are under tremendous pressure to get through the curriculum.

I met one teacher whose department chair insisted that this teacher get through the book by the end of the year. "Let the chips fall where they may," she was told. Unfortunately, these "chips" are people's children, and when they fall, they rarely do so quietly, and often will take us down with them.

At the end of the summer after my first year of teaching, I was offered a job teaching math to the five upper grades in a K–8 school. The staff greeted me with a warning that the eighth graders might be somewhat difficult. The majority of students in this class had not done well in math in years past and would probably not be eager to come around for one more year of failure and frustration. The content in the eighth-grade textbook did little to alleviate my concerns. After very few pages of review, the book jumped into complex concepts like multiples, factors, ratio, and square roots. These kids were in for a challenging year, indeed.

"Well," I thought, "let's see what these guys can do." I armed myself with a stack of teacher-made diagnostic exercises, sequenced according to district curriculum goals, to greet the students when they first walked through the door. When the kids arrived, it was obvious they did not want to be there. Even the presence of a young, enthusiastic teacher did not give them much hope. This was still math, and they were still going to fail as they always had. I shut the door and turned to find thirty-eight hostile, hulking teens, arms folded across chests, eyes glaring and suspicious. Fun.

"Okay kids, let's see what you remember. No grades—just do the best you can do." I wasn't terribly surprised to learn from this test that nearly half of the class faltered on addition problems that required regrouping. The few students who had mastered the basics were tested on more advanced concepts, but even the most skilled students were years behind where they were supposed to be according to the district standards.

As far as planning instruction went, I only had to look at these pretests to imagine how these kids would do on multiples or square roots. Now what? Do I stick to the book and a curriculum that is far beyond the capabilities of the class, or do I back up and start with what they actually can do? Clearly, there was more at stake here than an academic agenda: Imagine the kind of behavior I could expect from a group of students who could neither understand the lessons nor do the assignments.

> Do I stick to the book and a curriculum that is far beyond the capabilities of the class, or do I back up and start with what they actually can do?

Of course I felt considerable pressure to teach eighth-grade math to eighth-grade students, especially since a few of them were chronologically past driving age. On one level, it felt important that I expose them to skills they would encounter later on districtwide standardized tests. But I knew I'd only be exposing them to one more thing they were doomed to fail.[1] Their math anxiety, can't-do attitudes, and poor self-concepts hardly needed any reinforcement. Surely, attempting to teach math concepts when prerequisite skills had not been mastered would be pointless and self-defeating. I decided to start wherever was necessary for them to achieve, catching up as best we could. My immediate concern focused on helping each student to be better at math at the end of each week—regardless of where we had to start. (I also hoped to help them develop more confidence in their ability to do math, or at least wear down their resistance to coming to class and doing work there.) I announced that these students needed three things to succeed in this class: They had to show up, they needed a pencil, and they needed to produce, starting with whatever they could actually do.

GETTING AWAY WITH SUCCESS

There was some initial administrative concern that the majority of the students were still not in the district-assigned books after the first few weeks of school. But the pressure was not as strong as it could have been, because I had a number of things working on my behalf. I had the diagnostic evidence to back up my placements, and while it was likely that a number of these students might never catch on to the most complex concepts, every child in that room made tremendous progress in a very short period of time.

The increased success the students experienced was engaging. Overall attitudes improved and off-task behavior was at a minimum. Students were taking risks, trying new things, and beginning to believe that they could actually succeed in this class. I was even getting notes from parents, pleased and surprised to see their children bringing their books home and enthusiastic about math for the first time ever! And since my approach and my grading system were somewhat nontraditional, I made sure I included a list of math skills in each student's permanent record folder, checking off the skills each child had mastered in my class.

Of all the areas in which we could easily eliminate many discipline and attitude problems, the idea of increasing opportunities for larger numbers of kids to be successful seems to be one of the most difficult to accomplish. When we look back over the traditions from which our current school practices arose, we see a system that practically guarantees failure for at least a portion of our students, and failure pretty much guarantees discipline problems. Content-related pressures, real or self-imposed, exist in every teaching situation and with the most ideal students. When your students lack the skills necessary for school success, even our best lessons and instructional skills will fall flat. The cycle continues, with failure relentlessly feeding behavior, behavior feeding failure, on and on.

When student behavior interferes with learning or teaching, the pressure to cover content can become unbearable. Even without disputing the questionable importance of everything we believe all children should know or be able to do, the notion that we should be able to walk into any group of eighth graders, for example, and teach them all the same concept at the same time—and expect uniform mastery—is certainly not based in any reality I've ever experienced. Perhaps in light of this improbability, we developed a fondness for the good old bell curve, which allowed us to justify teaching to the middle—and accept a certain amount of failure in any class or group of students. In the meantime, we end up with a lot of kids left out of the loop, many of them acting out their boredom, indifference, anger, or frustration.

For the schools to continue to stress the importance of uniformity at this point in our information-age evolution creates far more problems than it solves. Nowhere is this value more evident—still—than in our obsession with standards and standardization. One of the unfortunate places to which these traditions lead is the expectation that teachers' evaluations reflect a normal distribution of grades.[2] As much as we may talk about wanting all children to succeed, you can be sure if you have too many successful kids in your class, somebody is going to be on your case for being too easy.

Nonetheless, there are things we can do to ensure success for larger numbers of kids.[3] I am continually inspired by the determination and resolve of teachers who manage to survive, connecting with kids academically, despite a soul-destroying lack of discretion about what they teach. I visited a district in which every ninth-grade student was enrolled in a required algebra class. If you already knew algebra, you took this class. If you couldn't subtract, you took this class. It was, for all intents and purposes, the only math class available at this grade level. To add insult to injury, every algebra teacher throughout the district was required to teach the same page on the same day. (The misguided belief was that this approach would prevent any student from being left behind. In reality, the majority of kids were failing algebra.) Yet there was this one teacher I observed who started her class by announcing, "I am required to teach Page 51 today. Bear with me. I will come around afterward and teach *you* when I'm done." She proceeded to teach the required lesson and then spent the rest of the class going around to work with her kids, wherever they were. (Win-win solutions apply to academics, too.) Even more fascinating were the number of students who came back to her class after school for additional instruction and remediation—not exactly the kind of commitment we generally get when we teach well over a student's head.

Even when I started teaching, there was tremendous pressure to "cover content," especially if it was going to be on "The Test." I learned early on that the more I could cover my bases—if not my backside—with lots of documentation, present fewer problems for the office, and generate increased support from parents, the more I was able to get away with an emphasis on teaching kids, not math. I'd love to tell you that my motivation was entirely noble and altruistic, but there certainly was an element of self-preservation there. I knew what kind of behavior I was in for from a frankly scary bunch of young people had I insisted on presenting more stuff they simply couldn't do.

Getting Away With Success: Tips for Teachers

- Assess what your students already know. If they can already demonstrate mastery, you can justify moving them ahead. If they lack prerequisite skills, you have something to back up your decision to teach what they need.
- Document like there's no tomorrow. Good documentation is more than a sign of professionalism and accountability. It also helps to protect your administration, whose support can be invaluable when matching your instruction to the needs of your students. Keep track of assessments, dates specific skills were mastered, work samples, and progress.
- Move along the lines of district-mandated curriculum. If you have to back up the content you're teaching or choose to include content that is not listed in the mandates for your grade level or subject area, working within what's already established in the system can give you more leverage than arbitrarily choosing skills or content to teach.
- Maintain high levels of performance as your criteria for achievement. Continue raising hurdles as kids make progress. You can fend off charges of "lowering the bar" or grade inflation when you keep pushing and refuse to accept inferior or substandard work.
- Back up decisions with research that will support your instructional choices—anything about how kids learn, or how they learn that particular content, can help.
- Build relationships and communication with your administration, department, support staff, and grade-level colleagues.
- Build relationships with parents. (See Chapter 23.) I never had a parent insist on a placement that would guarantee failure for his or her child. And once they saw evidence of success, achievement, progress, or even enthusiasm for my class, I found parental support to be one of the best weapons in the arsenal.
- Keep your intentions in mind. If you are there to ensure that your students gain knowledge and proficiency, you will choose very different behaviors than if you just want to barrel through the curriculum.
- Be willing to take a few hits. Bucking tradition can cost you some conflict or disapproval from colleagues.

TEACHING IN PRESENT TIME

Our greatest strides in developing win-win relationships and self-managing student behavior and a positive classroom climate can be sadly undermined by teaching content that is poorly matched to student abilities. It's easy to dismiss a success-oriented approach to instruction as being too easy. But in this math class, although we started with something the kids could do, we did not linger there. The challenge was continual, and from the first, the lessons demanded stretching beyond the comfort of previous achievement. Aside from a few practice laps, each successful trip around the track meant a higher hurdle to clear next time around.

As educational program developer and former principal Mark Ita advises, "Our job is not to document failure. Our job is to prevent failure." Learning will rarely take place unless students believe that success is within reach. The notion of toughening them up by letting them fail is a rather sadistic holdover from traditions of industrial-era structures. Students will have plenty of opportunities to mess up. Deliberately setting them up

> Learning will rarely take place unless students believe that success is within reach.

to fail is far more likely to slow them down, if not stop them cold. If we really want our students to make it in a tough world, they'll be far better served by practicing success than failure.

And what about the next year? Sure, some of those eighth graders would be hitting ninth-grade math classes without some of the skills of the eighth-grade curriculum. But they did have the advantage of the progress they made; at least they would not be starting without the skills from elementary math as well. They knew a whole lot more than they would have learned if I had insisted on teaching over their heads all year, simply widening the gap between what they knew and what there was to learn. Addressing present needs in present time allows us to make real and meaningful progress. One more year of failure and frustration at the eighth-grade level would hardly have made my students more successful the following year.

It's also hard to stay in present time when we are distracted by constant pressure to get our kids to perform on statewide or districtwide standardized tests. Although the value of the information provided by these tests is limited at best, when pressure to increase standardized test scores escalates, the more likely a teacher (or, indeed, an entire district) will be driven by academics and curriculum regardless of actual student readiness or progress. Even in the early 1970s, there was concern that my eighth graders would not be able to pass the square root problems on "The Test" because I wasn't teaching that skill to them. And indeed, I doubt many of my students did well on those problems. (I still contend that kids who couldn't add would have failed square roots no matter how well I might have taught that skill.) Nevertheless, the kids *could* do problems that demanded things like basic operations on whole numbers, fractions, and decimals—which meant that their performance on "The Test" was far better than it would have been had I simply presented them with more content they could not master.

We need to be careful that our concern for these tests (or next year) does not imbalance our intentions. We prepare students to succeed in the future with opportunities to succeed in the present, building the confidence and flexibility that will help them handle future difficulties more effectively. Authors Deborah Stipek and Kathy Seal agree that nothing motivates kids better than competence: "The more competent kids feel academically, the more interested they are in their schoolwork, and the harder they study. In other words, competence breeds self-motivation."[4] We never know when something in the content will just click for a child, or when appropriate placement will lead to a huge leap in learning. Surely we can't expect this kind of growth when we insist on presenting material that lies beyond their grasp. This brings up the whole point of why we're in the classroom in the first place. If our intention is for kids to learn, we'll choose very different teaching behaviors than if we simply want to cover content. In fact, if all we want to do is cover content, we don't even need kids.

REDEFINING "FAIR"

The goal of success orientation, whether in giving directions, feedback, or instruction, is to remove obstacles for success for all students. It is no longer acceptable to settle for adequate performance from the kids in the middle of the curve; high and low achieving students need and deserve to be challenged at a level at which they can learn and achieve as well. Even if the content is the same for everyone, there are things we can do to invite everyone to succeed.

When I taught spelling at the elementary level, I invariably had a handful of students who either flunked the test every Friday or barely passed. By simply following my same routine—which had only reinforced failure week after week for these students—what was the likelihood that their confidence or performance in this subject would spontaneously transform? Monday would come and they'd face twenty new words, Friday would come and they would fail the test. A new Monday only meant twenty more words they wouldn't learn. Something had to change, and chances were, their spelling performance was not likely to be any different until I changed my approach.

I remember sitting down with five or six kids to look at our options. They got so busy trying to convince me that "I can't spell" that the possibility of success never occurred to them. Trying to convince them that they could indeed spell, or at least do quite a bit better than they had done in the past, was meaningless in the absence of hard evidence. In desperation, I asked, "How many words do you think you can learn in a week?"

The group stared at me. A few shrugged or intoned an exchange I took to mean, "I don't know."

"How about five? Can you learn five?"

"I don't know."

"Let's give it a try. Get any five words right on the test and you get an A." For the moment, I also reduced the requirements of my minimally achieving middle group to ten words and asked my more competent spellers to agree on three words from the science unit to add to their list.[5]

When I relate this story to other teachers, I often get a somewhat shocked reaction. Even teachers who are comfortable with reading or math groups have more trouble with this strategy than my own students did: "Well, what if the students in the top group want to know why the other kids have to learn only five words?" they ask. "Simple! We tell them, 'It's because everyone is different, and everyone in this class gets to succeed.'"

In win-lose classrooms, where kids are routinely pushed into the deep end of the academic pool whether or not they can swim, it makes sense to assign twenty words to each child. Fear of protest by some students (or their parents) makes this practice easy to justify. But there's rarely a protest in a win-win classroom, because kids see, on a regular basis, the teacher's commitment to everyone's success. They quickly learn that fairness is not about uniformity, it's about uniformly accommodating, as much as possible, individual needs, abilities, and preferences. Where the factory equated "fair" with "same," in an information economy, fairness means, "equally appropriately challenged." (Besides, how is it fair for certain kids to fail week after week?) And parents who are kept current on policies and progress, particularly when contact focuses on positive aspects of their children's growth and behavior, tend to be far less adversarial than many teachers fear.[6]

> Fairness is not about uniformity, it's about uniformly accommodating, as much as possible, individual needs, abilities, and preferences.

The bottom line was that until I was willing to give each student a way to succeed in this subject, there would always be a small group who learned nothing each week beyond "I can't spell." (I did have one or two students over the years who asked to be moved, in the beginning, to a lower group. Although I believed they could do fine at a higher level, they lacked confidence, at least at first; it cost me nothing to consent. In nearly every instance, after a few days—if that—they each requested being returned to their original placement.) Some kids took a while to trust the possibility of success, but eventually each one stepped up to the plate. After a few weeks, I pulled the group back together: "You guys are doing great in spelling. Do you think you can learn seven words this week?"

"I don't know . . . ."

"Let's give it a try!"

Eventually everybody got up to twenty words. No, they didn't all become star spellers, but the improvement in skill and confidence sold me on the value of a teaching approach that accepts and begins with wherever students are in the moment, and continually challenges them at a point at which they each can succeed. Sure, it's easier and more convenient for the teacher to have everybody on Page 70 whether or not they belong there, but if students don't belong on Page 70, what we're doing is not teaching, at least not as far as those students are concerned.

Success-oriented planning leads to success-oriented instruction. In addition to thinking through the details and logistics of specific activities, planning also addresses what the kids can do, where their interests lie, and how to best reinforce the students' commitment, risk taking, perseverance, and belief in their own potential for achievement. Give kids a taste of success and you increase the odds that they might even love learning for learning's sake. But perhaps the greatest benefit of success orientation in a classroom is its ability to sharply reduce instances of disruption, confusion, frustration, conflict, off-task behavior, and wasted time that often occur when kids figure that as long as they're going to fail anyhow, they may as well have a good time. Success orientation won't eliminate every classroom problem we might encounter, but it will certainly help prevent the majority of discipline issues that arise when kids do not understand directions or content, or when they see no possibility for school success—regardless of how they behave.

Give kids a taste of success and you increase the odds that they might even love learning for learning's sake.

Save a Sub's Sanity

Make it easy for your substitutes to succeed, too. Create a file with emergency materials and activities, which can be especially valuable when they're available for a substitute who may have difficulty following your regular plans, pulling everything together for a more complex lesson, coming to your class in the middle of a unit, or getting the kids' cooperation. Keep emergency plans and materials in a "Substitute Survival Folder."

In addition to materials, I've met teachers who prepared their students for substitutes, first of all, by reframing the concept as a *guest teacher*. Several have assigned specific students to the job of host or hostess to help the guest teacher with routines, logistics, or the location of certain materials, for example. They report that with the students invested in the sub's success, their classmates tended to be more respectful. "If they were disrespectful to the sub, they were, in essence, disrespectful to the hosts, who were also their friends," one teacher claimed. Whatever you can do to make things go smoothly when you're not in school, it's a safe bet your efforts will be appreciated and lead to a better experience for the sub, the kids, and you on your return.

Activities

Here is a success-oriented planning list to help you evaluate activities and lessons before you implement them:

What materials do I need?

Do I have enough materials?

What do I still need to buy, assemble, make, or get?

How will I distribute the materials?

Will students have to move?

What changes in furniture or room arrangement will I need to make?

How can I make this transition as smooth as possible?

What will I be doing during this activity?

How free will I be to help answer questions or monitor behavior?

What resources, materials, and arrangements will help students solve problems without bothering me?

When is this activity supposed to take place?

Is that the best time for this lesson?

Do they need time to settle down from their last class?

Is it too close to the weekend or holiday to introduce something new?

What else might I need to contend with or compensate for?

What alternatives are available?

What are they most likely to misunderstand?

What else do I need to go over?

Do the students need to practice anything first?

What do they need to do, have, or get before they can begin?

What can go wrong?

What do I do if any of these things actually happens?

What is Plan B if this flops altogether? (Repeat all of the above for Plan B.)

Chart 17.1 Planning and Material Preparation

Backup Materials and Activities	Location of Materials	Readiness for Use	Special Instructions, Preparations, or Materials Needed

Use Chart 17.1 or create a similar chart on a separate piece of paper.

- In Column 1, describe the emergency or backup materials and plans you have for those occasions on which a particular lesson doesn't work, the materials you ordered don't come in on time, or the kids finish in half the time you anticipated.
- In Column 2, tell where the materials are located.
- In Column 3, tell if the materials are ready for use (if not, note what needs to be done).
- In Column 4, describe any special instructions, materials, or preparation the students will need in order to do these backup activities. If the students can get started as soon as they receive the materials, simply mark "independent" in this column.

NOTES

1. I often hear this term come up in rationalizations for presenting content kids simply can't do. I'm not sure how the notion of "exposing" kids to content for which they were cognitively, developmentally, or experientially unprepared ever came to be equated with teaching, much less good practice. Simply exposing me to advanced math or English composition or conversational German is far more likely to leave me frustrated, bored, and inattentive, if not feeling downright stupid if I don't have the more basic math, writing, or German language skills mastered. More often than not, "exposing" kids to content generally winds up being little more than an exercise in exposing them to failure.

2. The term *normal distribution* refers to the bell curve. The initial application, when first discovered in the early 1700s, involved odds in games of chance. Eventually applied (or misapplied) to social phenomena, the bell curve became an unquestioned staple in evaluation processes in educational institutions. Adapted and condensed from Ted Goertzel and Joseph Fashing, "The Myth of the Normal Curve: A Theoretical Critique and Examination of Its Role in Teaching and Research," *Humanity and Society,* 5 (1981): 14–31; reprinted in *Readings in Humanist Sociology* (Bayside, NY: General Hall, 1986). Available from Rutgers University Web site: http://www.crab .rutgers.edu/~goertzel/normalcurve.htm.

3. See sidebar, "Getting Away With Success: Tips for Teachers."

4. Deborah Stipek and Kathy Seal, *Motivated Minds: Raising Children to Love Learning* (New York: Henry Holt, 2001), 43.

5. I doubt that I would teach spelling as an isolated subject at this point in my career, but back then, this was what I knew.

6. See Chapter 23 for more information.

18

Learning Styles and Preferences

About sixty minutes into my full-day seminars, I ask the following question: "How many of you have been sitting longer in this past hour than you normally do in an entire day?" Nearly every participant responds in the affirmative. Their restlessness shows, even though we've had several opportunities for talking and interacting.

This is usually the time to introduce activities like drinking water (hydrating) and standing up to do an exercise that requires some cross-lateral movements (right hand to left knee, left hand to right knee) to help wake up their brains.[1] Afterward, practically everyone notices a significant difference in their level of alertness, although we're up and moving around for only a minute or so, if that. These are adults, trained for years in the cheerless art of sitting still for long periods of time. Imagine the implications for kids.

> We know, for example, that we can eliminate a large number of distracting and disruptive classroom behaviors when we ease up on our insistence on restricting kids' movement, limiting their interactions, and teaching in ways that make little sense to their nervous systems.

Among the considerations for factors that influence achievement and behavior, we've got to throw learning needs into the mix. We know, for example, that we can eliminate a large number of distracting and disruptive classroom behaviors when we ease up on our insistence on restricting kids' movement, limiting their interactions, and teaching in ways that make little sense to their nervous systems. This means learning a little bit more about how our students learn—or at least recognizing that not all students learn the same way.

I use the following quiz to help participants self-assess a handful of preferences, any one of which can influence how a student learns—and behaves—in a classroom. To continue, consider how *you* learn best and check the answer for each question that feels most like you.

	True	False	n/a
1. I study best when it's quiet.			
2. I learn more in a room with bright lights (or natural light).			
3. I listen better when I'm doodling, chewing gum, or playing with a piece of string.			
4. I'm more alert later in the day than early in the morning.			
5. I need to study in a relaxed position, with my feet up on the couch, or in bed.			
6. I remember things I *see* better than things I hear.			
7. I like a lot of freedom on my projects (structure and guidelines are okay).			

In my seminars and trainings, I ask participants to raise their hands in response to each question. Even with very small groups, we've never once had a group in which everyone responded the same way, even on any one question. In fact, part of the process of doing this activity is to have people notice the variations in preferences among the other people in the group.

The fact is, our students represent a wide range of preferences, learning needs, and ways of attending. Further, multitasking, dividing one's attention among a number of activities, has become increasingly common among children. (A 2005 study showed that while the amount of time that kids devoted to using electronic media was holding steady at six and a half hours a day, the amount of media exposure they were packing into that time was actually eight and a half hours a day,[2] and some believe the increase in "digital participation" is sharpening minds, not dumbing them down.[3]) To many adults, these students may not only appear inattentive, but also distracted, hyperactive, or even disrespectful.

One of the obstacles in actually reaching large numbers of these kids is our inclination to project our own particular habits and preferences on others, assuming that they need what we need when it comes to learning. Second, schools are generally set up to accommodate a rather narrow range of preferences. If you look at the kids who are best suited to succeeding when exposed to the most common, traditional approaches to teaching, you'll see characteristics such as an ability to sit still for long periods of time, take in information effectively through their auditory and visual channels, follow rules and instructions, respond quickly when called on, and an inclination toward linguistic and logical-mathematical intelligences and left-brain dominance (generally linear and logical in their thinking).[4] Now, this might be fine except for the fact that so few of us fit into this mold, including your humble author. In fact, if you want a little glimpse into how my brain works, look back at the aforementioned survey. All seven of those statements are true for me—and they're generally true in a big way.

> Doing things that required additional planning, time, and work, things that often took me way out of my comfort zone, was simply the cost of reaching learners and reducing restlessness and distractibility.

There are a couple of significant implications here. The first is the fact that, unless you also checked all seven statements as true, you'd probably have a hard time learning in an

The "Ideal" Student

Traditional classrooms tend to favor students with the following characteristics or strengths:[5]

- Left-brain dominant
- Strong in linguistic and logical-mathematical intelligences
- Academically on grade level (not too far ahead or behind)
- Learning preferences:
  - Prefers working in a quiet environment
  - Best time of day: Early morning, afternoon
  - Social: Prefers working quietly alone or in a group (limited need for interaction)
  - Can handle highly structured environment (seated in chairs, sitting up straight, not rocking or fidgeting)
  - Limited intake needs while working (food, drink, gum, snack)
  - Low mobility needs

- Modality strengths:
  - High auditory, high visual
  - Low kinesthetic (limited need for movement)
  - High verbal skills, ability to respond immediately when called on (rather than needing time to process quietly, internally, before responding)
  - Attending behaviors: Eye contact, little talking or movement (note taking is okay in linear, traditional form)

- Temperament traits:
  - High in adaptability, persistence, and regularity
  - Low in distractibility, intensity, and sensitivity to sound, light, smell, or touch
  - Low to moderate in activity or energy levels

- Personality traits: Concrete thinker, logical, rational, organized, prompt, and able to follow rules and procedures
- Studies show other factors (gender, culture, socioeconomic status, appearance, popularity, membership in highly valued groups or teams, for example) to also be relevant

How does the "ideal" student differ from the "real" students you encounter in your classes? How are they alike?

environment in which I imposed these preferences on you, teaching as if you learned the way I learn. This approach would certainly drive many people around the bend, which would end up as discipline problems for me! I learned early on that I needed to provide areas in my classroom with more subdued lighting or allow kids to turn their desks (or put their binders up in front of them) to shield them from distracting movements or visually busy bulletin boards and displays. I made my life easier by giving instructions in different ways. I avoided a host of problems when I could provide more structure than I would have thought necessary for students who froze if the project offered them too much latitude. In my training workshops, I had to force myself to work with overheads (and eventually pre-sentation software) because I was losing my visual learners without them, despite pages and pages of handouts. Doing things that required additional planning, time, and work, things that often took me way out of my comfort zone, was simply the cost of reaching more learners and reducing restlessness and distractibility.

The second implication concerns me—or kids like me—as a learner in your classroom. Whether you know anything about my learning preferences, imagine the level of engagement you could expect if you were simply willing to offer choices about where I could sit. If I knew that I could read or work curled up in a beanbag chair in a well-lit area, maybe drinking water or chewing gum, do you think I'd blow it by misbehaving or abusing these privileges? Not on your life!

Differences in learning styles can create stress in any relationship, which you probably already know if you're in a relationship with someone who profiles differently from you. My high auditory husband (who often swears he's told me things he's never actually said) has learned that I'm much more likely to remember things when he writes them down. I've learned that he's more open to ideas when he has far more information than I'd ever need ("It's red" usually works for me) and when he has more time to process and respond than I would generally take. But even if you've never lost your patience with someone you love just because he or she really *can* read and watch TV at the same time, you're probably well acquainted with the stress and chaos that can develop when we're dealing with dozens of kids with different learning needs in the same place and at the same time.

CHANGING LEVELS OF ALERTNESS

Throughout my teacher training, I remember hearing about the need to attend to children's cognitive, affective, and psychomotor needs, but other than this caution, I don't remember receiving much information on anything besides the cognitive domain. I've spent a good bit of time exploring the other realms over the years and, particularly with respect to body and brain, I'm continually amazed at the number of factors that can affect how a child physically functions in a classroom. I'd like to share some ideas I've learned—from research and seminars, from other educators, and from my own experiences and observations—in terms of specific ways we can help our students be physically comfortable in our classrooms, get information into their nervous systems, and maintain an appropriate level of alertness.[6]

Consider these suggestions in the context of the following: Human beings have a rather short attention span, even under optimal conditions, and our attention span varies with age, equaling roughly one minute of attention for every year of age. For preadolescents, that means switching gears every five to ten minutes to maintain their attention; most adolescents will lose their concentration after approximately ten to fifteen minutes. Even adult learners need a "brain break" every fifteen to eighteen minutes.[7] So with this information in mind, here are some things teachers across all grade levels are doing to help kids stay focused and to increase engagement and success.[8]

CHANGING THE VISUAL FIELD

Are your students sluggish and lethargic? Do you need their attention for a few more minutes? Try moving to a different part of the room and relating to students from there. Simply shifting their visual orientation to you can "wake them up" and improve their ability to attend. You can also have them turn their seats or desks to face a different part of the room for the remainder of the period. Other seat-changing strategies might include having your students switch seats with a neighbor or move over (or back) one seat, having them move to a different part of the room, or pulling a group or even the entire class to a specific space in the room that is different from where they've been sitting until now. You can also invite them to find a place where they'll be comfortable for a particular activity. Set a time limit if necessary (even the adults in my classes can take a minute or more to find a different space or seat when asked to move) and any conditions that will make this work for you.

Consider lighting needs and preferences. Light affects brain chemistry, and different people have different reactions to variations in lighting. (I left family, friends, and a good job to move to the Southwest for more sunshine; my husband can spend days with the blinds drawn.) Notice which kids gravitate toward the windows or the best-lit parts of the room, and which kids want to put their hoods up, keep their hats on, or sit under their desks or in darker corners. Provide full-spectrum lighting when possible. I've known a few children who were misdiagnosed as attention deficit when it turned out they were sensitive to fluorescent light. Some studies have shown that simply replacing fluorescent bulbs with full-spectrum bulbs can account for significant improvements in attendance and achievement, higher test scores, and a decrease in eyestrain, depression, illness, inattention, irritability, and hyperactivity.[9]

> Light affects brain chemistry, and different people have different reactions to variations in lighting.

Let them wear hats. I've heard from a number of teachers who have seen improvement in attention and behavior when students could wear visors or caps with brims in their classes, regardless of whether this represented light sensitivity or sartorial preferences. I don't recall ever having a problem in my classes because a student—kid or adult—was wearing a hat. Maybe this is just me, but it seems we've got bigger fish to fry than creating conflict, stress, and power struggles over kids wearing hats.

Another suggestion involves providing colored acetate sheets to place over text (or glasses with tinted lenses for kids to read through) for students who want or need them. For some students, color overlays can reduce print or background distortion, and glare or stark contrast of black ink on white paper. Many kids show significant improvements in reading comprehension and achievement when they were able to use overlays.[10] Since the brain craves novelty, it's likely that everyone will want to try one at first, so have enough overlays in a variety of colors for kids to choose, perhaps introducing this accommodation in small groups. Teachers report that after a couple of days, only the kids who really seem to benefit from the overlays continue to use them. Alternatively, several teachers have told me that their kids do better when they duplicate handouts or tests on pastel-colored paper.

> The brain craves novelty.

When you read to children, allow them to read along if they have their own copies of the book, or show pages of the book, or illustrations from the pages, with an overhead or computer slide presentation. And don't forget to provide instructions in written form, on the board or on paper, to support low auditory learners. Visual and spatial learners can benefit from actual examples or demonstrations.

CHANGING THE AUDITORY FIELD

Let kids listen to music when they're working independently. Although the majority (approximately seventy-five percent) of teachers need quiet to study,[11] many of our students actually perform better when they listen to music. I had one class nearly double their productivity when I let them play music during their seatwork time. Many teachers report observable improvements in attendance, cooperation, concentration, and on-task time, and a reduction in lateness and unpreparedness when they allow music.

We now have the technology to allow these young people to listen to music without bothering anyone else, so maybe it's time to consider lifting the ban on various forms of personal music players. (Some teachers get around this restriction using "listening posts" for small groups of students, or playing music for the entire group. Others have gotten "exemptions" for special activities, classes, or individual students with special needs.) I've seen teachers use this accommodation effectively, and when the kids knew that they could retain the privilege as long as they removed their headphones and turned off the players when the teacher needed their attention, they were inclined to cooperate rather consistently.[12]

There are many ways to handle the types of music you allow. Although most educators assume that only quiet or classical music is appropriate in a classroom, this may not be the case. While various classical pieces can help control anger or promote relaxation, some research suggests that kids labeled as attention deficit hyperactivity disorder (ADHD) show a significant decrease in motor activity when they listen to rock music through individual headsets.[13] In using music in my own classroom, I left the choice up to my students. If the music was played publicly, limits included keeping the volume low enough so that it didn't disturb any of the other classes and sharing music in which the lyrics didn't include anything "mean or obscene." Other teachers tell me that their classes have responded well to a variety of genres. In one instance, the kids alternated between the preferences of the school's two main social factions, in this case country music and heavy metal, with one day a week set aside for "teacher's choice."[14]

Some students experience improvements in reading comprehension (and other skills such as language processing, spelling, concept processing, attention to task, and speech and language development) when they hear what they are reading or can talk through what they are thinking about. Teachers report that even older kids benefit from using a "whisper phone," a commercial or teacher-made tube[15] that allows students to hear their own voices as they read or work, providing direct and immediate auditory feedback without bothering other students. This tool can also increase focus, reduce auditory distractions, and reduce the noise level in the classroom.

Other students will appreciate it if you respect and accommodate their need for quiet. I've met teachers who have collected large, heavily padded headphones and simply cut the cords; students wear the headphones to help drown out noise. Others have provided earplugs for study time, or brought in recordings of "white noise" (or used actual white noise machines) to add a level of sound that helps block out disturbing noises.

> If your kids are busy, a chime or a bell will create a gentle shift in the auditory field and reach their brains in ways your voice will not.

Vary auditory input to gain attention. If your kids are busy, a chime or a bell will create a gentle shift in the auditory field and reach their brains in ways your voice will not. (Changing the modulation in your voice can accomplish the same thing, but since that often involves increases in volume and anger, it can increase stress in the learning environment.) You can also move to a different part of the room to change the students' orientation to your voice.

And remember to provide instructions in auditory format or announcements. A number of teachers have told me that they've started reading their tests to the kids when they first distribute them to support their low visual learners.

TOUCH

Many low auditory students can listen far more attentively when they can do something else while they are listening. Much of what is often labeled hyperactive behavior or low impulse control can often be successfully channeled into tactile or kinesthetic activities such as playing with a "fidget toy" like a beanbag, a gel ball, a stress ball, clay, a pipe cleaner, a clothespin, paper fasteners, or even a piece of string while listening. (Invite me to doodle or knit while you're talking or reading to me and I'll not only sit, quiet and nondisruptive for hours, but I'll also hear, understand, and remember a lot more of what's coming out of your mouth.)

Tactile anchors can also help with sensory integration problems. I once had a sixteen-year-old sent to me at a day treatment center. I could not get this young man to respond or even sit up. Bored silly, I went out to my car and got a bag filled with fidget toys, sat back down, grabbed a beanbag, and offered the lot to him. He grabbed five different fidgets and immediately sat up, made eye contact, and started to talk like crazy—completely articulate as long as he had something in his hands. And one teacher told me how her district improved test scores by providing a stress ball for kids to use, if they wanted, during their standardized tests.[16]

Manage the use of fidgets as you would anything else. A primary teacher brought in an entire basket filled with beanbags she had made and explained that these were "in-your-hands, in-your-lap, or on-the-floor" beanbags. As long as the children were not throwing them around, they could even take two. Once the teacher started reading to her kids, several put the beanbags down on the floor so they could listen better. (Of course, the high tactiles picked them up, so everybody won!) Not all children respond well to fidget toys and will instinctively avoid them after the initial curiosity wears off. Other ideas include attaching Velcro strips (both parts, separated), three to four inches long, to the underside of the desk or seat for kids to touch while listening, or offering a variety of different-sized pens, pencils, and markers.

Many teachers have told me that some of their students like sitting in class wrapped up in afghans or comforters brought in for that purpose. The fact is, some kids can actually sit still and concentrate better when they have some weight on them. (This is sort of like needing to sleep with a blanket, even in the summer.) I suspect that many of the kids who like to keep their jackets on all year share this need. In addition to unweighted comforters or jackets, there are commercially available vests and blankets to which weights can be added. These items can be particularly helpful as sensory integration resources with kids who are easily distracted, hyperactive, and lacking in coordination, and can also assist in relaxation and sensory processing.[17] Teachers without the resources to purchase these products tell me that they offer similar accommodations by allowing their students to place five- to ten-pound sacks of beans or rice on their laps. (Backpacks can also work in some instances). Others use long athletic socks filled with rice, sometimes made by students, to place on the student's lap or shoulders.

> Some kids can actually sit still and concentrate better when they have some weight on them.

Even the most comfortable chairs in school can get pretty hard after a short period of time. Several teachers have told me that they've had great success putting foam cushions on the students' chairs. Many like the "egg-crate" foam, wedge-shaped pillows, or air-filled "fidget" cushions for comfort and proprioceptive input. Hit a few garage sales for alternate seating to bring to your classroom or have the kids supply their own. Beanbag chairs, recliners, or couches, for example, can accommodate kids who have a hard time sitting in traditional chairs, and many do well in seats with arms. (See the next section, "Movement," for more seating ideas.)

MOVEMENT

Few people can comfortably sit in one place for as long as we ask kids to sit. Get them up and moving. Deliberately allow for stretch breaks, and teach them when and how to move about the room without bothering others. Several teachers (at various grade levels) have told me about "pacing boxes" they taped off on the floor in the back of the room, and how much better their students behaved when they knew they could get up and just stand or walk around in this 2' × 6' area. Another described placing tape around a student's desk to confine the space within which the student was to move, stay, or keep her things.

Many teachers complain that the chairs they have in their classrooms don't even fit their students. Some young students can't touch the floor and older children can barely fit in their chairs, especially when they're attached to desks, or are behind desks that are too short. To whatever degree you can provide a variety of seat sizes, or types of seating, this is certainly an aspect of a child's school life that can have an effect on his or her learning, attention, and behavior.

Many kids instinctively find ways to move their bodies, tapping their feet or doing things with their hands. A number of my students liked to rock back and forth on the back legs of their chairs. Although rocking stimulates the vestibular system, which helps us take information in from our environment, kids rocking back on their chairs used to drive me crazy. While it may have been perfectly legitimate from a neurological standpoint, on our slippery floors, it generally meant that someone was going to get hurt. Several teachers report using tennis balls on the bottom of the back legs of the chairs to provide some traction and stabilization, a solution which, unfortunately, never occurred to me when I was in the classroom. (This strategy also helps to reduce noise made by chairs scraping on the floor when they are moved.)

If rocking in their seats isn't safe—or if it's just visually distracting to you—provide a place where kids can go to rock, or a seat cushion (foam or air filled) on which they can fidget and still keep all four legs of the chair on the floor. Provide seats that allow for movement. Many teachers have a rocking chair in their classrooms or provide chairs with wheels or with seats that rotate. You can also place a large rubber band, exercise band, or bungee cord around the front legs of the chair to provide resistance, something against which the students' feet can push. I recently heard from a teacher who cut Styrofoam "pool noodles" into smaller lengths his students could roll under their feet as they sat at their desks. Not only can this keep some kids focused, but it can also reduce talking in some students as well. (This may be true for many of the strategies that involve putting something in kids' hands.)

Exercise balls (with or without stabilizing "feet") can also be used as chairs, as can beach balls for younger children. I had an occupational therapist explain that using a ball as a seat helps students recruit their core muscles, which may explain why a number of educators have reported that using these seats helps improve their kids' handwriting!

Provide cushions, "sit-upons," or carpeted spaces to work on the floor. I had elementary and middle school children who couldn't sit in a regular chair for five minutes but could work, sitting or lying on the floor, for more than an hour at a time. Also, create a space where students can work standing up, if they prefer. And if they want to kneel on chairs while they're working, and they're not bothering anyone or blocking the view, encourage this option as well.

Movement also includes taking notes or writing, and many kids will maintain their attention by putting information down on paper—sometimes as words and sometimes as drawings. As a highly tactile learner, I find that I need to be writing (or taking notes on a computer when the noise of my typing isn't bothering anyone) or my mind tends to wander, although if I'm knitting or doing needlework, I will remember just as well. Like many compulsive note takers, I rarely look at my notes again. For some of us, the act of writing is the piece that helps cement the information in memory—not the content of our notes. Other outlets might include drawing, doodling, playing with a fidget toy, knitting or other handcrafts, or using certain "touch" surfaces like Velcro or sandpaper glued to the sides of the desk or seat.

Give kids a chance to talk, interact, and change affiliation. Every few minutes, ask them to turn to someone, even if only for twenty or thirty seconds, just to share something they've learned or their reaction to

> Give kids a chance to talk, interact, and change affiliation.

what you've just presented. Even if they don't specifically stay on topic, the movement alone helps anchor what you've just shared. Remember, kids can focus their attention for only a few minutes at a time, so break up your instruction with different types of movement, including a few short breaks for social interaction. Use a bell or chime to get their attention back.

If your kids tap on their desks or books with their pens, the noise can drive you to distraction. I've heard of teachers who have brought in sponges, small carpet squares, or mouse pads for each desk; who have taped felt around the tops of the pencils or pens; or who have provided pipe cleaners so the kids could tap without making any noise. One particularly win-win high school teacher invited his kids to get to class on time so they could spend the first three minutes of class tapping! He said that it got pretty silly about a minute into the noise, everyone had a laugh, and that was pretty much the end of the disturbances (particularly those that might have been deliberate).

PUTTING SOMETHING IN YOUR MOUTH

Of all the strategies listed so far, these tend to be the hardest to sell. I've seen unbelievable amounts of valuable instructional time wasted on scolding, warning, punishing, giving students detention, or sending students to the office because of eating in class or chewing gum. The argument always maintains the necessity of punishing this particular behavior to discourage students from putting food or gum where it doesn't belong. Does it not make more sense to teach kids to use these accommodations properly?

Many people, including a large number of special education teachers and occupational therapists, describe how gum chewing seems to anchor some of their kinesthetic learners (and many students identified as attention deficit or hyperactive). The chewing, they claim, channels some of the students' energy and actually helps them concentrate and stay on task, especially when the students had to sit or study quietly for extended periods of time. Generally speaking, the teachers who make the least fuss over gum chewing report having the fewest problems.

Be very clear about the conditions under which kids can chew gum in your class. Show them how and where to throw it away. (Do you think they befoul their homes with gum? Let's give them an investment in the classrooms so they're not using gum vandalism as a way to get power or revenge.) Frankly, as long as I couldn't see it, hear it, or smell it, my students were allowed to chew it. This was a very big deal for some of them. Do you think they'd allow one another to interfere with this privilege by putting gum anywhere other than the trash can, wrapped in tissue or scrap paper, when they were done? No way!

Follow through if a child messes up, but leave the door open for him or her to get it right later. Whenever I noticed a student absentmindedly cracking his gum or blowing bubbles, simply pointing to the trash can was the only signal necessary—for that student, the privilege was lost for today. We'll try again tomorrow, no big deal. (Someone in a workshop once asked me what to do if the kid sneaks another piece of gum in his mouth. Well, if he can chew it without violating the boundary, let's call that learning and just move on. If not, point to the trash again. This was one privilege the kids didn't want to lose, and one I never had to revoke.) This privilege can help develop behaviors that extend beyond your classroom. I've had a number of teachers tell me that their students were much less likely to contribute to gum or other litter throughout the building or campus when they developed a sense of ownership and accountability in their rooms.

Find alternatives if gum really doesn't work for you. Win-win teachers who find the habit personally offensive, or those who encounter or anticipate a great deal of stress from other staff members, can minimize problems with a simple admission that gum chewing is distracting or problem producing to them, and providing other positive outcomes for their students. These might include straws, commercially available oral-motor stimulators, coffee stirrers, or even rubber surgical tubing. I've heard the latter used—again, with all age levels—in several different ways, including cutting off a 4″ to 6″ piece and putting it on the end of a child's pencil, or running a string through a piece to make a necklace. One teacher said her middle school kids concentrate better and talk less when they're working if they have their necklaces available.

Encourage your students to stay hydrated. This is one of the most basic, brain-friendly and inexpensive strategies we can use. Water helps the body communicate with the brain (and vice versa). It maintains the electrical balance in cells and improves our ability to concentrate. Water can counter the negative effects of caffeine, sugar, stress, and low frequency electromagnetic fields. Oddly, if not surprisingly, one of the most effective selling points about increasing hydration is the likelihood that test scores tend to be higher among hydrated learners.[18]

> Encourage your students to stay hydrated.

And yes, they'll have to pee. It takes the kidneys about a week to adjust. Let's get our relationships and power dynamics in order so kids don't constantly ask to leave the room to get their power or attention needs met. Many teachers, including myself, have found that the less we try to micromanage this aspect of the kids' lives, the more successfully they can self-manage. (They do at home.) Many teachers discover that when students know they can "go" any time they need to, even the ones who ask for the pass most often hardly have to go at all. Set contingencies as need be. Many teachers request that the kids not leave while the teacher is talking to their group, and insist that the pass is available only as long as the students aren't creating problems for anyone else—in or out of the room. Also remember that offering opportunities for kids to move within your classroom will eliminate the frequent requests to leave the room from kids who simply can't sit still another minute longer.

> Let's get our relationships and power dynamics in order so kids don't constantly ask to leave the room to get their power or attention needs met.

A number of teachers report improved performance on tests or activities when their kids' brains are stimulated by flavored candies. Several swear by peppermint, cinnamon, or lemon drops; a few have had the freedom to use scented oils or candles in their classrooms. (Please be considerate of students who may have allergies or sensitivities to fragrances.)

I've met several occupational therapists who encourage teachers to allow kids to have food in the classroom. They recommend chewy foods, crunchy foods, or thick liquids sucked through a straw. I remember once sitting in on a high school language class in which every student had a can of soda or water bottle, and most had snacks. They enjoyed this privilege and were as careful about cleaning up as any adults I've met. As always, the key is teaching kids to use whatever accommodations appropriately and with consideration for others.

SUPPORTING THE LOW VERBAL LEARNER

So much of what we do in school involves calling on kids and having them respond verbally. If students don't reply fairly immediately, we assume they either are not paying attention or that they do not know the answer. While traditional classrooms include high verbal ability among the characteristics of ideal learners, many of our students do not fall into this category. Low verbal learners may include students who need more time to process information before they are able to articulate an answer, highly introverted students, or kids who simply find sharing, much less standing up in front of a group, to be an uncomfortable—if not excruciating—experience.

If a child freezes when you call on him, you can tell him to think about it for a minute (or even look it up if he has to) and signal when he's ready to share. Under stress, our weakest channels get even weaker. Backing off and giving him some time can relieve some of the stress and put him in a place, neurologically, where he'll be able to retrieve the information and articulate it. (I've had some teachers give the child until the next day to look up the answer to a particular question and start off with an answer he's had the entire night to rehearse.) A high school teacher got her kids talking more by starting with their journals, using her responses to their writing to encourage them to share their insights and experiences verbally with the rest of the class.

Keep your intentions in mind. Why are you calling on this person? If you just want to see if he or she understands a concept, you can find out in a one-on-one conversation, casually asking what the student thought of the second act of *Romeo and Juliet.* If the child hasn't read it, ask him or her to come talk to you after it's been read. Calling on students to "wake them up" or embarrass them is generally stress-producing and counterproductive, not just for the kids being addressed, but for the others in the class as well.

A biology teacher once told me that eighty-five percent of her students' grades came from an oral report they were required to give. The low success rate she encountered may reflect the fact that speaking publicly is one of the most common fears among all human beings, regardless of their age. Many of the adults in my seminars claim that they would much rather offer the information requested in a written report, computer slide presentation, or video, for example, than stand up in front of others. The anxiety is so strong for some that many would just as soon drop the class or take a failing grade (or, say, get their teeth drilled) than stand up in front of their peers. While the opportunity to do an oral presentation may be very exciting for some of your students, why not offer other options for checking mastery as well?

I'm all for coaching kids out of their comfort zone and believe that part of our job is to encourage them to try things they may not love to do. I also do not believe that we all have to be pushed to do all things, and if there was ever a place to cut a kid some slack, this might be a good place to start. Teachers who feel pressure to push all of their students to do an oral report because state standards require them from everyone—there's that pesky uniformity again—have encountered success by allowing their students to choose whether they wanted to do the report in front of the entire class, a few friends they select, the teacher alone, or even, when resources allowed, as a privately recorded audio presentation, or in front of a video camera in an otherwise empty room. Let's keep in mind that there are many highly successful, productive, and well-educated adults who will never voluntarily stand up and speak in a room full of people, nor should they have to. I'd much rather see us devote our energies to helping kids develop the talents they do have rather than the ones we think they *should* have.

ALLOWING ACCOMMODATIONS IN SCHOOL

Look at photos of factory workers one hundred years ago and you'll often see rows of workers all doing the same thing. It's not surprising that the constraints of this setting translated to a school structure in which children sat in straight rows, with expectations for teachers to get them all into uniform postures (backs straight, feet flat, eyes forward, hands folded, mouths closed).[19] Despite the sharp decline in factory work environments, and despite the fact that only a very small percentage of students can actually learn or attend sitting in this position, we still interpret departures from this posture as inattentive or disrespectful. (In a testament to the persistence of these factory-era expectations, I encountered a group of teachers all too recently whose district had just purchased a curricular program that insisted that the teachers not start teaching until the students had "assumed the position" previously described. And of all the classrooms I've visited, I still see the overwhelming majority configured to factory-era, straight-row designs.)

Clearly, we have got to stop evaluating teachers on the basis of how quietly and still their students are sitting. But this trend has been slow to change. I've had numerous teachers tell me of supervisors or administrators who sent them to workshops on learning styles and then later wrote them up for implementing what they had learned there. But keep in mind that administrators and colleagues—and parents as well—may be more open to less traditional approaches when the behavior in that classroom is not disturbing other classes and when the kids are engaged and learning.

> Clearly, we have got to stop evaluating teachers on the basis of how quietly and still their students are sitting.

The key for many teachers is learning to respect and accommodate people who learn in ways that differ from their own patterns, preferences, and profiles. With so many factors that can influence a learning profile, including temperament and personality traits, modality strengths, brain dominance, and environmental and social preferences, to name a few, trying to reach all students with a handful of techniques that might work with a very small slice of the population no longer makes sense. We need to get a lot more comfortable letting different students demonstrate mastery in different ways. We need to be willing and flexible enough to explain things more than once, and in different ways, if a child isn't getting it. We need, above all, to refuse to accept the long-cherished belief that it's normal and acceptable for some kids to consistently fail.

One teacher kept a sign on her bulletin board to remind her, "If they don't learn the way you teach, teach the way they learn."[20] Still, accommodating needs for things like kinesthetic outlets, increased mobility, or alternative types of seating is new territory for a lot of people, and the thought of introducing these accommodations, especially into a group of kids who are challenging to begin with, can be unsettling at best. Fortunately, there are ways to make this work—and often, these very strategies, scary as they may seem, can actually bring order and stability into a classroom setting. (See sidebar: "Making These Strategies Work.")

Making These Strategies Work

- Choose options you can live with and those your students can handle. Nothing will compromise trust faster than blowing up at your students for doing something you've allowed or encouraged.
- Find ways to stretch your comfort zone. If you are distracted by movement, create specific locations to accommodate mobility needs of individual students or allow breaks for kids to move as a classwide brain break. If you're having a hard time with the idea of gum, try other oral-motor stimulators.
- Introduce new options one or two at a time. As your class becomes more self-managing, add new or different accommodations. And be sure you have your power dynamics and win-win relationships well-established before introducing these resources (although certainly, accommodating learner needs can help bring student behavior in line). Even the best behaved students can become distracted and unruly when too many new ideas and materials are offered at once. I can't stress strongly enough the value in starting slowly.
- Certain accommodations will work better with different students (or classes) and during different types of activities. If you notice certain students getting so absorbed in the accommodation they're using that they're no longer hearing you, back up and try a different outlet. I once saw a second-grade teacher intervene when a student got so involved in drawing that he didn't even notice that the class had been dismissed for recess. All she said was, "This isn't working. Let's try something different tomorrow." Although drawing during story time was no longer an option, he was encouraged to find other kinesthetic outlets that would allow him to focus and attend to the lesson.
- Be cautious about possible sensitivities or allergies to certain foods or products (many kids are sensitive to certain foods like wheat, milk, corn, peanuts, soy, chocolate, eggs, yeast, citrus, and sugar, and certain food additives can have a huge impact on a child's attention and behavior).[21] Latex is also a problem for some individuals, and fragrance-sensitive students could be negatively affected by scented oils, candles, or air fresheners.
- Let parents and administration know what you're doing and why. Look to your district's special education teachers and coordinators, occupational therapists, or school nurses, for example, for resources, ideas, and support. There is plenty of research to back up these strategies. Collect data about your students (from learning style inventories, interviews, anecdotal records or other types of assessment) as well as information about differences in how kids learn. These records can help you justify decisions you make about the types of strategies you use and accommodations you offer. Also, being able to document improved behavior or performance, and having more kids on task, will almost always work in your favor.
- Start small and with accommodations that are less likely to raise suspicions or feel like a threat to other adults in the school. Even in very restrictive environments, teachers have managed to bring in things like colored transparencies or seat cushions without much fuss or objection from others. Use the improvements to leverage greater flexibility and consideration for other accommodations from the administration and other staff.

(Continued)

(Continued)

- If school rules are a hindrance, work to change them or ask for special exemptions or accommodations. One coach got permission for a "trial run" for her students to use personal music players during track and said she suddenly had kids who had previously refused to leave the benches up and moving when they had music to listen to as they walked or ran. In another instance, a first-year elementary teacher took a stack of research on hydration to the superintendent and successfully persuaded him to revoke a rule against water in the classroom.
- Invite the students to petition for rule changes and for assuming the necessary responsibilities that go with it. I had a group of teachers tell me how their middle schoolers convinced the administration to install juice machines by committing to keeping the campus clean, which they did.
- Look for results: Accommodating students' learning preferences can improve their performance and behavior, sometimes dramatically and immediately. If the quality of work or behavior declines, remember the phrase, "This isn't working." Withdraw access to the resource or activity for the time being and look for something else (or try again at another time). This tends to work best when we can continue to offer these privileges contingent on cooperative, nondisruptive participation by the students.
- Stay positive and optimistic. These and other strategies are working in classrooms, helping countless children—and their teachers. They can work for you and your students as well.

Conditions With ADHD "Look-Alike" Symptoms

- Highly kinesthetic or tactile learners
- Strong in bodily-kinesthetic, spatial, and musical intelligences
- Auditory dominant
- Communications-limited (needs time to process, retrieve, and articulate information)
- Sensory integration dysfunction
- Depression
- Bipolar disorder
- Asperger's syndrome
- Absence seizures (petit mal epilepsy)
- Chronic middle ear infection, sinusitis
- Visual or hearing problems
- Sleep disorders
- Lack of natural light, sensitivity to fluorescent lighting
- Scotopic sensitivity syndrome
- Seasonal affective disorder (SAD)
- Too-warm temperatures
- Thyroid problems
- Poor diet, food allergies, sensitivity to food additives
- Chemical or environmental sensitivities
- High extrovert, processes through social interaction, talking, writing
- Emotional problems
- Posttraumatic stress disorder (trauma or abuse survivor or witness)
- Lack of clear guidelines or instructions
- Inadequate feedback

- Inadequate instructional stimulation (lack of novelty, relevance, choices, or autonomy)
- Fetal alcohol syndrome or effect
- Obsessive-compulsive disorder (OCD)
- Child abuse and neglect
- Reactive attachment disorder
- Oppositional-defiant disorders, conduct disorders
- Temperament-related patterns (oversensitivity to sounds or sights, difficulty sequencing movements or processing visual or auditory input, or a tendency to be distracted by details)
- Use of stimulants
- Deliberate misbehavior: Better to be perceived as "bad" than "dumb"

These conditions are often misdiagnosed and treated as attention deficit hyperactivity disorder (ADHD). This information comes from a variety of sources as reported in my book, *Creating Emotionally Safe Schools,* with additions to this list as suggested by readers, workshop participants, and e-mail correspondents. The ever-increasing length of this list and growing number of kids being referred, diagnosed, and treated as attention deficit disorder (ADD) or ADHD suggest the very real possibility that many, many children are being misdiagnosed, and that, in many cases, alternate and often less-invasive interventions are in order. I include this list as a plea to rule out other possible causes of the symptoms before automatically jumping to a diagnosis of ADD or ADHD. (This goes for Asperger's syndrome, another popular diagnosis.) If you know of any other conditions that might be mistaken for ADD or ADHD, please contact me. Check my Web site at http://www.janebluestein.com/handouts/adhd.html for an up-to-date listing.

NOTES

1. These are two of the four basic Brain Gym exercises. (The other two are usually introduced a bit later in the day.) For more information, see Paul E. Dennison and Gail E. Dennison, *Brain Gym, Teacher's Edition* (Ventura, CA: Edu-Kinesthetics, 1996), or visit the following Web sites: www.braingym.com and www.braingym.org.

2. Claudia Wallis, "The Multitasking Generation," *Time* (March 27, 2006): 50–51.

3. Steven Johnson, "Don't Fear the Digital," *Time* (March 27, 2006): 56.

4. See sidebar, "The 'Ideal' Student."

5. Assembled from a number of resources and reported in Chapter 13, "How Does Your Garden Grow? More Diversity, More Discrimination," Bluestein, *Creating Emotionally Safe Schools.*

6. With particular thanks to Mary Sue Williams and Sherry Shellenberger and their book *How Does Your Engine Run?* (Albuquerque, NM: TherapyWorks, 1996) for their organization of these suggestions into the categories represented in next five sections of this book.

7. Martha Kaufeldt, *Teachers, Change Your Bait! Brain-Compatible Differentiated Instruction* (Norwalk, CT: Crown House Publishing, 2005), 54; Joseph LeDoux, *The Emotional Brain* (NY: Simon & Schuster, 1996), 270–271; David Sousa, *How the Brain Learns* (Reston, VA: National Association of Secondary School Principals, 1995), 14–15. Kaufeldt notes, "It has been estimated that, in general, there is a one-year to one-minute correlation for children's attention spans, give or take two minutes. An average twelve-year-old, therefore, might be able to attend to your presentation for 10 to 14 minutes. Of course, this is true only if the student is well rested, has had proper nutrition, and is not on any medications; it may be diminished if the student is coping with an attentional disorder."

8. Many of these suggestions have come from various occupational therapists, physical therapists, kinesiologists, school nurses, counselors, social workers, and special education teachers, among others, focusing on the needs of nontraditional learners, as well as contributions from workshop participants and Web site visitors. Although Web site addresses tend to change frequently, I have mentioned a few in the footnotes in this book. You might want to check my Web site for links to various multisensory or brain-friendly sites: http://www.janebluestein.com/links/index.html.

9. "The Many Effects of Daylight," *Pure Facts,* newsletter of the Feingold Association of the United States (March, 2000): 1–5; Carla Hannaford, *Smart Moves: Why Learning Is Not All in Your Head* (Arlington, VA: Great Oceans Publishers, 1995), 148; also Dale Dauten, "Lighting Deserves a Look," *Albuquerque Journal* (January 25, 2000). Hannaford also noticed a decrease in agitation in students when the conventional fluorescent lights were turned off, and Dauten also cites studies that show that natural lighting (in this case, from the addition of skylights) also reduced accidents in warehouses and increased sales in stores.

10. Excerpted from *The Australian Journal of Learning Disabilities* 9, no. 2 (June 2004): 14–22, and an article by Gail Martin in *The Charlotte Reporter,* reported in *The Irlen Institute Newsletter* XV, no. 2 (June 2005): 8. These students were reportedly tested for scotopic sensitivity syndrome and provided "optimum color overlays," according to test results. However, many teachers have told me that even without testing, they saw increased levels of engagement, longer periods of time on task, improved participation, and improved achievement when they provided various colors of acetate sheets and allowed their students to select the color they wanted to use. For more information, visit http://www.irlen.com and http://www.hale.ndo.co.uk/scotopic/definition.htm.

11. Hannaford, *Smart Moves*, 191.

12. One concern involves the potential for loss or theft of personal music players. Schools and teachers using this accommodation effectively simply treat these items as they would anything else the students might bring from home. They establish an understanding with the students (and their parents) that they, the students, are responsible for keeping track of any materials or equipment they bring from home, including music players or other expensive items. The choice is left to the students and their families whether to bring these items to school.

13. Sheila Ostrander and Lynn Schroeder, with Nancy Ostrander, *Superlearning* (New York: Delacorte Press, 1979), 63; Thomas Armstrong, *The Myth of the ADD Child: 50 Ways to Improve Your Child's Behavior and Attention Span Without Drugs, Labels or Coercion* (New York: Dutton, 1995), 98.

14. This teacher withheld judgment about the kids' preferences and, on "his" day, deliberately brought in a comically wide range of choices, including opera, show tunes, and things like yodeling records, brilliantly challenging his kids to be tolerant and respectful of differences in others.

15. Teacher-made Whisper Phones are most commonly made from PVC pipe and two or more ninety-degree elbows. A simple Internet search led me to a number of resources including several with directions for making your own. Please check the Multisensory Links on my Web site at http://www.janebluestein.com/links/multisensory.html for these resources.

16. I don't know that I'd recommend *introducing* fidget toys during a test. I suspect that this district had used these fidgets in classes to help kids identify if this was indeed a help or a hindrance.

17. From the *In Your Pocket/Abilitations* Web site: http://weightedvest.com/why_use.html. Although there is limited research in this area, many therapists and educators have found a weighted vest may also assist with reflex maturity, body position awareness and coordination, balance, eye-hand coordination, spatial perception, and hearing and speaking skills. See also Carol Stock Kranowitz, *The Out-of-Sync Child* (New York: Berkley Publishing Group, 1998), and http://www.sensoryint.com/or http://www.kid-power.org/sid.html for more information about sensory integration dysfunction.

18. Hannaford, *Smart Moves*, 138–145; Sharon Promislow, *Making the Brain Body Connection* (West Vancouver, BC: Kinetic Publishing, 1999), 36, 57; Dennison and Dennison, *Brain Gym, Teacher's Edition*, 24.

19. These are generally the characteristics expected in classrooms throughout the United States. Teachers in other countries have described variations on these characteristics, but the expectation that every student would assume a particular posture—and could not possibly be paying attention otherwise—was consistently affirmed regardless of the nature of the posture these teachers demonstrated or described.

20. Peggy Corcovelos, quoted in Bluestein, *Creating Emotionally Safe Schools.*

21. Jane Hersey, *Why Can't My Child Behave?* (Alexandria, VA: Pear Tree Press, 1999), 19–20, 48; various articles from Feingold Association of the United States newsletter. For more information about allergies and sensitivities to foods, additives, and other products, visit http://www.feingold.org. I've seen work samples done by students with food sensitivities. There were several grade levels' difference between writing and drawing exercises, for example, that were done when the students were exposed to the foods or additives to which they were sensitive and work done when they adhered to a diet that excluded these items.

PART VI

Increasing Positivity

19

Changing Your Focus

As we saw in earlier chapters, schools can be pretty negative places, and the majority of feedback kids (and adults) get tends to focus on problems, errors, omissions, or mistakes. It will always be easy, especially in a negatively oriented environment, to find something wrong with anything we observe. Fortunately, we have a tremendous amount of control over the way we look at any given person, event, item, or experience.[1]

The type and quality of information we offer to our students can have an enormous impact on their motivation and progress. Consider how powerful a positive perspective can be. Any time we can find something to criticize, if we're looking through the right lens, we can probably find something to recognize in a positive way.

Never underestimate the power of encouragement. "A lot of times, a little push helps us get started," says author Jonathan Scott. "A little guidance helps us stay on track and a lot of cheering helps us finish up strong."[2] To illustrate, a teacher received a paper from one of her second-grade students. The drawing on the paper was little more than an angry black scribble. Instead of a story, there was a sentence fragment without a capital,

> Never underestimate the power of encouragement.

no punctuation, and not one correctly spelled word. Attempts to erase stray pencil marks had left several holes, and the paper had been crumpled at least once in frustration.

The teacher had acknowledged each of the other students' papers with a sticker and some positive comment about the work. But this paper was something else. Naturally, the teacher's first instinct was to take out the red pencil and go to town. Her only hesitation was not knowing where to start, but that gave her a few seconds to think. Here was a product that had "I can't" written all over it. What would her criticisms contribute?

She made a note to work with this student on capital letters and spelling and to show him how to use an eraser without mauling the paper. And then, as she had done for the other students, she placed a sticker on the top. Finding something positive was a challenge, although shifting back to that goal enabled her to see the one thing the student had not messed up. She returned his paper marked "Magnificent Margins!"

What did this teacher communicate to the student? At no point was she saying that fragments instead of sentences were okay or that crumpling the paper was acceptable. But instead of seeing these problems as something to criticize, punish, or even mark wrong, she chose to see them as skills he still needed to master. Her primary intention was to encourage this child to continue learning. Simply deducting points for his mistakes would not be anywhere near as constructive as taking the time to teach him the skills he'd need to improve his work—and his attitude. So she started by looking for what he had done right and developed a plan to teach him the rest.

The student was delighted with his sticker. The positive focus helped him begin to turn his "I can't" perceptions around. Building on the pride and accomplishment of his magnificent margins, with further instruction, encouragement, and a little time, his work steadily improved. The shift in the teacher's focus allowed her to break the failure loop that had simply strengthened his self-defeating beliefs.

> The shift in the teacher's focus allowed her to break the failure loop that had simply strengthened his self-defeating beliefs.

A success-oriented focus means that the time we take to evaluate our students' work has a greater purpose than simply coming up with numbers to put in little boxes in our grade books. The only real reason to bother looking over the work our students have done is to determine what they already know (or have learned) and what we need to teach next. This is quite different from our traditions in which our assessment goals focus more on determining a score—some letter, number, or mark which, depending on the task and the teacher, can represent a dispassionate percentage of correct answers or the teacher's opinion of a student's achievement, effort, or behavior.

WHAT DO GRADES TELL US?

In one of my classes, I had three kids who had failed math the previous year. It took me a while to discover what these grades meant. As it turned out, one of the students was quite capable as far as math skills went. He had just never turned in much work in that class. The second student was not so fortunate and needed a great deal of instruction to catch up on skills. Evidently, his grade indicated that he was performing far below grade level. The third student seemed to have received an F more on the basis of his behavior than his mastery of math—which, incidentally, wasn't too bad. Aside from this experience providing a great argument in favor of preassessment (and not making decisions based on last year's grades), it clarified just how arbitrary and capricious our feedback and judgments about a student's performance can be.

We sometimes use grades to motivate students, although many teachers claim that students have become increasingly resistant over the past few decades to this form of motivation. Nevertheless, grades may still be effective as motivators with high achieving students who see high marks as meaningful and accessible or to students whose self-worth depends on the approval and validation they derive from good grades. However, grades will rarely motivate students with a history of low scores and negative self-perceptions. (It's hard to be motivated by things that have consistently been beyond our reach.) And they will not inspire students who simply do not care about grades—regardless of their potential or prior achievements.

In general, our grading practices reflect the perfectionism of factory-era standards: Only by making no mistakes can students avoid red marks on their papers. (Many teachers report improvements in attitude when they switched from red ink to some other color, but if the focus of the feedback is exclusively negative, ink color becomes rather beside the point!) And if our on-paper responses to students simply address what the student did incorrectly, imagine the fate of a student who hands in an assignment done completely wrong. In the win-lose classroom, the teacher probably gives the child a zero and rationalizes, "I already explained this twice," or "Well, she should have been listening." In the win-win classroom, the student can get some credit or acknowledgment for her efforts, remediation for her misunderstanding, and, most likely, a chance to correct her errors and get it right.

> In the win-win classroom, the student can get some credit or acknowledgment for her efforts, remediation for her misunderstanding, and, most likely, a chance to correct her errors and get it right.

Grades are very much a part of a win-lose tradition. They tend to be competitive, limiting the number of A's available and ensuring that at least some kids will fail. (How many classes are set up for all students to be able to get A's? And what happens to the teacher if each student does indeed complete the requirements for this grade, even when the requirements are pretty stringent and the achievement well documented?)[3] Grades rarely reflect effort or progress. They are almost always influenced, consciously or unconsciously, by a student's behavior, or by the feelings a teacher has about a student. In win-lose classrooms, poor grades are often used as a powering technique to punish uncooperative students, which can simply feed the cycle of indifference and failure.

Negative feedback can undo even the greatest breakthrough. Something clicked for one of my reading groups after their reading time was rescheduled for later in the day—when these particular individuals were more alert and functional. They suddenly made huge strides, going through an entire year's worth of material in a few months. They were excited about reading, doing huge quantities of excellent work; there was no way anyone could say they weren't earning A's and B's. Or so I thought. Unfortunately, my principal had a different agenda, and personally changed their report card grades to C's and D's because the students were still reading slightly below grade level. Not surprisingly, I didn't get much from those kids for the rest of the year—not only in reading: The quality of their work and attitude declined in other subjects as well.

Legitimate feedback, guidance, and instruction are necessary for learning, but how much of these do grades actually offer? As a solitary form of feedback, grades are extremely limited and simplistic. Unless our criteria for grading each assignment are sharply focused and well communicated, the grades we give our students tell very little about what they know or can do. A grade of B– on a writing assignment says little more than "This is not as good as the one that got the B+." This grade certainly does not tell students which concepts they misunderstood, where they needs additional work, or what they might have done to achieve an A. A grade of seventy-six tells students that they understood seventy-six percent of the content on the assignment or that they can do a particular skill seventy-six percent of the time. What value does this information have in terms of learning needs?

Grades, in fact, tell us so little about what a child knows or needs to be taught that many teachers and schools have turned to more descriptive forms of feedback. But useful or not, for the majority of teachers, grades are a rather intractable fact of life. The fact that grades are a familiar tradition, accepted without question and understood by parents and administration, certainly lends to their appeal. And grades are attractive because they are far easier to record, communicate, and keep track of than descriptive evaluations. If we have to live with grades, then let them work for the student as well. I've known teachers in settings that supported their efforts to base their grades on a combination of student progress and productivity. Almost always, copious, solid documentation, along with communication with administrators and parent support were factors in their success. Let's keep our focus on what the student is doing right and use the evaluation process predominantly for noticing areas that need improvement and determining what we need to teach and reinforce.

LEAVING THE DOOR OPEN

Early in my career, a fourth grader who had a habit of testing me wrote a long, wonderful story for a writing assignment. One of the criteria for this task was that the final product be presented in cursive handwriting. Nonetheless, this student handed in three pages in his neatest printing.

I was at a crossroad—Do I lower his grade for printing and disregard all the writing he had done, or do I ignore the printing? Not comfortable with either option, I read the story, which was excellent, and told him it was a "great first draft!" I told him that I'd be happy to accept it when it was completed. He could still turn it in at that point if he didn't mind losing points for printing (although he would get credit for a great story), or he could rewrite the story for full credit. He had a choice; either option was okay with me. I made it clear that I appreciated and enjoyed the work he did and, of course, still valued *him* regardless of his choice.

Offering students the chance to renegotiate a grade puts a great deal of responsibility on the student, requiring more time and effort devoted to learning, correcting, and redoing. This choice leaves the door open for greater success (in terms of deeper understanding, better grades, and advancement to new content) while also allowing the student the choice of accepting the grade for the effort he or she made. In this way, grades are simply a reflection of how the student is doing on this particular project so far—feedback the student can use in making decisions about personal learning goals.

I once had the privilege of observing a small group of high school students doing reports on various world religions. Each was to have created a large drawing or diorama and to present certain bits of information regarding traditions, holidays, foods, cultural influences, and so on. The first five kids did a great job. However, it was obvious in the final presentation by a young man reporting on Hinduism that he hadn't put a whole lot of time into this project. His drawing was crude and incomplete, which didn't trouble me nearly as much as his detailed—and quite serious—description of the Hindu castle system. It took me a minute but I managed to respectfully inquire if he might actually be referring to the *caste* system. "No," he insisted. "Their buildings are *way* different from ours."

When I reported back to the teacher, I mentioned this exchange. The teacher just sighed and said, "Okay. I'll drop his grade ten points."

Yeah, that's what we do. And in all fairness to this wonderful, harried teacher, this kid hardly deserved full credit for the work he'd done. But think about this: If our intention is, for whatever reason, that this young man have a clearer grasp of the Hindu caste system, is the student not likely to learn more from some more time online or in the library than he will from the loss of ten points?

> Is the student not likely to learn more from some more time online or in the library than he will from the loss of ten points?

Let's leave the door open for kids to do their work over and learn from their mistakes. In computer classes I've taken, I've learned more from correcting the errors in the code I've written than I ever did from the stuff I got right the first time. Understand that there will be students who will be satisfied with a lower grade. But make the option available whenever you can. I've had teachers taking my master's-level classes who were perfectly happy to turn in the minimum requirements to just pass the class. That may not be my first choice, but I've certainly got to respect that some people take these classes just to get credit so that they can recertify or qualify for a raise, even if they had no interest in the content. And I've met a number of professionals for whom the opposite is true. They learn a great deal from classes just by attending and participating, and several have done the equivalent of the requirements but didn't want—or bother—to register for the class or hand in the assignments. The credit may not have been important, but the learning was.

FOCUSING OUR INTERACTIONS

A positive focus need not be solely reflected in our evaluations of our students' work. A high-school teacher made it a point to individually greet as many of his 150 students as possible each day. He met quite a few at the door as they were coming in and spoke with the others by walking around the room during their independent work time. His comments may not have been terribly elaborate, ranging from a simple "Hi," or "How was your weekend?" to "I really enjoyed reading your essay last night," or even just, "Glad you're here." Yet he found that connecting with his students, finding something positive to say to each one, helped improve the overall classroom climate, his relationships with his students, and his attitude and feelings about the kids he was teaching. He was able to notice positive qualities in even the most difficult students. He learned to appreciate something in each student and was able to communicate his appreciation for the special contribution each one made. He still had his boundaries and required students to operate within the limits he established, and he still corrected errors in work and intervened in the infrequent disruption. But the general atmosphere of the class was quite positive and inviting, and each student felt valued and accepted at the same time.

There seems to be a certain automatic, even unconscious quality to the way many adults interact with children. Certain courtesies we extend to other adults seem extravagant, or at least unnecessary, in our interactions with kids. I recently surveyed several hundred teachers, asking them how they typically responded when they discovered that a student lacked a skill necessary to work with content they were about to assign. The majority of these teachers were appalled to realize the frequency with which they responded with impatience, criticism, or shaming: "Why didn't you pay attention last year? You should have learned this by now!"

By the same token, children learning to walk rarely get yelled at or punished when they stumble—or so one would hope. Indeed, quite the opposite is true. The child takes that first tentative step and out comes the video camera to capture the moment. Within seconds, we're on the phone to grandparents, neighbors, and the media! Helping children learn to walk is a process of pure encouragement and celebration. (Can you imagine the impact on literacy rates if kids learned to read with the same support they receive when they're learning to walk?) Yelling at children because they cannot subtract does not improve their math skills. If it teaches them anything, it's only that they're not particularly safe in this classroom or with this teacher, and that they're not very capable

> Can you imagine the impact on literacy rates if kids learned to read with the same support they receive when they're learning to walk?

when it comes to math. And yet this pattern is so deeply ingrained, that for some teachers, it's hard to imagine that kids will learn without negative or critical feedback.

Nonetheless, the win-win notion of not making children wrong can also apply to their mistakes and incorrect responses. I once observed a technology teacher explain a particular procedure with great emphasis on the importance of selecting an item in a graphics application before any of the menu commands would work. One after another student sought help for problems that would not have occurred had they remembered this caution. Yet this teacher responded to each student patiently and positively: "I'll bet you forgot to select the item. Ask me how I know." By admitting that she, too, had made the same mistake when she was learning to use this software, she created a very safe environment in which the students were enthusiastic and highly focused and quite willing to take risks they might have otherwise avoided had they feared recriminations for lapses in memory or errors in process.

A positive focus can also help us maintain a certain levity and defuse potential conflicts and confrontations. One day, when I was detained for a minute on my way back from lunch, I returned to thirty-five loud and disorderly students. Although I had a get-started assignment on the board as always, they were completely distracted by a classwide dispute over who had won the game in gym. They were so wound up they barely noticed me, so much so that they did not hear my request to take their seats until I finally blew up and yelled at them to sit and put their heads down!

They were quite surprised. This was not my usual way of dealing with this normally cooperative and—by this point in the year—self-managing class. Startled and suddenly quiet, they immediately took their seats. Just as I was beginning to calm down, I noticed that one of the kids hadn't made it to class. That was the clincher! I could feel myself slipping out of control. At that very moment, this student ambled into the class, looked at her classmates with their heads on their arms, and before I had a chance to jump all over her, said, "What are we playing?"

I was on the edge: Had I not burst out laughing, I surely would have said or done things I'd later regret. To this day, I'm not convinced that the decision was entirely conscious, but it certainly broke the tension and averted what could have created some really ugly energy in that classroom. We were able to move on to more important (instructional) matters with a safe and positive climate restored.

BECOMING MORE POSITIVE

All-or-nothing thinking is likely to trigger objections if someone mistakenly assumes that making schools more positive means accepting or applauding any and all student behavior. Nonsense! Even the most positive teacher doesn't pause, while little Joey is tormenting the jade plant, to make a mental list of his great qualities. Our focus does not keep us from immediately intervening to correct negative behaviors—in this case, protecting the plant. It simply enables us to remember that Joey is more than the distasteful behavior he is exhibiting at the moment.

Because negative patterns may be painfully familiar, a conscious shift toward a more positive focus can pose a real challenge. There are a number of things you can do to help maintain your own positive attitude, from creating a pleasing and comfortable physical environment in your classroom to becoming more mindful of your language and behavior. Commit to noticing a student you haven't spent much time with lately. Proclaim a positive period in which your written comments on student papers give feedback only on what they've done correctly. (You may want to extend this positive period indefinitely.) Make a point to recognize something positive in another teacher—and let that person know it. Promise yourself to not complain or make one negative comment about a student, teacher, parent, administrator, or administrative policy during your lunch break, in the teachers' lounge, or during a faculty meeting. You can even ask your students for feedback on what *you're* doing well. (You may be pleasantly surprised by what they notice and appreciate.) One middle school teacher claimed to have been helped by putting little plus signs around her classroom (and even at home, and on her mirror, in her purse, on her car's dashboard). Not only did the cards serve to remind her that she had a choice about her focus, but they even started encouraging her students and her family toward a more positive outlook as well.

Retired football coach Dave Triplett would tell his players, "It only takes one negative person to convert seven people to their negative thinking. But it takes seven positive people to convert one negative." There will be times when it seems perfectly reasonable to blow up, worry, or complain, but these reactions cost us—socially, emotionally, and even physically. Just being around negative people can wear us down very quickly and in the midst of an ordinary busy day, a commitment to positivity can quickly disappear.

> Even in the most stressful situations, we have choices about how we perceive and interpret what's happening, and how we will respond.

But even in the most stressful situations, we have choices about how we perceive and interpret what's happening and how we will respond. (Sometimes pausing for a few seconds can help, not only to avoid doing or saying something that might hurt or alienate, but also to remind us that we have other options.) The more frequently we remember to take the more positive route, the greater the benefits. We can build trust and avoid conflict in our interactions with others, reduce our own stress levels and symptoms, and increase the amount of satisfaction and contentment in our lives—and work—as well.[4]

Chart 19.1   Possible Responses

Negative Situation	Negative Response	More Positive Response

Use Chart 19.1 or create a similar chart on a separate piece of paper.

- In the first column in the chart, describe several occasions or situations that evoked or tempted a negative response from you.
- In the second column, describe either your actual negative response or a possible negative response.
- In the third column, describe a more positive response you could have used instead.

Reflection

- In what ways is your verbal feedback to students positively focused and success oriented?

- In what ways is your written feedback to students (grades, items checked on papers, comments on written assignments, essays, tests, and so on) positively focused and success oriented?

- What sort of information do you collect and record to keep track of student progress and performance (letter grades, percentages, anecdotal records or other descriptive data, skill checklists, and so on)?

- In what ways does your evaluation of student progress and performance influence your teaching decisions (pacing, materials, review, assignments, and so forth) for individual students in your class?

- What opportunities do your students have to change, improve, or renegotiate grades?

- What have you done to maintain a positive focus in the classroom?

- What have you done to encourage your students to maintain a positive focus about themselves, school, their friends, their work, and other aspects of their lives?

NOTES

1. If you're thinking that a positive orientation is naïve and unrealistic, you're not alone. This point is a hard sell for a lot of educators (and parents, as well). Most of us grew up with a great deal of negativity and may have come to believe that criticism, for example, is necessary for learning. Let me encourage you to watch out for all-or-nothing thinking here and assure you that the strategies in this section may produce some of the most powerful and positive results. Your willingness to wrestle with the ever-prevalent negative mind-set will make it easier to implement the ideas in this book.

2. Jonathan T. Scott, *Fathering From Love: How to Rediscover One of Life's Greatest Treasures* (Sierra Madre, CA: Proud Parent Publishing, 2006), 125.

3. The college classes I've taught were always set up with a list of criteria and requirements for anyone who wanted to get an A in the class. If you wanted a B or a C, those options were also listed. The opportunity for everyone to get an A was there—although I often had someone in these classes ask, "What's the least amount of work I have to do to still pass?" (Incongruously, this question was asked in a class on motivating kids, among other things.) I suppose I should be grateful for these underachievers, because even in college classes, there exists some question about the validity of instruction and assessment when every student achieves the highest grades.

4. More information on supporting yourself in Chapter 25.

20

Creating Congruence

Throughout my teacher training, I kept hearing about the importance of being consistent without anyone ever getting around to explaining what the term meant. I suppose I understood how consistency could contribute to structure, and I've often seen how its absence could provoke student insecurity, distrust, and chaos. But I've started to wonder if maybe consistency is a bit overrated. In many ways, the notion of consistency is rooted in the uniformity and sameness of industrial-era values. We say we need consistency to achieve our behavior management goals, but the appeal is often superficial and can quickly turn to stubbornness and rigidity. Rather than using the notion of consistency as a way to try to get everyone to buy into (and enforce) the same rules or teach the same page on the same day, let's take a commonsense approach to the idea of creating congruence in our work with kids.

Clearly, if our students are accustomed to working at a certain noise level without censure during a particular work time every day, it's not fair to yell at them just because we happen to be in a bad mood or experienced something on the way to work that is currently limiting our ability to deal with things that wouldn't ordinarily bother us. And we can prevent unnecessary resentment, surprises, or conflicts by simply warning the kids ahead of time that at least for today, the rules have changed. (Have you noticed how flexible, even protective, kids can be when you've got a good relationship in place and you're just having a really bad day?)

Likewise, we allow different behaviors on a playground than in a library, and special events like field trips or guest speakers may require considerations not normally required by everyday classroom activities. But if we suddenly lash out at previously accepted behavior just because the principal is in the room, you can be sure that we've also strained the emotional climate in the classroom, violated trust, and compromised safety. When different activities, situations, or circumstances require a departure from the normal structure, it's only fair that we adequately prepare our students by letting them know beforehand the new limits that apply.

I suspect that the early admonitions to "be consistent" may have actually had more to do with following through than imposing "sameness." How often, for example, is the comment "I'll only say this once" actually an introduction to something we repeat all afternoon? Do we spend time warning, reminding, and nagging? Do we interact with students who are at our side seconds after asking them to stay in their seats? These inconsistencies erode our credibility with our students. As we saw in previous chapters, a boundary or contingency is only as good as our follow-through. Kids learn more from our actions—doing what we say we'll do—than from any verbal warning, threat, or reminder. Breaking out of these self-defeating patterns requires awareness and practice.[1]

One of the most common issues in my workshops has to do with consistency between our behavior and the other teachers in the school. We can count on our students to lean on

> We can count on our students to lean on us about any inconsistencies that don't work in their behalf.

us about any inconsistencies that don't work in their behalf: "But Mr. Peterson never gives homework!" The rules and privileges extended by different teachers reflect differences in personalities, tolerances, and personal needs. These differences are not inconsistencies. We do not control other people's behaviors. Trying to model their behavior, adopt their limits, or imitate their teaching style for the sake of consistency is silly and self-defeating. If we don't need absolute silence in our room, why demand it just because the other chemistry teachers do? If our kids get their seatwork done while listening to music, if they prefer to work with a partner, or if their chewing gum doesn't get on our nerves (or anywhere else), applying someone else's standards will work only to meet that person's needs—not our own. Additionally, we're more likely to be careless about following through on values, rules, or limits that are imposed on us unless those conditions have meaning and importance in our lives.

Sure, the standards and limits that apply to our personal needs may require our students to shift gears when they go from one class to another because it's likely that our boundaries will demand a slightly different set of behaviors than some other teacher's. Not all teachers are similarly distracted or provoked by noise, movement, lateness, slouching, or a student's preference for working on the floor, sitting with a friend, or writing with green ink—nor do they need to be! Even very young children are far more flexible than we often give them credit for. (I once saw a two-and-a-half-year-old who rarely went a minute without his pacifier at home, unquestioningly spit it out to leave it in the car when he arrived at his nonpacifier preschool.) Besides, our students will certainly encounter a variety of people throughout their school careers (and lives); let's help them develop the flexibility they'll need to relate to—and succeed with—these different personalities. (See sidebar, "Helping Your Students Deal With Different Teachers.")

WALKING THE TALK

Perhaps the greatest value of consistency is in regard to our role modeling, that is, the kinds of behaviors we exhibit for our students in our interactions with them and with others. To what degree is our behavior congruent with the standards we hold for our students? For example, are we on time as frequently as we would like our students to be? When we mess up, do we take responsibility for our mistakes, catching ourselves before we make excuses or cast blame? Do our desk, handwriting, and appearance reflect the degree of order, readability, and neatness we want our students to demonstrate? If we

Helping Your Students Deal With Different Teachers

If your students seem to have a hard time dealing with differences in the needs, limits, or tolerances from one teacher to the next, you might want to involve them in various discussions about individual differences and similarities, not only about their teachers, but also, perhaps, about their siblings and friends. Some possible discussion starters might include the following:

- Tell me something you really like about each one of your teachers.
- What are you allowed to do at home that you can't do in school?
- In what ways are your friends alike? How are they different?
- How are your teachers alike? How are they different?

What else can you do to help students understand differences in standards, values, and freedoms from one teacher or situation to the next?

forbid eating or drinking in the classroom, are we willing to leave our coffee cups and snacks in the teachers' lounge?

These examples make some teachers very uncomfortable, but they're well worth a second look. Our behavior sends powerful messages to the students in our lives, teaching them a great deal about what is appropriate or acceptable in various situations. Thomas Lickona advises, "If we want to teach character, we have to display character."[2] It's hard for kids to take us seriously, or respond with the trust and respect we desire, when we aren't willing to walk the talk, or when we exhibit behaviors we would not encourage in or tolerate from them.[3]

Modeling desirable behaviors in the way we talk to our students can have a significant impact on the quality of the relationships we develop with them. Do we use the same tone, posture, body language, and words with our students as we do with adults? Would we feel valued and respected if another adult talked to us the way we talk to our students? If we hear ourselves speaking in a way that would provoke anger, resentment, shame, fear, defensiveness, or embarrassment in us, it's a safe bet that our students are hearing—and feeling—the same things. Kids can see through a double standard. A commitment to maintaining congruence between what's acceptable for us and what's acceptable for them builds consideration and respect.

INTERNAL CONSISTENCY

Other areas of consistency are somewhat tricky and more subtle. They involve the relationships between our feelings, values, and language and are crucial to the quality of classroom climate and our relationships with students. Matching our behaviors to our feelings can be challenging, particularly in high stress situations. For example, have you ever had a child rock a little too far back in his or her seat and then come crashing down on the floor? What did you feel at that moment? You were probably startled by the noise and frightened for the child's safety. How did you react? If you're good at this, you might have asked if the child was all right and then said, "Wow! That really startled me! I was afraid you might have been hurt!"

But is that how most of us react? Our fear and frustration (how many times have we told this kid not to rock back in her seat?) may come out instead: "You're so clumsy! You can't even sit in a chair right!" Worse still, we may even punish this child by disallowing sitting privileges for the rest of the period.[4]

The danger in this type of inconsistency is that the child tends to create meaning from the words and can misinterpret our reaction. It's highly unlikely that this student will be thinking, "Gee, my teacher must really have been startled. She's only yelling at me because she's having difficulty reconciling her fear for my safety." What she hears is simply another vote for her clumsiness and inadequacy—and this on top of whatever physical pain or embarrassment the fall may have caused.

> It means that we think about what we're really feeling before the words come out of our mouths and that we learn to take responsibility for our anger, fear, and frustration without personally attacking the child.

Recognizing and modifying inconsistencies between our feelings and language demands that we wait a few seconds to respond—not react—to emotional or high stress situations. It means that we think about what we're really feeling before the words come out of our mouths and that we learn to take responsibility for our anger, fear, and frustration without personally attacking the child.

There are also some subtle issues to consider when we start looking at consistency between our intentions and our requests. For example, asking students to "please pick up the blocks so that no one trips over them" conveys quite clearly that we want the student to clear the floor. Asking them to "please pick up the blocks for me" or saying "I feel angry when you leave the blocks on the rug" may get the same results but for an entirely different reason (caretaking and teacher pleasing). If seeing the blocks all over the rug really upsets us, or if we believe our students will respond only if we're highly reactive, we might respond with an attack: "You are so thoughtless and inconsiderate! Get over here and pick up these blocks this instant!" If all we care about is getting those blocks off the floor, then it probably doesn't matter which approach we use. But if we not only want to have the blocks put away but also want to reinforce self-management and preserve emotional safety, then we certainly want to use language that motivates without anger or neediness.

Keep coming back to purpose and intention. Bridging the gap between information-age priorities and industrial-age behaviors begins with an awareness of and commitment to our win-win objectives. From that point on, we have a standard against which we can check the behaviors and language we're tempted to choose. We can examine our behaviors and ask if the particular feedback we have offered reinforces independence, if the structure we have provided encourages self-management, and if our response to a student's comments or actions promotes empowerment and self-worth.

The words and actions we choose will either help us achieve what we say we want or create obstacles for reaching our goals. Consistency requires of each of us, as adults working with children, a certain degree of consciousness and deliberateness, a willingness to notice and be responsible for the language, behaviors, and attitudes we bring to our relationships. Over time, it gets easier, and each attempt brings us closer to the positive, cooperative climate of a win-win classroom.

Activity

1. List five or more behaviors you want your students to demonstrate.

2. Now identify how consistently you demonstrate the same behaviors. Rate yourself on a scale of 1 (*rarely*) to 5 (*almost always*). For example, if you've listed "be on time" or "come prepared," how regularly are you on time and prepared?

3. Describe an instance in which you were challenged to maintain consistency between what you expect of your students and your own behavior.

   a. How was that situation resolved?

   b. What are you doing to maintain consistency at this level?

4. Describe an instance in which you were challenged to maintain consistency from one day to the next.

   a. How was that situation resolved?

   b. What are you doing to maintain consistency at this level?

5. Describe an instance in which you were challenged to maintain consistency between your feelings and your language (words, tone, facial expression).

   a. How was that situation resolved?

   b. What are you doing to maintain consistency at this level?

6. Describe an instance in which you were challenged to maintain consistency between your language (requests, directions, or feedback) and win-win objectives (such as student responsibility, initiative, internal motivation, or self-management).

   a. How was that situation resolved?

   b. What are you doing to maintain consistency at this level?

NOTES

1. Outside observation and feedback, or a video or audio recording of your teaching, can be immensely helpful.

2. Thomas Lickona, *Educating for Character: How Our Schools Can Teach Respect and Responsibility* (New York: Bantam Books, 1991), 117.

3. Consider this: How do the teachers you know behave in meetings or staff development seminars?

4. I would love to say I was above this practice. But no matter how well I justified the logic in my response, there was no getting around the fact that whatever positive energy existed before this incident was soured by my reaction. I doubt that much learning took place during the remainder of the period, not just for the child involved, but for most of the others as well.

21

Keeping the
Good Stuff Going

Over the years, I've seen few ideas as misunderstood or misapplied as the concept of reinforcement. While I certainly appreciate those of us working to get past the negative focus and make an effort to strengthen positive student behaviors, I've noticed a tendency to use what we think are reinforcement strategies at inappropriate times or convoluted ways. And when our efforts don't yield the results we hope for, we throw up our hands and dismiss the concept as frivolous and unimportant.

Sadly, I can personally relate to nearly every misguided approach I've seen. Let's go back to my first year of teaching, which seemed, at times, to be more of a laboratory to discover what doesn't work in a classroom than anything else. Over one weekend early in the year, I channeled my creativity and frustration into developing a system of giving out tokens for what I considered good behavior. I collected all sorts of prizes to give out as awards—colored pencils, erasers, key chains, inexpensive games or toys, and even candy. I put a price tag on each one and made up about a million little construction paper tickets, which I planned to distribute throughout the week to be used during a shopping period at which time the kids could exchange their tickets for prizes. In my mind (and desperation), it seemed like a good idea at the time.

I'd give an assignment and walk around the classroom dispensing tickets to kids who were on task, kids who finished their work, kids who weren't disruptive. They got tickets for turning in homework, for getting quiet, for being prepared, for being on time. Want to guess how much teaching I did that week? Not only that, but this system seemed to create its own set of disruptions: tears over lost tickets, accusations and fights about stolen tickets, and lessons interrupted with questions about prizes or purchasing or earning extra tickets. The clincher came a few days later when I asked them, at the end of the day, to settle down for dismissal and someone queried, "Are we gonna get a ticket?"

"Enough!" I thought—and into the trash went all the tickets along with any shred of hope or optimism I might have had left.

Token reinforcement has its place, and I've seen teachers use tokens successfully, particularly when used infrequently, when it was conceivable that any student in the class could earn the token (and not just the first or the best), and when the criteria for receiving these tokens were very specific. Giving stickers, stars, or points, for example, for a special project or completion of a particular assignment, for progress on a checklist, or even just for fun, can be quite useful at times, as long as it doesn't drive you—or your students—to distraction. However, management of token systems can be a real nightmare and most often verbal, social, or activity reinforcements are far more effective.[1]

> Giving stickers, stars, or points, for example, for a special project or completion of a particular assignment, for progress on a checklist, or even just for fun, can be quite useful at times, as long as it doesn't drive you—or your students—to distraction.

SUBJECT TO MISUSE

When teacher education programs address the concept of positive reinforcement, they often focus on using praise, either to motivate or reinforce cooperative behavior. This emphasis probably grew out of the intention to discourage negative teacher behaviors, such as yelling and criticizing. Unfortunately, the times that teachers are inspired to yell and criticize generally are not conducive to using positive reinforcement. Furthermore, the processes of motivation and reinforcement are not interchangeable. Teachers who attempt to use reinforcing techniques to motivate cooperation will often run into (or create) other problems in their relationships with students.[2]

I became aware of the frequent misuses of this technique when I began observing beginning teachers in their classrooms. During the first week of school, I walked into a classroom to see Ms. Harding standing in front of the room, trying to get her twenty-five first graders settled down so she could continue with her lesson. Despite her firm and patient requests, the students were out of their seats, wrestling on the rug, fighting over toys, throwing game pieces across the room, or running through the language center. Ms. Harding began to feel the panic of being out of control and frantically thought over the tricks she'd learned in student teaching. She managed to focus on the one student who was still, thankfully, in his seat.

"I like the way Bobby is sitting," she announced.

With that, Bobby perked up and sat at attention, beaming. Although one or two other students stopped to look at Bobby, the chaos continued.

Ms. Harding tried again: "I *really* like the way Bobby is sitting."

Bobby sat up even straighter, folded his hands and smiled proudly. Again, the rest of the students were barely distracted from their fun. And as Ms. Harding continued, louder and more intense in her praise for Bobby, his behavior got better and better while the rest of the class continued to fall apart. Ms. Harding was literally saved by the lunch bell, which got the students' attention long enough for her to furiously proclaim that unless they all took their seats that instant, they would never leave that room again!

"So much for positive reinforcement," she thought.

And that's too bad, because positive reinforcement does work. The technique is logical and well founded. Why, then, does it seem to lose so much in its translation to the classroom? Part of the problem is timing. For a reinforcer to work, it must *follow* the desired behavior, which means that the student has to somehow initiate the behavior. In other words, we can't reinforce a student's handwriting if she hasn't written anything, and we can't reinforce her quiet behavior if she won't clam up.

Positive reinforcement encourages the student to continue or repeat a particular existing behavior. Frustration and disillusionment with the technique can occur when teachers attempt to use reinforcement to *evoke* (or motivate) a desired behavior that does not yet exist. Ms. Harding discovered this problem when she found that the reinforcer (her praise) had a positive effect only on the student she reinforced. Praising Bobby did not inspire the other students to settle down and imitate him.

PROBLEMS WITH PRAISE

When I share this story, many teachers, especially those working with younger children, argue that very often, praising Bobby is quite effective in getting Susie to sit down. (Although we don't usually hear this specific language in secondary classrooms, our behavior can just as clearly communicate our conditional approval in these settings.) But even when this approach appears to work, praise has its price. Let's take a look at how this process works—and what it can cost.

Positive reinforcement can come in the form of a grade or a sticker, a written comment, an earned activity or privilege, academic progress, or a nod or smile from the teacher, for example. As long as it *follows* the cooperative behavior and is meaningful to the student, it works as a reinforcer, increasing the likelihood that the exhibited behavior will continue or reoccur. Now, certain reinforcers such as praise are more likely than others to communicate conditional teacher approval. When these reinforcers work, they do so because they appeal to a basic human need to feel valued and worthwhile. Since many of our students value our approval, and since praise is probably the most immediately familiar strategy for communicating our approval, we'll be tempted to use praise as both a motivator and reinforcer.

By stating, "I like the way Bobby is sitting," Ms. Harding conveyed her approval of one student whose sitting was good and teacher pleasing. Had Ms. Harding really wanted to reinforce Bobby's behavior—for Bobby's sake—she would have privately recognized how quickly he got quiet or acknowledged the fact that he was ready. The fact that she proclaimed her approval of this one student to the rest of the class is a good indication of her desire to get the other students to act like Bobby (so she would like them, too).

Even little ones can grasp the negative implications of praising one student to try to evoke performance or cooperation from others. Praise of Bobby becomes a criticism of anyone who isn't acting like Bobby, with the additional hint, "If you act like him, you will be good and please me, too." But such statements build dependence on external approval and can actually interfere with the development of responsibility and self-management. This focus on the pleasure we take in our students' cooperation encourages them to be good just to make us happy and suggests the potential for rejection and disapproval if they do not. There are serious risks in using this approach, not least of which is the fact that students really have to care an awful lot about our happiness for this to work!

So many of our apparently positive attempts to motivate students are actually critical throwbacks to the industrial-age tendency to promote uniformity, which also inspires win-lose competitiveness and discouraged, "I-can't" attitudes that are hardly ideal for a win-win classroom. For example, we imply criticism when we praise an unrelated event or situation:

"Your brother was such a good student" or "But your other papers were so neat." Announcing to the class that "José wrote the best story in the class" simply informs everyone that they aren't quite up to José's talents. And since praise reinforces an externally defined self-concept and a dependence on others for one's feelings of self-worth, after a while, even the *absence* of praise can be perceived as a criticism.

Further, not all students are comfortable being singled out. Our approval is effective only as long as it's important to our students. The need for teacher approval often conflicts with their desire for peer approval. Sometimes even typically cooperative students, feeling pressured or embarrassed, respond to praise with disruption or withdrawal. (And how long would it take Bobby to realize that the other kids were having a whole lot more fun than he was?) Finally, praise can seem redundant to nondependent students who did what was asked because they simply wanted to do the task or because resistance never existed in the first place.

Often implicit in praise is the expectation that once demonstrated, there is no reason for the behavior to diminish or discontinue. We might communicate this expectation subtly ("See, I knew you could do it!"), directly ("Why can't all your papers look this good?"), or even sarcastically ("Well, it's about time!"). If our praise even remotely suggests ". . . and you'd better keep it up," it may actually have the opposite effect. Children can be extremely sensitive to our motives, whether we're clear on them ourselves, and even very young children can detect insincerity and manipulation. One kindergarten teacher reported having a student ball up a paper she had just gushed over. "She just does that to get you to be good," she heard him tell his friend.

If we tell our students that they're smart, for example, in order to get them to act smart, they'll see right through our maneuvers. Such flattery does not build confidence or commitment, regardless of the sincerity of our intentions. A student who doesn't feel smart will certainly hear our praise with suspicion, believing either that we just don't understand or that we must not be so smart ourselves. That student might even attempt to prove that we don't know what we're talking about. Either way, our endeavors will probably be more successful at eroding trust than anything else.

The fact that praise sounds so positive has led many a teacher to believe that these kinds of statements held the key to a students' self-concept. But a positive self-concept does not mean "I am great because my teacher thinks I'm great." If we can only feel adequate and worthwhile when we're receiving praise, what happens when the person on whose praise we depend forgets to appreciate us? And what happens, heaven forbid, if we make a mistake or have a bad day?

Self-worth is an inside job, but we, as educators, can certainly contribute to its development. If we can create an environment in which lower level needs for things like structure, acceptance, success, and, very importantly, power or control are being met—conditions which are far more critical to the development of self-concept than outside approval—we can support a well-grounded, highly internalized sense of self-worth. This is a goal we will never achieve using praise.

> Self-worth is an inside job, but we, as educators, can certainly contribute to its development.

AN ALTERNATIVE TO PRAISE

Positive verbal reinforcement can be a legitimate and highly effective tool in any win-win classroom when we do it right. We help ensure repetition of positive behaviors without fostering dependence on outside approval or reinforcing people pleasing. To reach this goal, we switch to recognition statements, which offer a healthy alternative to praise. These statements use a two-step process to strengthen existing positive behavior: First, we describe the behavior; next, we tell the students how their cooperation pays off for them.

The second part of the recognition statement, connecting the performance or cooperation to the positive outcome, will challenge us to differentiate between our needs and those of our students. Our own needs are almost always tied to the requests we make. We all want our students to write neatly so that we'll be able to read their work. We want them to put the materials away so that we won't be stuck with a mess. But when we can shift our focus to the benefits to the students, we help kids see the connection between their choices and the outcomes of their choices, supporting their perception of having the ability to influence their lives in positive ways.

Consider the following examples: "I see you got all the materials in this center put away. Now you can go to lunch." "Super! You got your college applications in today. Now I'll have time to write a really good recommendation for you." Statements like these allow us to see how recognition differs from praise in a number of ways that are significant to the goals and objectives of a win-win authority relationship.

For example, praise typically connects the worth of the student to the student's behavior, or the value of the student's behavior to the teacher: "You're so good! You remembered your library book," or "I'm so happy when you come prepared." Recognition statements, on the other hand, connect the student's behavior to positive outcomes that benefit the student: "You remembered your library book! Now you can take another one home." Neither the worth of the student nor the teacher's feelings are a factor here.

> Neither the worth of the student nor the teacher's feelings are a factor here.

Recognition tends to be more specific than praise: "You put all the art materials away before you left the center" rather than "You were good today." It's also more descriptive and less judgmental than praise: "Look at how neat your handwriting has gotten!" instead of "I like the way your handwriting has improved." When recognition uses valuing words, the value is connected to the performance or achievement, not the person: "The ending to the story was really exciting," or "You're making great progress in biology." Recognition can also express appreciation: "You really added a lot to our discussion," "Nice try," or "My, you really worked hard today!" Even short, nondescriptive comments like "Well done!" or "Good point" communicate appreciation for the value of the child's contribution without emphasizing the benefit to the teacher (or the worth of the student).

These examples may sound far more impersonal or detached than they actually are. But recognition can be expressed with great fervor and excitement and still not emphasize the teacher's needs, values, or judgments. (Please watch out for black-and-white thinking here. I once had a graduate student seriously misinterpret my cautions against using conditional approval. The day after our class, she ran up to me saying, "Boy, am I glad I'm in this class. I almost gave someone a compliment yesterday!" Remember, we want to use as much positive feedback and encouragement as possible.) In a win-win environment, we are certainly free to be generous with compliments and enthusiastic acknowledgements, provided that our sentiments are genuine, spontaneous, and not designed to influence or manipulate behavior. It's entirely legitimate to tell students that they look great in certain outfits, that we missed them when they were absent, or that we're just glad that they are in our class. In a nonconflict setting, when we have no attachment to particular outcomes and no agenda other than the desire to share a particular sentiment, such statements can communicate a great deal of respect and appreciation.

MEANINGFUL CONNECTIONS

As with motivators and rewards, it's easy to trip over personal values and preferences, projecting what's important to us and assuming that the same things have similar meaning to the students. As innocent as they may seem, statements such as "You must be proud" or "I'll bet you're happy now" presume that a student feels a certain way, although the experience may hold an entirely different meaning or value to him. Instead of suggesting how a student should or must feel, we can acknowledge our observations ("You're obviously excited about this" or "You seem pleased"), ask students how they feel, or simply recognize the accomplishment ("You worked very hard on this!").

We also need to be careful that we don't connect the students' positive behavior to something they perceive as negative. (How would you feel if I recognized the great job you did cleaning my bathroom by saying, "Now that you're finished, you can iron!"?) For our statements to actually reinforce, they must have value and make sense to our students. Connections that promise "Now people will think you're neat" or "Now you can take care of the fish" may not be exactly punitive, but a child who doesn't need to be perceived as neat or one who has no interest in the fish will probably shrug in response. "That will help you get into college" will be meaningful only to a kid who is striving for that goal, perceives it as accessible in some way, and is generally close enough to achieve it.

The best verbal reinforcers are those tied into the actual (or realistically possible) experiences of our students. For example, consider the following statement: "You remembered to put the caps back on the markers. Now they won't be dried out when you go to use them tomorrow." These comments will have a greater impact on a child who has actually tried to write with a dried-out marker than one who has never had this experience. Still, the reinforcer maintains its validity; even if the student can't imagine the negative consequences, we're still reinforcing the cause-and-effect nature of his or her behavior.

> Even if the student can't imagine the negative consequences, we're still reinforcing the cause-and-effect nature of his or her behavior.

If the positive outcome of a student's behavior is too remote or abstract, we can still reinforce the behavior by connecting it, as we did in setting up our boundaries, to something more immediate and concrete. For example, learning to regroup in addition problems has a number of positive outcomes, but most of them are related to being able to do something more complex in math at some point in the future. When children experience a breakthrough in this process, it may be quite reassuring to tell them that now they'll have an easier time with the next lesson, but we'll probably see an even more powerful effect by stating, "Now that you understand this skill, you can work with these new math puzzles and games (which will allow them to practice their recent accomplishment)." So long as it is meaningful and available within a reasonable amount of time, reinforcement increases the probability that the behavior will recur. Period.

THE POWER OF POSITIVE OUTCOMES

This is where we begin to appreciate the value of using boundaries instead of rules. When we promise positive outcomes that are meaningful to the student, we motivate the behavior we want: "As soon as you finish the assignments in your folder, you can work on one of the enrichment activities." We've established the connection between what we want and what the students want. Now we can simply revert to this same language to reinforce their cooperation: "Way to go! You finished all your assignments. Now you can work on an enrichment activity."

Yet regardless of the values of verbal acknowledgement, there is probably no stronger reinforcement than allowing kids to experience the benefits our boundaries promise. The privilege of helping in the kindergarten, going on to the next lesson, or working on an enrichment puzzle when students finish their work builds commitment and good work habits. So does being able to continue to listen to music, hear the story, sit on the floor, or work with a friend as long as their behavior reflects the requirements previously established. Actual access to positive experiences increases the likelihood that their cooperation will continue and, over time, become habituated and internalized. It strengthens the students' sense of personal power and their ability to make their lives work. Verbal reinforcement can provide additional support even in cases in which the student has access to a tangible reward or privilege, but it is usually the actual experience of an earned privilege or reward that carries the most weight.

And yet, despite the efficacy of correctly used positive reinforcement, our factory-era training can get in the way. Much as there is some resistance to motivating children, there is often a similar reluctance to reinforce with rewarding activities or privileges. But the desire for a payoff is built into the experience of being human, not something we teach with reinforcers. Remember that there is no such thing as unmotivated behavior. Experiencing a rewarding outcome does not teach kids to expect positive outcomes any more than eating teaches them to be hungry.

> Experiencing a rewarding outcome does not teach kids to expect positive outcomes any more than eating teaches them to be hungry.

The use of reinforcers and recognition statements can present a challenge to teachers at all grade levels. Elementary or preschool teachers typically struggle with changing praising patterns, especially the habit of relying on "I like the way. . . ." And the need for recognition seems to be harder to sell to some secondary teachers, who may equate reinforcement with gushy praise. But this need applies to students of all ages and may be even more effective in the upper grades, where some students are so starved for any type of positive exchange with meaningful adults in their lives that even the simplest acknowledgement can go a long, long way.

Even when we tie the behavior to an outcome that is not inherent in the task itself ("Since you finished your work early today, you can take this note to Ms. Compton if you'd like"), we are still increasing the likelihood that the desired behavior will recur. Perhaps along the way, the desired behavior will become more automatic or intrinsically valuable. But either way, we are strengthening the kinds of desirable student behaviors that contribute to learning, self-control, and an environment that everyone can truly enjoy.

Hot Tips for Reinforcing Positive Behavior

- Use positive reinforcement—verbal or nonverbal (interactive, token, or activity) to acknowledge and strengthen already-existing behaviors. Avoid attempting to use reinforcement before the desired behavior has occurred.
- Watch for a tendency to use praise to help students solve problems or feel good about themselves. Flattery can appear manipulative even to a young or needy student. Such messages are superficial at best and will not contribute to the student's genuine sense of self-worth.
- Avoid using teacher approval as a means of reinforcing desired behavior. Learn to distinguish between reinforcers intended to maintain a particular student behavior and genuine expressions of appreciation, affection, or enjoyment of your students. In a win-win classroom, behaviors such as a smile, touch, nod, or wink—which obviously communicate the fact that the teacher is pleased—are not used as expressions of conditional approval. Although they may sometimes be used as reinforcers, such behaviors may also appear randomly, regardless of the student's performance or behavior, as expressions of appreciation or affection.
- Phrase reinforcements as an affirmation or acknowledgement of a behavior the student has demonstrated and the positive consequences now available (not as "if . . . then . . ." statements, which are more useful for *motivating* behavior that has not been demonstrated).
- Remember that reinforcements may be effectively communicated in either oral or written form.
- To reinforce a desirable behavior, first describe the behavior that took place. Be specific and concrete and avoid making judgments about the behavior or the worth of the student.
- Whenever possible, attach a comment that connects the immediate benefits of the student's behavior to the student (or the group), making sure the outcome is positive and meaningful. Avoid projecting your own feelings and values, which may or may not be relevant to those of the student, or suggesting how the student should feel.
- Look for the positive. You can almost always find something to recognize in any performance. Reinforce what was done right and work to correct or improve the rest.
- Perhaps because of the rigidity of roles during the factory era, there was a tendency for teachers to recognize certain behaviors in boys (such as strength, mechanical skill, and ability in math and the sciences) more frequently than girls (who are more often reinforced for neatness, creativity, attractiveness, and writing and artistic abilities). In recognizing students, be aware of any tendencies to promote stereotypes.

Chart 21.1 Recognition and Outcome Connection Statement Development

Desired Behavior	Recognition Statement	
	Description of Behavior	Payoff for Student

Use Chart 21.1 or create a similar chart on a separate piece of paper.

- In Column 1, identify five specific desired behaviors—that is, behaviors you want your students to exhibit.
- In Column 2, imagine that the student has just demonstrated the desired behaviors you identified in Column 1. Write the first part of a recognition statement, describing what the student has done (without judging the value of the behavior or the student).
- In Column 3, write the second part of the statement to connect the student's cooperation to a positive outcome (what's in it for the student).

Activity

1. Identify several positive student behaviors you acknowledged (after the behaviors were demonstrated) during the past two or three days:[3]

   a. How specific were your recognition statements in describing the desired behavior?

   b. How successful were you in avoiding personal judgments and teacher approval?

   c. How successful were you in avoiding attempts to use praise of one student to elicit a cooperative behavior from another?

   d. How successful were you in avoiding attempts to use praise to dismiss a student's problem or make the student feel better?

2. Describe some of the instances in which you were able to connect the student's behavior to the positive outcomes of his or her behavior:

   a. How well were you able to focus on (and communicate) the immediate benefits to the student?

3. In what ways are you satisfied with the reinforcement strategies you currently use?

4. In what ways would you like to change or expand these strategies?

NOTES

1. Jane Bluestein, *Being a Successful Teacher* (Torrance, CA: Fearon Teacher Aids [Frank Schaffer Publishers], 1989), 146; D. Keith Osborn and Janie Dyson Osborn, *Discipline and Classroom Management* (Athens, GA: Education Associates, 1977), 35.

2. This chapter focuses on strengthening or *reinforcing* positive student behavior. For more information on *motivating* these behaviors, see Part IV, particularly Chapters 11 and 12. The connection between reinforcement and motivation, particularly with regard to boundaries, is explained later in this chapter.

3. You may want to tape record a lesson or ask a colleague to observe. In either case, the object of this activity is to identify specific language: what you say to recognize positive behavior and also how you connect it to the positive consequences to the students.

22

Supporting Emotional and Social Development

Although my preservice and subsequent training offered occasional directives about appreciating the affective dimensions of our students' lives, the reality of the school systems presented a rather different perspective. Whether in the counsel of veterans who advised the new teachers to tell our students to "check their feelings at the door," or in the mountain of test scores that seemed to define our purpose and effectiveness, the overriding emphasis on cognitive performance was unmistakably clear.

We receive very limited training—if any—to prepare us for the practical aspects of dealing with the emotional dynamics that occur in a classroom. And once we begin our work in the schools, how many of us are evaluated for our ability to listen or support a child in crisis? In fact, efforts to accommodate emotional and other noncognitive learning needs are often perceived as superfluous or soft, distractions from the "real" job of teaching

> How many of us are evaluated for our ability to listen or support a child in crisis?

content. In general, the emotional components of children's lives are either relegated to some separate, unintegrated, spare-time activity in school, or they are ignored altogether—at least until some fairly severe event occurs. But as surely as the brain needs motion to function, it needs emotion as well. Emotion drives attention, which, in turn, drives learning and memory. (Think of how clearly you remember the emotionally charged events you've experienced or seen in the news.) Strategies that engage students' emotions are powerful learning tools.[1]

Unfortunately, if emotion seems to be the *only* thing happening in your classroom, teaching and learning will suffer. Feelings and pressures in children's lives can ultimately affect learning and classroom behavior. Don't imagine that the students' needs or demands on instructional time will be limited to cognitive development or that trying to distract them with academic demands will make their affective lives disappear. Feelings and problems are a part of life, and no amount of devotion to content curriculum will keep them out of your classroom.

We may not wish—or need—to devote our entire careers to our students' emotional lives, but that doesn't mean we can ignore them either. We know we can avert many conflicts and outbursts by providing constructive, nonhurtful outlets for feelings that would otherwise be—or become—distractions. Unfortunately, schools rarely even offer physical space, let alone psychological or emotional space, for processing feelings that can interfere with learning. Perhaps if students could indeed leave their feelings outside our classrooms, this would make sense. But as long as we're working with human beings, we're going to be working with their hearts as well as their heads.

Schools don't have a great track record for providing the kind of emotional support that would eliminate many of the problems that can emerge as a result of unresolved emotional issues, and kids quickly learn that feelings in general—and strong feelings in particular—are neither welcome nor acceptable in school. (When a case of the giggles in a high school study hall landed me in detention, it became obvious that even being too happy was unacceptable in school.)

When the overriding message tells children that feelings aren't okay, they learn to stuff their feelings and pretend that they are "fine" rather than risk an adult's criticism, impatience, or other negative reaction. These children typically grow up to become adults who are uncomfortable with children's feelings, adults whose responses often add stress to the situation, making it unsafe for children to express feelings. Even adults who *want* to really be there for kids in need often feel awkward and unskilled at handling kids' crises effectively. So we end up perpetuating this cycle of nonsupport, creating school environments with no real provisions for dealing with affective needs.

A PLACE FOR FEELINGS

The more upset students are, the less effectively they can solve problems and make rational decisions. The cognitive aspects of problem solving require parts of the brain that are difficult to access when the body is flooded with stress hormones, so kids generally don't do a very good job of "figuring things out" until they are physically and neurologically calm and grounded. We can help support kids who are emotionally wound up by listening and validating their experience, but sometimes they need a few minutes to calm down a bit first.

Creating a space for kids to simply *have* feelings can often become a space in which kids don't have to act them out. Many teachers have quickly defused conflicts, averted problems, and redirected destructive energy by giving kids a means of getting the feelings out in nonhurtful ways. Is there someplace in your classroom or school where students (or teachers, for that matter) can go when they feel a need to cry? What can students do to get rid of strong feelings without harming property, other children, or themselves? Sometimes, a few minutes out of the classroom, a brief walk around the playground or gym, or a chance to go get a drink of water can shift the affective energy a bit and help kids regain their focus and concentration.

> Creating a space for kids to simply *have* feelings can often become a space in which kids don't have to act them out.

A high school teacher in one of my workshops gave each of his students a little card that read, "I'm having a bad day. Leave me alone." He not only understood that we all have good days and bad days, but also provided an outlet for those *really* bad days, one each semester, when being able to manage normal classroom demands was just too hard. He found that for most of his students, just knowing that outlet was there was comfort enough. He also saw incredible discretion in the use of these cards, and when one came out, it was a sure bet that the crisis in that child's life was pretty significant.

Without the skills, outlets, or sense of safety necessary for expressing feelings in non-hurtful ways, kids often end up repressing, or "stuffing," their feelings. While this may seem to serve the teacher and the class, the long-term effects can be very destructive to everyone involved. Repressed feelings often come out explosively, sometimes at the slightest provocation, or in hurtful, destructive, or self-destructive behaviors. And despite every admonition to "just say no," to a child invested in avoiding painful feelings, any mood-altering substance or behavior that appears to offer relief can become quite attractive. If nothing else, our most creative lessons and enthusiastic presentations are likely to be lost on stressed-out kids who are focused on their feelings—or struggling to hold their feelings inside.

Regardless of the outlet you provide, your willingness to acknowledge students' feelings and help them channel those feelings nondestructively can significantly reduce disruptions and arguments in the class and ultimately contribute to the children's ability to self-manage both feelings and actions. Additionally, any outlet that does not create problems for others is far more consistent with the values and objectives of a win-win classroom than an insensitive, invalidating, or repressive reaction.

Unfortunately, our best efforts to help tend to skip the feeling part of the process. Most of us are inclined to see an upset child (or adult, for that matter) as simply needing a solution. The truth is, a child who trusts us enough to share that he or she is having a problem may not be looking for answers as much as a safe space just to be upset.[2] We get so busy wanting to analyze, advise, or fix the problem—which are all cognitive processes—that we bypass the affective demands of the situation entirely. Even worse, we may compound the students' problems when we respond to their needs with annoyance or impatience.

We can certainly help students develop constructive and independent problem-solving skills (described in the following chapter), but we need to help them deal with their feelings first. And we need to recognize that these are two very separate situations, each requiring different types of adult intervention strategies.

LISTENING

In many cases, we can be the greatest help by lending a much-needed ear. One of the most common complaints among kids, regardless of their age or background, is that no one is listening to them. And although this may not be your primary role, your students may take great comfort in simply knowing that your door is open if they need to talk.

But our willingness to sit and listen needs limits. Students often need to talk when it's not convenient for us. Sometimes we try to assess the urgency of the student's needs, asking, "Is it important?" Now, of course the student will think so. What we're really asking is for the student to determine whether it's important enough to interrupt the teacher. If it's not a good time for us, we don't need to ask. We simply let the student know when we'll be available. (The question will be equally superfluous if the student is in the obvious throes of a very serious trauma or physical distress that require immediate attention.)

If you're not available at the moment the student needs you, as will often be the case, set a boundary that acknowledges the child's desire for your attention and also lets him or her know when you'll be available: "This is important. I need to explain this assignment to this group. I'll be free to talk to you in about ten minutes (or when the big hand is on the three, when the bell rings, at lunchtime, or even after school)." Rarely will a child thus acknowledged not be willing to wait. Your desire to take care of yourself and still accommodate the child as soon as possible can go a long way toward building a child's patience and respect for your time and priorities.

Even when you're not available, there are a number of ways you can accommodate students who need some support until you're free to listen. One kindergarten teacher posted a picture of a storybook character on the bulletin board and invited the students to "Tell Mrs. Murphy" if they had a problem when the teacher was too busy to talk. If she saw a student spending an unusual amount of time whispering to the picture on the board, she would make a point to check in with the child later to see if everything was okay. More often than not, the student would assure her that "Mrs. Murphy took care of it."

A counselor used a stuffed bunny with great big ears for kids who needed a friend who would listen when an adult wasn't around. Live animals can provide a similar resource. (Several high school teachers found their students drawn to the animals in the science lab, including mice, lizards, and a couple of tarantulas.) And a middle school teacher accomplished a similar objective by drawing a picture of a big ear and taping it to the bottom half of the door in the back of the room. The fact that there always seemed to be a student back in that corner made it clear that the need to deal with feelings is critical at any age. And teachers at nearly all grade levels report success when making journals available for their students.[3]

If you're not in the mood to listen or if your patience is questionable, your tone of voice and body language will make that clear. Be honest ahead of time: "I'm too busy (tired, angry) right now to give you the kind of time and attention you deserve." Then give the student a specific time to return: "I do want to talk to you. I'll be finished with this group in ten minutes. Let's talk then."

When we finally do have a chance to sit face to face and talk with a student, let's revive the lost art of listening. This means letting *them* talk, resisting the urge to interject advice or, say, personal experiences. We can communicate our attention and concern with validating behaviors such as eye contact, nodding, and encouraging comments: "Uh-huh," "I see," or "Tell me more." Often, the less we say, the more helpful we can be. Just offering a chance to unload can help kids process the various dimensions of the problem well enough to see a solution for themselves.

ACCEPTING THEIR FEELINGS

We need to learn alternatives to trying to make the problem go away, making the child wrong, or fixing the problem for the child.

Keeping these channels open will depend on how we respond to our students. Nearly every adult who claims "I want my kids to come to me" also has a well-practiced litany of nonwelcoming, nonsupportive responses that tend to block or shut down communications. If this is truly going to work, we need to learn alternatives to trying to make the problem go away, making the child wrong, or fixing the problem for the child. This doesn't leave much besides resisting the rather counterintuitive urge to *do something* in favor of simply listening and accepting that the child has a feeling.

You'll know that you're providing this support when you're not responding in a judgmental, critical, dismissive, or otherwise unaccepting way. This is no small feat. Let's face it—some of their problems can seem pretty strange or even silly to us. I once had a student approach me on the verge of hysteria, claiming that one of the other students had called her a camel. Sometimes trying to take these incidents seriously can be a challenge, but the pain and stress the students experience are very real to them. Learning to respect and accept a child's reality, especially when it is very different from what ours would be under similar circumstances, may be one of the greatest gifts we can give that person. (This goes for other adults as well.)

We've clearly got a long way to go in this regard. When I've polled teachers about what this child would probably hear in response to her complaint, among the most common responses were those that dismissed or trivialized her feelings ("Don't be ridiculous. You can't possibly be upset about that!"), those that were sarcastic or attempted to distract the child ("Why aren't you this worried about your math grades?"), or those that criticized, blamed, or showed anger ("Can't you get along with anyone?" "What did you do to her?" or "That does it! I'm calling your parents.") Is it any wonder that kids can be very cagey when it comes to opening up to even the most well-meaning adults? (See sidebar, "Hot Tips for Supporting a Student in Crisis.")

Also common and, in its own way, equally destructive is a tendency to ask a student, "Why does that bother you?" For one thing, this question assumes that the child knows why something is troublesome and, at the very least, requires the student to shift from an affective process (experiencing feelings) to a cognitive one (explaining them).[4] Second,

---

Hot Tips for Supporting a Student in Crisis

- As much as possible, avoid the following nonsupportive responses:[5]
  - Dismissing or Minimizing: "That's nothing to be upset about." "So she called you a camel. Big deal." (Devalues the significance of the event to the student.)
  - Excusing: "She didn't mean it." "He didn't know what he was saying." "She must be having a bad day." (Suggests that it is okay for people to do hurtful things as long as they have an excuse.)
  - Denying: "Oh, you don't really feel that way." "That doesn't really bother you." "Teachers don't hate their students." (Tells students that they aren't feeling what they are feeling. Dismissive, confusing, and just plain "crazy-making.")
  - Distracting: "Well, at least you're passing your other classes." "You're lucky you didn't get detention." "Cheer up. You should be happy." (Does not validate or accept the reality of the student's experience. Confusing and irrelevant.)
  - Medicating: "This cookie should make you feel better." "Just get busy." (Uses some form of substance—usually food—or activity to distract students from their feelings.)
  - Attacking or Shaming: "I told you that would happen!" "How could you be so stupid?" "Don't be such a baby." "Nice girls don't say words like that." "You're just too sensitive." "Can't you get along with anybody?" (May also include sarcasm, disappointment, impatience, criticism, or contempt. One of the best ways to build walls and stop communications in any relationship.)

(Continued)

(Continued)

- o Blaming: "What did you do to her?" "That's what happens when you don't put things away." "Well, if you had just put the caps back on the markers, this wouldn't have happened." "You got what you deserved." (Compounds the initial problem and builds intense mistrust.)
- o Challenging: "Why does that bother you?" (Requires students to defend their feelings to convince the teacher that the feelings are legitimate, thus securing the teacher's conditional acceptance.)
- o Enmeshing: "That wouldn't bother me." "Your problems drive me crazy." "I really like this topic." (Confuses the teacher's reactions or reality with the student's.)
- o Commiserating: "Well, he's just a jerk." "You don't need her." "You're so unlucky." (Denies student's responsibility, is dismissive, and can suggest that the student is a victim or is disempowered, in the situation or in general.)
- o Rescuing: "I'll go talk to her about it." "I'll tell her to stop picking on you." "What's your excuse?" (Relieves the student of responsibility, either by the teacher taking responsibility for the problem or by providing a loophole in a boundary.)
- o Advising: "Just ignore her." "Go tell her you're sorry." "Go play with someone else." (Relieves the student of responsibility for finding a solution because the teacher is telling the child how to solve the problem.)

- Get clear on your role. In the long run, it is far more helpful to teach children to protect and defend themselves and to find their own solutions to problems than it is to do these jobs for them.
- Listen. If you're not available when they need you, let them know, as specifically as possible, when you will be free. When they're talking, make eye contact and minimize the amount of talking—and interrupting—you do.
- Distinguish between feelings and behaviors. There's a difference between wanting to hurt someone and actually hurting someone. For example, it really is okay to want to drop out of school or punch a classmate—although actually doing either one has serious consequences. Accepting students' rights to their feelings does not give them permission to exhibit hurtful or destructive behaviors.
- Accept the students, their feelings, and their rights to have their feelings. Your acceptance will be conveyed by the absence of judgmental, shocked, critical, impatient, or disappointed words, looks, or body language. Even if you disagree with their feelings or don't understand them, resist the desire to make kids wrong for their feelings.
- Validate the student's reality. Anything you say or do that gives children permission to have feelings will validate the experience. Again, the absence of disagreement or judgment will help, as will comments like, "I see," "I understand," or "Of course you're angry about that."
- Maintain your boundaries. Let your students know when you'll be available to talk or help. Watch the tendency to take responsibility for their feelings or problems by trying to fix the situation or cheer them up (fix them) or by rescuing or advising.
- Trust their ability to solve problems independently and provide instruction and support necessary to do so, preferably in a nonconflict setting. Model and teach conflict management, demonstrating nondestructive ways to have and express feelings and building skills for setting and maintaining boundaries.
- Provide healthy, nonhurtful outlets for feelings (and meeting needs).
- Ask—don't tell. When students are ready to start looking for solutions, use questions to guide them and help them identify and evaluate options available and anticipate probable outcomes. Caution: Watch out for questions that disguise criticism or advice, such as "What were you thinking?" or "Why don't you tell her how that hurts your feelings?" (See Chapter 23.)
- Respect the fact that the student may not want to talk about it right now, or may not be comfortable talking with you. Leave the door open for future discussion. Look for or suggest other resources (such as the school counselor, a student support group, or an outside agency) if the student would prefer or if you are personally not comfortable discussing a particular topic.

asking why something is bothersome requests that children explain or defend their feelings, with the implicit message that our acceptance of the feelings and the children's right to them is conditional, requiring that they have a good enough reason for being upset. In a supportive, emotionally safe classroom, it doesn't matter whether children are upset because they have an inexplicable fear of large, exotic mammals or because their best friend called them a name. Children don't need an excuse for their feelings, nor do they need to name or describe them; they just need to know it's okay to have them.

How many of us try to comfort a student by making excuses for the other person? Saying things like "Oh, she didn't mean it" (which probably isn't true) or "Well, you know his parents are getting a divorce" (which suggests that it's okay for the child to be cruel or abusive since he's got an excuse) can surely violate trust and block future communications. I know it's tempting to want to make unpleasant feelings go away, but in most cases only the *child* will go away, feelings hidden or stuffed (but likely to show up later in some destructive or self-destructive behavior).

Probably the most common way of handling student problems is by giving advice (telling the student how to solve the problem). Even teachers skilled in avoiding other destructive and nonsupportive reactions have a hard time with this one. It's nearly impossible to resist stating what seems like an obvious solution to us: "Just ignore her." "Well, go play with someone else." "Have you told her how you feel?" Remember, children in crisis aren't always looking for solutions—sometimes they just need a safe space to have a feeling, which is often a critical step in just getting to a place where they can find solutions on their own.

There are major drawbacks to giving advice. For one thing, advising immediately draws us into the problem, making us responsible for it and its solution. For another, our advice can sometimes create new or additional problems and also makes us vulnerable to blame if we're wrong. Further, children need confidence and skill in their ability to take care of problems on their own—after all, there won't always be an adult around to tell them what to do. Giving advice not only deprives the student of the opportunity to develop problem-solving skills, it also suggests that the child is incapable of doing so (often heard as "too dumb").

> Giving advice not only deprives the student of the opportunity to develop problem-solving skills, it also suggests that the child is incapable of doing so.

The greatest challenge for many teachers in these situations is resisting the seduction of being needed. Often, disengaging will require reframing our role in the lives of our students. If we believe that part of our job is to protect students from problems and conflicts, it'll be hard to resist the temptation to say, "Well, I'll go have a talk with her," when one student has a problem with another. But we then need to be prepared to wind up in the middle of endless conflicts, wasting time and energy trying to fix blame or determine "Who started it?" If, on the other hand, we see our role as helping students learn how to take care of themselves in conflicts with others, we will, so long as their immediate safety is not at stake, assume a much different role.

It's true that much of what we've learned—and much of what continues to be modeled around us—is not as supportive as we might like. But replace these nonsupportive responses with listening and validation—and remember, we're still not working on solutions[6]—and we move that much closer to achieving our win-win objectives.

VALIDATING THEIR REALITY

One of the easiest ways to validate other people's reality is to agree with them. Of course, if a child complains, "I'm really stupid," this does not mean we should respond by saying, "Yes you are!" In cases like this, validate the frustration, not the opinion: "You're having a hard time with this assignment" or "Wow. This was harder than you expected."[7] The student whose friend called her a camel happened to come to me a few days after I had attended a conference workshop that dealt with accepting and validating feelings. Lucky for her, because my typical, automatic reactions were, in retrospect, pretty negative and nonsupportive. I remember fighting my natural inclination toward impatience—especially with this particular student, who had done her share of name calling herself—biting my lip so I wouldn't say anything while she was talking and thinking very hard about how I wanted to respond. When she said she was upset, I simply agreed: "Sometimes it hurts when people call us names."

> One of the easiest ways to validate the other people's reality is to agree with them.

She stared at me for a second and then concurred: "Yeah." That was it. She walked back to her desk and sat down and got back to work. For that moment, she didn't need a solution. Simply being heard and having permission to feel bad was all she apparently needed, after which she had no need to hang onto her hurt feelings—or use them to justify hurting back.

You can check or communicate your understanding by restating what they have said in your own words, without evaluating, judging, interpreting, or commiserating: "You're saying that her teasing bothers you." "You weren't expecting him to do that." "You asked her to stop and she ignored you." This strategy can help your students feel validated and understood, gain understanding of the problem, and find their own way out. And as we develop our ability to objectively reflect what we are hearing, we can also avoid more familiar, negative responses.

Sometimes this response is enough. You have acknowledged their concerns, validated their feelings, and let them know that you understood what was being said to you. Your lack of criticism, disappointment, judgment, or impatience have made clear your unconditional acceptance—both of the students and their right to have their feelings (even if the feelings seem silly, frivolous, or incomprehensible to you). You have also left the responsibility for the solution with the students because your response did not involve you in the cause or solution of the problem. This is support in the truest, kindest, and most helpful sense of the word.

**Things to Remember About Creating a Safe,
Supportive, Emotional Environment in the Classroom**[8]

- Students have feelings in and out of the classroom. Teachers will encounter students' feelings from time to time no matter how much curriculum we have to cover and no matter how far behind the students may be.
- Teaching children to deal with their feelings and problems independently and in healthy, constructive ways will ultimately leave more time for teaching content.
- It's okay for children to have feelings without explaining or defending them to anyone. Cheering students up may make us feel better, but it rarely addresses the issues kids have or teaches problem solving. (No matter what, this is definitely *not* the best time of their lives.)

- Feelings are not behaviors. Feelings are never right or wrong, but behaviors that hurt other people are not okay. Teachers do not need to protect other people from a child's feelings, but we may need to intervene in hurtful behaviors.
- It's okay to express feelings as long as doing so does not hurt anyone or create problems for others.
- Most children (and many adults, for that matter) do not have healthy, nonhurtful outlets for expressing their feelings, especially anger or frustration. Nearly all students can benefit when we discuss and present options available to help kids externalize their feelings—or get them out—without hurting themselves or others, especially if we do this proactively, before there is a problem, and at a nonconflict time.
- Possible nondestructive outlets for the children may include the following: talking to a stuffed animal or picture when you're not available, drawing a picture or writing a letter about how they're feeling—and then tearing it up, writing in a journal, going for a run, or going down the hall for a drink of water and a chance to catch their breath. Simply distracting them with work is not the same thing.
- Teachers and students are distinct, separate individuals. It is not necessary to feel someone else's feelings or own his or her problems to show that person we care.
- Teachers are not responsible for changing or controlling the child's feelings. It's more loving and supportive to communicate that a child's feelings are heard, respected, and taken seriously—even when we don't understand them.
- Children learn to deal with feelings more effectively when they don't have to stuff or hide them to protect a critical, guilt-ridden, or overreacting adult.
- Teacher responses that interfere with children's ability to own, feel, express, or process their feelings can block communications, teach children to mistrust their own feelings and perceptions, and interfere with the development of their problem-solving capabilities.

Are You a Safe Adult?[9]

Some students are fortunate enough to have parents, relatives, neighbors, coaches, religious leaders, or other adults in their lives that they can turn to for support and guidance. However, many students do not have safe and supportive adults in their lives. One of the most important factors in ensuring students' success—in school and in life—is having at least one adult in their lives they can count on for support no matter what. Are you that person? Here are the characteristics of a safe adult. Which ones describe you?

- Safe adults tend to lead balanced lives. They are not always in a state of crisis.
- Safe adults are consistent. Although they have good and bad days, they do not listen to students patiently one moment and then yell at them the next.
- Safe adults are good role models. They act the way they want their students to behave and treat students with the same respect they would like in return.
- Safe adults take responsibility for their actions. They do not blame students (or others) for lapses in their own behavior.
- Safe adults are not looking to be seen as cool by their students. They understand that they are adults and are not looking to be a part of the students' peer group.
- Safe adults can clearly communicate that they do not like something students have done while still letting the students know that they are valued.

(Continued)

(Continued)

- Safe adults do not always tell students what they should do. They give them choices and help them think through the possible consequences of each choice.
- Safe adults respect a student's need for confidentiality and will make clear the times they will be obligated to share something a student has shared.
- Safe adults do not make students feel uncomfortable. They are not sexually or emotionally inappropriate with them.

NOTES

1. Robert Sylwester, *A Celebration of Neurons* (Alexandria, VA: Association for Supervision and Curriculum Development, 1995), Chapter 4; Terence Parry and Gayle Gregory, *Designing Brain Compatible Learning* (Arlington Heights, IL: Skylight Publishing, 1998), 14; Marilee Sprenger, *Becoming a "Wiz" at Brain-Based Teaching* (Thousand Oaks, CA: Corwin Press, 2001), 83.

2. Therapist Jared Scherz concurs: "They are rarely looking for answers and if they are, they increase dependency, not self-sufficiency. It may be more economical, time-wise, but only in the short run."

3. Not all students will find this outlet the most satisfying or productive way of processing or reporting feelings, but some will find it absolutely indispensable. For some journaling resources for kids, check out *Creative Journal for Teens: Making Friends With Yourself,* by Lucia Capacchione (Franklin Lakes, NJ: New Page Books, 2002); *Totally Private and Personal: Journaling Ideas for Girls and Young Women,* by teen Jessica Wilber (Minneapolis: Free Spirit Publishing, 1996); or Lorraine M. Dahlstrom, M.A., *Writing Down the Days: 365 Creative Journaling Ideas for Young People* (Minneapolis: Free Spirit Publishing, 2000).

4. Even asking students to *name* their feelings requires a cognitive shift to analysis and identification, something few people can do in the middle of an emotional hijacking. I'm not convinced that we need to name a feeling in order to process it. Oftentimes these details don't become clear to us until we've had a chance to sit with our feelings for a while, if then. In the moment, sometimes it's just enough to feel.

5. These nonsupportive responses were originally described in my book, *Parents, Teens & Boundaries: How to Draw the Line* (Deerfield Beach, FL: Health Communications, 1993). They are reprinted here with the permission of Health Communications, Inc., www.hcibooks.com.

6. See the next chapter for helping kids with problem-solving strategies.

7. This is a great way to defuse and discourage a constant need for attention and reassurance. It's also much more effective than arguing with a student ("You are *not* stupid!") or retorting with a sarcastic, demeaning, or otherwise nonsupportive response.

8. Adapted from Jane Bluestein, *Parents, Teens & Boundaries: How to Draw the Line* (Deerfield Beach, FL: Health Communications, 1993).

9. Adapted from Jane Bluestein, and Eric Katz, *High School's Not Forever* (Deerfield Beach, FL: Health Communications, 2005), 226–228.

23

Building Problem-Solving Skills

Once an upset student calms down and actually has access to the more rational, cognitive parts of the brain, we can start looking at ways to help the child resolve a particular problem. This process will often bring up issues of personal responsibility and problem ownership. When it comes to building independence and problem-solving skills, one of the greatest challenges for adults is reflected in our ability (or inability) to simply get out of the way. There is a great rule of thumb for problem solving in a win-win classroom: The person with the problem is responsible for solving the problem—without making it anyone else's problem. Yet, regardless of our commitment to these goals, it's still easy to get hooked by our students' needs, even when we're not really needed.

Adults frequently mistrust kids' problem-solving capabilities, rushing to help before help is needed. For one thing, we've usually got the clarity and perspective that would make it easy for us to see how the problem could be resolved or avoided. Or perhaps we simply see solving other people's problems as part of the job. If our students have sold us on their helplessness, assuming responsibility for their problems can be especially tempting if we're inclined to want to protect them. Add to that our need to be needed, important, wise, influential, and powerful, and it's easy to see the difficulty in separating ourselves from our students' problems.

Falling into this trap serves no one. Our involvement robs our students of opportunities to develop the confidence and skill that come from taking responsibility for their own problems and learning from the experience. Certainly, our students' problems will, at times, compete with our ability to concentrate or stay on task. How often do we jump in out of impatience or frustration, thinking if we just solve this problem for them, maybe it will go away? But mediation in the name of expediency often ends up reinforcing helplessness and teacher dependence, opening the door for future interruptions to occur. After a while, the interruptions and lack of self-management are bound to get on our nerves. Whether it's the nature of the problem or the teacher dependence itself, when our patience wears thin, our reaction is likely to be neither helpful nor supportive.

Factory-era hierarchies obliged leaders to be aware of and involved in aspects of the groups' functioning, which, in a win-win classroom, are often left to the individuals in that group. Students are encouraged to take the initiative for solving their problems within whatever limits allow teaching and learning to continue. Of course, if you need to protect property or a student's physical safety, or if you simply need to keep a situation from getting out of hand, by all means, intervene. But the majority of classroom problems do not require our involvement. Our role, then, requires shifting from ignoring, dismissing, solving, or becoming enmeshed in our students' problems to listening, encouraging, and facilitating their ability to solve the problems themselves.

PROBLEM-SOLVING STRATEGIES: LAYING THE GROUNDWORK

Success-oriented problem solving requires some groundwork. To begin, we need to let the students know—from the start—that there will be times in which we will not be able to help them with their problems, and that our insistence on their finding their own solutions does not mean that we don't care. To maintain a win-win atmosphere, we also need to remind them that solving their problems cannot create problems for anyone else, and we may need to teach them to work independently and help one another in nondisruptive ways if they haven't already demonstrated these skills.

Further, we need to be sure that there are options available within these limits by which the students can indeed resolve their conflicts on their own. As author Becky Bailey asserts, "self-control cannot be learned until an opportunity to exercise self-control occurs."[1] For example, if students are upset that other students are bothering them or interfering with their ability to do their work, are they allowed to move their desks or find another place to work? If students do not have necessary materials, do they have the option of asking around before class starts to borrow a pencil or share a book? If students get uncomfortable or fidgety in their chairs, is there somewhere else they can do their work? Without positive ways to generate solutions to their problems, students will surely find negative routes. And the place we may see this pattern most often will be in interactions between students, especially those whose problem-solving skills—and social skills—could use a little work. Many of the discipline problems we encounter begin with student-to-student conflicts, and as part of our preventive efforts, we can pretty much count on having to teach kids some of the skills they can use to prevent and resolve conflicts.

> Without positive ways to generate solutions to their problems, students will surely find negative routes.

THWARTING THE TATTLETALE

Good boundaries will help minimize the number of interruptions we experience when students feel compelled to report on the behavior of their peers. Tattling can drive anyone to distraction, and I don't mean reports of a fire in the library or a stranger in the bathroom. (You can be sure that no matter how strict your no-tattling limits are, you will hear about the serious stuff.) And I'm also not talking about incidents in which a student is being threatened, harassed, or hurt by others.[2] I'm talking about the annoying attempts to drag us into non-life-threatening conflicts with peers: "Dodi was looking at me," "Garry said a bad word," or "Kendra kicked my chair." What do we do when we've set everything up to encourage student self-management only to find a child tapping on our shoulder because "somebody stole my pencil"? How can we resist allowing these problems to become our own? (Yes, these examples are more common in lower grades, but how often did my older kids try to involve me in situations just to get one of their classmates in trouble?)

One third-grade teacher told her students that she had simply gotten too busy to listen to them tattling and supplied them with a Tattling Form until she was available.[3] By assuring the students that she was truly concerned, despite her unwillingness to become directly involved in their conflicts, she put the responsibility back on their shoulders, communicated her faith in their ability to resolve their conflicts, and put herself in the role of facilitator, not rescuer. In addition, by saying, "I want to hear about this in a little bit. Fill out this form so I'll have more information," she removed herself from the temptation of automatically reacting with habitual, nonsupportive responses. Further, by providing a constructive outlet with the Tattling Form, she made it possible for students to be heard, and to work through their feelings on paper, evaluate their options, and choose positive alternatives to negative situations. Finally, she not only avoided being drawn into problems she did not own, but she also bolstered the students' confidence in their own ability to resolve conflicts and get their needs met without creating problems for anyone else.

There are times students will tattle as an excuse to talk to the teacher, times they just need that connection or attention. Win-win teachers will find ways to accommodate the students' needs, even when they aren't physically available to listen, just as the aforementioned teacher was able to do. I've been in classrooms that had an unconnected telephone, tape recorder, or suggestion box for reporting events and concerns. One first-grade teacher told me she selected various helpers who each wore a button that said "I want to know" and had the other students report to them. After a while, everyone had a chance to be a helper. It did not take long for the students to gain a fair amount of discretion once they were on the listening end.

Another teacher, totally frustrated with an endless stream of tattling sixth graders, finally exploded: "That does it! From here on in, no more tattling unless somebody dies!" The students got the point, had a laugh, and still, on occasion, forgot her directive. However, from then on, any time a student came up to complain about another student, all the teacher had to do was remind the complainer that since the other student was still alive, they'd have to work the problem out peacefully among themselves.

Nonetheless, if students are new to solving their own problems (or insecure about their ability to do so), there will be times when they will come to you in the hopes of having you fix the situation. Even when you have set the stage for personal responsibility ahead of time, your refusal to get involved may add to their frustration. Some students need a little time to get used to the idea of being responsible for solving their own problems, and when you really do need to intervene, there are ways to support them, and truly be there for them, even if you aren't doing the work for them.

> Some students need a little time to get used to the idea of being responsible for solving their own problems, and when you really do need to intervene, there are ways to support them, and truly be there for them, even if you aren't doing the work for them.

There are various versions of a tattling form that encourage kids to take responsibility for solving their own problems, rather than reporting them to the teacher. One that was initially shared by a third-grade teacher (and which, frankly, could be adapted for use at any grade level) included the following questions:

Tattling Form

1. Your name:

2. The name of the person who is bothering you:

3. Something nice about that person:

4. Describe the problem:

5. What are you going to do about the problem?

WHEN TELLING *ISN'T* TATTLING

There will be times when we *will* want to know, particularly when a student's physical or emotional safety is at stake. The good news is that students are more likely to report serious problems when they know that they can trust us to take them seriously and not respond in a nonsupportive way (which includes not becoming reactive, punitive, or hysterical). Creating the dynamics found in win-win classrooms will help us avoid situations in which even well-intended reactions actually cut kids off from the support they need.[4] As one researcher found, "Typical adult responses to allegations of harassment in schools almost always discouraged students from further reports, seldom curbed harassment, and left kids feeling as though they had no place to turn for help."[5] And yet, students are in a prime place to prevent bullying and harassment as well as more serious problems when these channels are open. Of nine separate plots to do violence in schools in the spring of 2006, all of which were discovered before the incidents had a chance to occur, violence was averted in a number of cases because students reported what they had heard was going to happen. In fact, a separate article, referring to potential incidents, confirms that "student reporting is the most effective way to prevent school violence."[6]

This is an enormously important issue and deserves more space than this book can adequately provide. Nonetheless, I firmly believe that there are things we can do, as teachers, not only to create the type of environment in which students feel safe enough to come to us when there is a problem, but also to create the type of environment in which these types of interactions—whether harassment, teasing, hazing, bullying, excluding, gossiping, rumor spreading, or other types of emotional and physical violence—are far less likely to occur. Creating classroom and school communities in which students' needs for dignity, respect, belonging, and autonomy are being met is a great place to start. Modeling behaviors like asking directly for what we want, managing our anger effectively, setting good boundaries, refusing to engage in abusive interactions, and learning to not take things personally help to model options for students besides lashing out. And let's also invest some time in helping students build independence, problem-solving skills, and strategies for preventing and peacefully resolving conflicts with peers.[7]

BUILDING SOCIAL COMPETENCE AND STUDENT SELF-CARE

There are so many students who lack the basic skills for sticking up for themselves in nonaggressive ways that their social interactions can become yet another source of classroom conflicts and discipline problems. Regardless of the grade levels at which you teach, you may need to work with individuals or groups of students, preferably at a nonconflict time, to build positive social skills such as sharing, politeness, and taking turns, or teach behaviors involved in conflict resolution, impulse control, and alternatives to blaming and excuse making. If you can involve parents or a school counselor (should your site be fortunate enough to have one[9]), so much the better. Instructional activities such as round table discussions, brainstorming sessions, or role-playing, along with dialogue addressed to resolving specific problems, can help build social and emotional development in such a way that, in the long run, you'll have much more time to devote to academics.

Social Skills That Help Reduce Conflict and Discipline Problems

As students develop the competencies that follow, we are sure to see fewer behavior incidents that stem from negative social interactions.[8] Imagine the difference the following skills will make as your students improve their ability to

- listen and really hear what their peers are saying.
- manage their own stress and anger.
- develop a tolerance and understanding of differences.
- treat others fairly.
- use given or chosen names (call others the names they wish to be called).
- take responsibility for their actions.
- make amends when they've hurt someone.
- anticipate consequences of their behavior.
- stick up for themselves in nonhurtful ways.
- look for win-win solutions that are fair to all concerned.
- address, rather than ignore, difficult issues.
- have empathy and compassion for others.
- treat others fairly and appropriately.
- be honest, forthright, and trustworthy in their interactions with others.
- defuse negative comments from peers.
- distinguish between healthy and unhealthy friendships.
- recognize abusive and disrespectful behavior for what it is.
- refuse to watch, join in, or encourage fighting.
- be a friend or advocate for someone being excluded or bullied.
- learn when it really is time to go to a safe adult.

We can also prevent many classroom conflicts when we model and teach good boundary setting skills. Even preschoolers can learn to say no, walk away from someone who is being mean, and refuse to participate until their classmates play nice. Unfortunately, many of the popular techniques taught to children have side effects we may not realize. For example, teaching students to ask a classmate, "Why did you take my crayons?" invites excuses, blame, and arbitrary acceptance or judgment. If kids want to protect their stuff, teaching them to say, "Please ask first" or "I'll be happy to share if you ask me" is far more assertive and direct.

We also have a tendency to encourage kids to "Tell him how that made you feel." This approach has often been packaged in a formula called "I-messages," which attempts to use one's feelings to change how others act.[10] Now I'll admit to a certain amount of enthusiasm for this technique at one time. After all, "When you . . . , I feel . . ." certainly sounded a lot more positive than attacking and name calling. But it didn't take me long to realize that children who say, "When you call me names, I feel hurt and angry," for example, actually project themselves as the emotional victims of the name caller. While these I-messages appear to structurally shift the emphasis to *me,* they are—literally and energetically—still "you-messages," statements of blame that put the responsibility for one's feelings on someone else. (This really contradicts the notion that these I-messages encourage problem ownership.) Of even greater concern, they give a great deal of power to someone who may not have the student's best interests at heart, and they effectively reinforce what may well have been intended as hurtful behavior in the first place. ("Cool. It worked!")

Perhaps the most serious flaw in promoting the use of phrases that suggest "When you . . . , I feel . . ." is the assumption that the other person is significantly invested in the emotional well-being of the person using this statement or is unaware of the emotional impact the behavior is having on that person. (This isn't always the case in intimate adult relationships. How likely is it going to be true in a school hallway or on the playground?) And despite the argument that I-messages are meant as positive exchanges, I fail to see anything positive in the accusation and disempowerment inherent in telling someone "you caused my feelings."

In a win-win environment, individuals take responsibility for their own feelings and learn how to ask for what they want. "I'm really angry," which expresses a feeling without blaming, projecting, or self-victimizing, is quite different from "You make me angry" or "When you (do this), I feel angry."[11] Author and educator Naomi Drew recommends using a type of I-message that focuses on your needs without letting blame creep into your voice, which, again, is a terrific alternative to the "When you . . . , I feel . . ." statements that are the more familiar construction. She recommends statements like "I want a turn, too. I've been waiting a long time," or "I'm not going to stand here and listen to you insult me," both of which are strong, assertive, honest, and likely to command far more respect than talking about how someone's behavior makes you feel.[12]

We have the right to be treated well—and to ask to be treated well—and there are ways to do this without ever bringing our feelings into the arena. For example, if one person wants another to change his or her behavior, that person simply asks, "Please stop calling me names" or "Let's talk (or play) when you're not calling me names." One preschool teacher shared a response she overheard from a student who was being teased about her hair. Imagine a three-year-old confident enough to tell her classmate, "You're not in charge of my hair!" If we can teach children to say, "When you . . . , I feel . . . ," we can certainly teach them to set boundaries to ask for what they want. Indeed, I would rather have students say, "I don't date people who hit" than talk about how being hit makes them feel.

We can also give them permission to not engage with a hurtful person or even help them learn ways to agree with that person ("You could be right" or "No kidding!") and then change the subject.[13] Let's look for ways to help kids stick up for themselves without being emotional victims of someone's behavior and to help them demonstrate respect for others without obliging them to become emotional caretakers.

ASK—DON'T TELL!

The time for resolving a problem is generally *not* when a child is in crisis. A child in crisis needs support for his or her feelings, as described in the previous chapter. Once the feelings have been acknowledged, felt, and worked through, and the student has shifted out of the immediate affective experience, then it may be time to explore options and find solutions. We can play a valuable role in this process, even when we aren't specifically telling students what to do. As our role shifts from problem solver and rescuer to encourager and facilitator, we start doing much more listening than talking. Instead of blaming, giving advice, or getting in the middle of their problems, we help them find answers by asking them questions, shifting the responsibility for problem solving back to the students. Leading and open-ended questions also help them process, explore, and resolve their conflicts; build decision-making skills; and demonstrate our belief that they are indeed capable of working things out.

What's Wrong With I-Messages?

Description

Formula for expressing feelings in conjunction with another person's behavior: "When you _____, I feel _____ (and I want you to _____)" to get the other person to act differently.[14]

Problems

- They are still "you-messages," literally (verbally) and energetically, carrying a message of blame: "My emotional state is the result of your behavior" ("victim" talk).
- They put the responsibility for your feelings and emotional well-being on someone else.
- They assume that the other person is invested in your emotional well-being and would be willing to change his or her behavior to take care of you. This is especially not true of typical playground or hallway social dynamics.
- They give a great deal of power to someone who may not have your best interests at heart, someone who may, in fact, be hoping to cause you discomfort, embarrassment, inconvenience, or pain.
- If someone's intention is, indeed, to hurt you, I-messages tell that person that his or her strategies are effective and, in fact, working!
- Few child relationships have (or should have) the intimacy required for dealing with the emotional impact of behaviors—and such intimacy is neither necessary nor relevant for generating cooperative, respectful behavior.
- Kids who are willing to change their behavior so other people won't feel sad or angry often have a hard time making good decisions on their own behalf, looking instead to the reaction (or potential reaction) of others when making choices. Their caretaking behavior patterns carry their own dangers and risks.
- There are other, better ways to generate cooperation from others, regardless of their personal feelings for you.

Alternatives to I-Messages

- Dealing with confrontation by agreeing with the other person and changing the subject.
- Requesting different behavior (or that a certain behavior stop): "Please stop kicking my chair." "Please don't touch the stuff on my desk." (No need to justify or explain why.)
- Stating a preference or limit: "I don't care to discuss that." "I don't like that word. Please don't use it around me." "I don't like to let other people wear my stuff." (And then cheerfully changing the subject, redirecting the discussion.)
- Setting a boundary, if possible, using a promise with a positive consequence: "I don't play with people who call me names." "I'll let you borrow this CD when you return the one you already have." "I'll be happy to continue this discussion when you stop yelling at me."
- Simply refusing to engage or respond is also appropriate in some instances.
- Telling a safe adult. Note: If adult intervention does not seem to have any impact, or actually makes things worse, please tell kids not to give up. As educator Jo Ann Freiberg advises, "Adults don't always have all the answers. Some adults might blow you off because they don't know what to do. If you get a blank look, a brick wall, or a response that you don't like, tell somebody else. There *is* a caring adult out there. Keep trying, keep trying, keep trying."[15]

For example, rather than automatically telling students who complain about the teachers who constantly pick on them to "just behave better in his class," we ask questions: "What's going on?" "How would you like the teacher to treat you?" "What have you tried so far?"[16]

The process of asking questions does not need to be particularly time-consuming. Many times, one or two questions are all that's necessary. In fact, many teachers eventually get to the point where they simply say, "What do you need to do about that?" or "How are you going to solve that problem?" to get the students focused on taking constructive action. Even very young children can respond—or learn to respond—to questions aimed at helping them solve their problems. True, it's expedient to say, "Just ignore her," but if you've gotten this far in this book, you probably want to accomplish more than reinforcing order taking or just getting this child out of your hair.

Each question you ask puts the responsibility back in the child's hands. Of course, some students will be disappointed, shocked, or even angry when this happens. They are so accustomed to getting advice or being told what to do, they often have no idea how to respond on their own and feel abandoned when we refuse to take responsibility for solving this problem. (And, don't forget, if they can get us to tell them what to do, they can also blame us if our advice doesn't work out.) As the one doing the asking, you may, from time to time, find that getting constructive responses from children can be quite a challenge. There are few things more aggravating than setting time aside to talk to a child who responds to every question with a shrug. One principal, who often had students respond to his questions with "I don't know," would further challenge them by asking, "Well, what would you say if you *did* know?" At this point, it's also appropriate to say, "I understand. Why don't you think about it for a bit? We can talk later if you'd like." In this way, you make it clear that you are willing to help the child solve this problem, although you have no intention of either solving it yourself or giving attention to indifference, indecision, or irresponsibility. What a wonderful way to be supportive, encouraging, and present in a troubled youngster's life! This process leaves little question about who is responsible for solving the students' problems or about the amount of faith we have in their ability to work things out.

> If they can get us to tell them what to do, they can also blame us if our advice doesn't work out!

Sample Questions

The questions that follow are provided to help with the mechanics of mastering the technique of "asking—not telling," an effective alternative to giving kids advice that encourages independence and problem-solving competence. The questions are in no particular order and will neither be relevant nor appropriate for every child or situation you encounter. Read through the list to familiarize yourself with the language and possibilities and to ground yourself in the process. Use what works for you. Add to this list as you think of other questions or want to note ideas that work.[17]

The purpose of these questions—and this process—is to allow you to put the responsibility for solving a particular problem on the child, almost like throwing a ball back to him, over and over, even though it will almost always seem easier to just catch the ball (the problem) and run with it yourself. Remember, you want to get a dialogue going, one in which your students do most of the talking and you do most of the listening. You want to help them get a better grip on what's going on in a particular situation and to determine what they want, which options are available (and won't create additional problems), and what they're ultimately going to try to make it better or make it right.

This process is only as good as your ability to listen and respond to what you're hearing. Please do not "drill" your students or get impatient to ask the next question. This is not a script, and the questions are not the issue—the process is!

Some Sample Questions

- What would you like to happen next?
- What do you think will (or might) happen next?
- How do you think you'll feel later (or afterward)?
- What have you tried so far?
- What have you tried that's worked in similar situations (or with this person)?
- What are you risking by doing that?
- Is it worth it?
- What seems to work for the other kids?
- What do you think the other person wants?
- How are you going to prevent this problem in the future?
- What are you willing to do differently?
- What will happen if you don't (pass this class, get the part, stay in this relationship, make the team)?
- How will you know if that's a good choice?
- What do you wish you could say to this person?
- Would you like to talk to someone else about this?
- Can you live with that?
- What parts of this situation are beyond your control?
- What parts of this situation are within your control (or influence)?
- What would that sound like?
- If the situation doesn't change, how can you take care of yourself?
- What bothers you the most about this situation?
- What other questions could I ask?

How will I remember to *ask* (or just listen!) the next time I'm tempted to give advice?

Activity

When a problem occurs in the classroom, it is always best if we can evaluate the situation before acting—or reacting. To practice, think of a problem one of your students recently shared with you or asked you to solve.

Describe the problem.

In what way could this be (or become) your problem?

What do you need to do to prevent it from becoming your problem?

What options does the student have for solving this problem on his or her own?

What other options might you make available for similar future incidents?

In what way have you acknowledged the student's needs and feelings?

How did you help the student solve this problem without making it your own?

How successful were you at avoiding a negative response (advising, asking why, criticizing, scolding, moralizing, trivializing, being sarcastic, etc.)?

Which negative responses are most difficult for you to avoid?

In what ways have your students shown growth in independence and problem-solving skills?

In what ways have you become better able to separate yourself from your students' problems (and turn the responsibility back over to them)?

What are your plans to further enhance your growth (and theirs) in this area?

NOTES

1. Becky Bailey, *There's Got to Be a Better Way: Discipline That Works* (Oveido, FL: Loving Guidance, 2003), 192.

2. This section addresses things teachers have done to avoid taking responsibility for problems their students could solve on their own or finding ways to accommodate a student's need for teacher attention until the teacher was actually available to listen or help. There's more information on strategies for supporting kids who are experiencing peer harassment, bullying, or worse in the next section, "When Telling *Isn't* Tattling."

3. See sidebar, "Tattling Form."

4. See "Guidelines for Supporting a Student in Crisis" in the previous chapter.

5. Charol Shakeshaft, Laurie Mandel, Yolanda M. Johnson, Janice Sawyer, Mary Ann Hergenrother, and Ellen Barber, "Boys Call Me Cow," *Educational Leadership* 55, no. 2 (October, 1997).

6. ABC News Web site, "Recent Incidents of Thwarted School Violence," http://abcnews.go.com/ (April 24, 2006); "Reporting Trouble Works! Prevents School Violence," presented by HealthNewsDigest.com (2005) and reported on the DentalPlans.com Web site.

7. See sidebar, "Social Skills That Help Reduce Discipline Problems."

8. Includes ideas from Bluestein and Katz, *High School's Not Forever* (Deerfield Beach, FL: Health Communications, 2005), 52, 63, 84–85, 112; Naomi Drew, *The Kids' Guide to Working Out Conflicts* (Minneapolis: Free Spirit Publishing, 2004); Jo Ann Freiberg, "Elements of Respect: Translating Respect Into a Playground Code of Conduct" (handout); plus personal correspondences with Naomi Drew and Jo Ann Reagan.

9. Also school psychologist, social worker, or other support staff at the school or district level.

10. Yes, there are many ways to use the word *I* very assertively in a sentence without using the "When you . . , I feel . . ." formula (with or without a third part that is often taught, one that asks the other person to behave differently: "and I want you to . . ."), and I will mention them later as very effective ways to deal with conflict. In this section, I am *only* referring to the aforementioned formula which, frankly, is the structure most people learn—and think of—when they hear the term *I-messages*.

11. If the anger is connected to (or was triggered by) someone else's words or actions, the focus is on the angry person's reaction and interpretation, which often has little to do with the other person's behavior. For example, a teacher who feels hurt, discounted, or invalidated because a student says a lesson is stupid is very likely to be up against much larger issues, such as the need for approval (the student's and others') or a fear of failure or inadequacy, or the feelings probably wouldn't have come up. This isn't about the students or the lesson.

12. Drew, *The Kids' Guide to Working Out Conflicts* (Minneapolis: Free Spirit Publishing, 2004), 54.

13. My thanks to Peggy Bielen for "You could be right," and to Lynn Collins for "No kidding." I've used these responses in potentially volatile situations and have found them to be immediately disarming, particularly when I simply refused to engage in any further dialogue or explaining. (Changing the subject sends a powerful message in itself and is another technique we can teach students of all ages.)

14. Once again, this refers *only* to statements constructed as in this description. For more details, see the free article on my Web site, http://www.janebluestein.com/articles/whatswrong.html.

15. Quoted in Bluestein and Katz, *High School's Not Forever*, 102.

16. See sidebar, "Sample Questions."

17. In the interest of space, I've selected a relatively small number of examples. For a more extensive list of sample questions, visit my Web site at http://www.janebluestein.com/handouts/questions.html.

PART VII

Working the System

24

Backup
and Support

Creating a win-win classroom is all about building positive and mutually respectful relationships, and up to this point, this book has focused on the relationships between teachers and their students. Although teaching can sometimes leave us feeling isolated from everyone *except* our students, these relationships extend beyond the walls of our classrooms. Let's keep in mind that each of us is also a part of an adult school community that includes administrators, support staff, other teachers, and parents. Even if our contact is infrequent, the quality of these relationships can have a very real impact on

With support from the adult community, even the most difficult students seem less challenging. . . .

our attitude, performance, sense of belonging, and mental health. With support from the adult community, even the most difficult students seem less challenging; on the other hand, lack of support can make us feel completely alone. And negative relationships with other adults can make life miserable, even with ideal classes.

Building a support network involves consciously connecting with other adults—not just for solving problems, but also for feedback, encouragement, and renewed perspectives throughout the year. It means applying the same win-win objectives and behaviors to preventing and resolving conflicts with other adults. And it means being there for others as a resource as well. Each school community operates by a set of complex social and (often) political dynamics. Exploring the school community—the one that exists outside our classrooms—can help us discover who's out there, which resources are available, and how the system works. We can learn about other people's expectations and the approaches and information they need (or don't need) and ways to interact to maximize the support that's available to us.

PARENTS PLAY A PART

Parents[1] can be an ace in the hole when it comes to support and reinforcement. A good relationship with the parents of your students can mean the difference between a great year and one fraught with stress and obstacles. Unfortunately, parent-teacher relationships rarely attain their maximum potential. Often, both parties complain of a lack of contact unless there's a problem. If this has indeed been the case with the parents of your students, imagine how effective a more positive approach can be.

You probably have already seen that parents are likely to be far more enthusiastic and positive in their support (or at least less likely to complain or interfere) when they see their children being successful, challenged, and excited about school and when they believe their children to be safe and valued by the adults in their children's lives. Likewise, when parents feel informed and included, when they feel welcomed in our classrooms, and when their interest in their children's well-being is respected, the likelihood of strong, supportive relationships increases significantly.

Teachers with good relationships with parents don't leave much to chance. Many bank on getting acquainted early in the year, either by note, phone, in-school conferences, welcome meetings, or home visits, and keeping first meetings positive. They attribute their success with the students' parents to keeping in contact on a regular basis, often with "good notes" or phone calls to report progress and improvement, or with occasional newsletters to keep parents informed about new projects, activities, policies, and objectives. (If the newsletter or report has been prepared by their children, or includes work, stories, poems, puzzles, or drawings made by their kids, it's a safe bet it will get home—and be read.) Frequent positive contact is the key! Hearing on a regular basis about what their kids are doing well forms a strong foundation for a relationship. Whether the parents receive handwritten notes, forms or reports, telephone calls, e-mail, or face-to-face contact, the effort that goes into informing them about their children's progress and performance reflects well on the teacher.

Whether we're reporting specific progress or simply something we appreciate about the child, parents generally will take note of the extra time and care we put into communicating with them. I often found that sending home weekly checklists not only kept parents informed but also encouraged greater commitment and more positive behavior from even my most challenging students. In designing your reports, be sure to choose easy, observable skills, things that every child could conceivably do, such as "takes care of materials," "comes to class prepared," "is caught up on homework assignments," and even basics like "says please and thank you." This is a great way of letting parents know your priorities and a way to indicate patterns—good or bad—that could eventually show up on the report card. Change the skills you list as student behavior improves and as your needs change, and commit to checking off as many skills as possible each week, with no child ever going home with fewer than three of the skills marked. (If the student is having a really bad week, this note will probably not be the only contact you will have with the parents.)

You can even have the students write their names on the forms (or have one student fill in all the names), and then you fill in the rest. The few minutes you invest in this task each week can build amazing connections with the other adults in your students' lives. As a bonus for all concerned, take a few extra seconds to write a little note on the bottom or back. Imagine how the parent will feel seeing that you took the time to write: "Big breakthrough in fractions," "Great sense of humor!" or (what may well be the best thing you can say to a parent) "I love teaching your child!"

The kids can become surprisingly attached to feedback like this. The one Friday I got too distracted to finish these reports, my eighth-grade class actually held the bus up while

I frantically finished my notes, telling their parents what their kids had done well that week. These reports can shape student attitudes and behavior, even with kids we'd think would be too old—or too cool—for "good notes." Even if your usual correspondences never seem to get home, somehow these messages manage to get there. (If you teach several classes, select one or two you feel would benefit most from parent support. This strategy is particularly effective with "difficult" or at-risk kids whose parents rarely hear anything positive from teachers or other school personnel.)

One middle school vice principal told me that he made a point to call the parents of each child in his school at least one time each semester, just to say something positive. He kept a list of the entire student population; as he spoke to teachers and heard or observed something positive about a student, he would make a note and call the parent that evening. He insisted that even with a large student population, this was entirely feasible, and took no more than about ten minutes a night.[2] Imagine the impact on the culture of a school in which the staff is constantly on the lookout for *good* things to report!

Regular, positive contact builds good home-school relationships and invites positive parent involvement. If problems arise, we can then approach the parent in the context of an already-established relationship, one that's been created in a positive context. We never want our first contact with parents to be about something problematic. However, when we do need to call parents to let them know about a problem, let's state that as the purpose of the call, describe the incident without anger or judgments, and inform them of our goals and plans for solving the problem. Above all, we'll do well to avoid blaming, unloading, or suggesting that we expect them to solve the problem for us. This is between teacher and student. We can invite ideas or suggestions, but we undermine our professionalism, accountability, and personal responsibility when we try to make this their problem as well. It's important that we keep parents informed about incidents that could affect a child's performance or success in school. However, parents rarely appreciate being called as a punishment for their child's misbehavior, and they do not enjoy being asked to scold or punish their child for a behavior that they did not witness.[3]

In all instances, let's keep relationships and interactions professional. We'll probably have the greatest success if we can focus the discussions on the child's behavior (not character), avoiding judgments about personalities or values and not discussing other students, parents, or professionals. If a student is experiencing difficulty, either with the work or in his or her social behavior, or if the student is demonstrating behaviors that are interfering with his or her potential success in school, parents need to know right away. There are few things more embarrassing or unprofessional than having to explain why the parents weren't informed before the behavior became enough of a problem to affect the student's grades, progress, placement, or graduation. Finally, it's always a good idea to document contact we've had with the parents, either in a contact log or in the student file itself, noting the date, the purpose of the contact, what was discussed and resolved, and intentions for follow-up.

ADMINISTRATIVE SUPPORT

A good relationship with school administrators can afford tremendous support and resources for the decisions we make in our classrooms. If we have a difficult or antagonistic relationship with the office, our work and attitudes will suffer the stresses of having our authority, goals, and intentions continually undermined. One of the key differences between these two situations is how we regard the administration when it comes to student behavior and discipline issues. Generally speaking, our willingness to assume responsibility for conflicts with or between students will work in our behalf. One of the most common complaints from administrators concerns their teachers' reliance on them to take care of their discipline problems. Many principals resent being called on to punish students, especially for things like chewing gum, talking, being unprepared, behaving disrespectfully, or acting out as the result of the teacher's negative or hurtful behavior.

> One of the most common complaints from administrators concerns their teachers' reliance on them to take care of their discipline problems.

But even if the principal enjoys playing disciplinarian, we are not well served by relying on him or her to take care of misbehaviors. For one thing, it's nearly impossible for someone outside the actual incident to intervene in a fair, meaningful, related, or win-win manner. Sending a child to the principal's office is a win-lose, punitive reaction intended to hurt or retaliate, a response that hearkens back to the "wait 'till your father gets home" mentality of the industrial era. As common and accepted as this practice may be, it really will not serve us to follow a tradition that essentially communicates—to the administration, the staff, and the students themselves—that we are unable to handle the students or resolve our own problems. (If we're sincere about building responsibility and accountability in our students, do we really want to model a dependence on someone else to fix our problems for us?) If we need to get the student out of the room in order to defuse or break up a conflict, the office may be a fine place for the student to go to calm down, but beyond requesting the use of that space for that specific purpose, the principal need not be involved in the intervention or resolution. (If the principal cannot resist getting involved, another classroom, the library, or the hall may be a better option.)

If you have a good relationship with your principal, you can invite him or her to observe you (or your class), make recommendations, point you to the best resources, clarify available options, or help you brainstorm solutions. If such an invitation would instead end up opening a door for unwanted scrutiny, criticism, or having an agenda imposed on you, you might try this with another colleague, one with whom you have built a strong, trusting relationship. If you decide to approach your principal for help, proceed with a plan. Present specific information about the problem, your objective, and what the administrator can do to help. The more information you can provide, the more help you're likely to receive. (This also applies to working with other support personnel.) A diverse, detailed student file with work samples, interest inventories, anecdotal records,[4] or other forms of documentation adds to your professionalism and is far more likely to get positive results than simply telling the school psychologist that "Dylan is driving me nuts." Be clear that this is *your* problem and that you could just use a hand sorting things out. When you bear the burden of responsibility for what's going on in your classroom, administrators and support staff are far more likely to be supportive when you really need them.

Even if the administration is not particularly (or initially) supportive of your win-win intentions, certain attitudes and behaviors will give you a much better chance of minimizing resistance. Little things can go a long way. For example, make sure the office gets a copy of anything you send home (such as announcements, newsletters, or general correspondences). Administrators also appreciate documentation. Any time you keep track of parent contacts, incidents with students, or student achievement, diagnoses, placement, and progress, you are also protecting them. If you are maintaining contact with parents as previously discussed, let the principal know what you're up to. It's also a good idea to inform him or her of special activities or events you have planned. The fewer surprises that end up in the office, the more supportive the administrator will probably be. Anything you can do to keep kids (and their parents) out of the office will work to your benefit. If you aren't causing problems for the administration, even a significant difference in philosophy and approaches to motivation can help you avoid drawing fire from above.

BEING A PART OF THE SCHOOL COMMUNITY

Any adult member of the school community can make a great difference in the quality of your life at school, so you have a great deal to gain by building strong relationships with your colleagues. In any school, you will find existing relationships, power structures, and traditions, and some adults are more willing than others when it comes to sharing materials, taking an interest in your ideas, or offering encouragement and support when you're having a bad day. There are still plenty of holdovers from the days when "looking good" was a critical part of teacher survival. Even in a healthy school culture, building (and becoming a part of) a support community can require a certain amount of savvy and discretion.

> Even in a healthy school culture, building (and becoming a part of) a support community can require a certain amount of savvy and discretion.

Too often, teacher stress and burnout involves problems with other adults, and problems will arise from time to time wherever people are working together. Learning when and how to respond can save you from personal feelings of anger, frustration, powerlessness, or self-righteousness, and can also help you avoid ending up on the receiving end of suspicion, alienation, or hostility. As in any relationship, win-win basics apply. We will always fare better when we treat others the way we wish to be treated, when we take the time out to show our appreciation, when we are willing to ask directly for what we want, and when we are willing to give in return.

When something comes up, be direct. Many people dance around a problem, never getting close enough to actually resolve it. One of the best skills we can develop—and teach our students—is the ability to ask for what we want and to do so without attacking or making anyone wrong. Unfortunately, we have very few healthy models for dealing with conflict, and a regrettable array of harmful approaches.

For example, how often do you see people perpetuate conflict by complaining about it? Complaining—especially when it involves triangulating,[5] gossip, and back-stabbing—is more likely to compound problems than solve them. Of course, these approaches can seem more attractive than actually confronting or even acknowledging a problem directly, particularly if we fear that a more direct approach might put us at some risk: "He'll have a fit!" or "She won't like me." Fear of anger and disapproval makes for some rather convoluted and dysfunctional interaction patterns. (This is another argument for avoiding the use of these reactions as a discipline or motivation strategy.)

Notice, too, how often people assume that the other person knew—or should have known—what they wanted. We are all products of individual experiences, and what's important to us may not even be coming in

> Self-righteousness may feel good for a time, but it's not much of a relationship builder.

on another person's radar. Self-righteousness may feel good for a time, but it's not much of a relationship builder.

Many indirect approaches are masks for a belief system that does not include the perception that we actually have the ability to change things. Successful relationships don't mean that we never have any problems with people, but they do require a belief in our power to influence our life and our interactions. We will always have choices about our own behavior and reactions, and this fact becomes especially clear in the language and tone we select when we do confront someone directly.

If someone else's behavior is keeping you from doing or enjoying your job, the first response is often reactive and emotional. It's hard to be objective when the noise from next door hinders your teaching, or when someone has exhausted the supplies you needed, even though these events are probably not personal assaults. While it may be natural to get upset when someone is using equipment or a space you specifically (and proactively) reserved, you still have options.

You could certainly demand that this person vacate the room. After all, you have the schedule on your side. But regardless of how justified you feel, you have just backed the other teacher into a win-lose corner, and it can cost you plenty, even if you win. This powering approach considers only your needs; it's likely to create hostility, resentment, and strong resistance with someone who might otherwise have tried to work through the problem.

The possibility of making a scene—or an enemy—can lead to the opposite win-lose scenario. In this instance, you decide to not mention it, either because you believe it probably wouldn't do any good or it would just create greater problems. In the meantime, your needs fall by the wayside. But the "why bother?" approach is an adequate response only as long as you can live with the consequences of not bothering—quietly and happily. Assuming a victim role often disguises the same "how dare she?" feelings that prompted a powering approach and can manifest as passive-aggressiveness, ineffective complaints, helplessness, or attempts at manipulation.

Then again, you can try win-win, taking responsibility for meeting your own needs while considering the needs of another person: "I think we have a problem. I signed up to use the room this period. I won't have another opportunity to do this activity and we can't really do this anywhere else. Is there some way we can work this out?" You identify the problem, giving the other teacher additional information in a way that puts you both in a position to cooperate. If the other teacher has any flexibility, especially if you have a win-win history with this individual, you'll probably get the room. But even when you don't get the resolution you'd like, you probably won't burn any bridges either.

As in teacher-student relationships, the best way to resolve a problem with other adults is to prevent it from occurring in the first place. Anticipation and simple courtesy can help avoid problems arising from assumptions that no one has conflicting needs or that no one cares. Ask ahead of time if neighboring teachers will be bothered by a noisy activity in your room after lunch. Find out when the library will be free for your students to use next week. Consistently modeling respect in your adult relationships might even help your colleagues become more considerate of your needs and how you might be affected by their plans and the choices they make.

> As in teacher-student relationships, the best way to resolve a problem with other adults is to prevent it from occurring in the first place.

Finally, look for opportunities to support others. I don't think I've ever met an educator who complained about getting too much recognition or appreciation. As with kids, never pass up a chance to let others know when they've done a good job. Genuinely acknowledging how much your students love someone's class, or how effectively he or she handled a difficult situation, can not only make that person's day, but also provide a badly needed boost in the face of whatever job stress and emotional fatigue that teacher may be experiencing. Offering to take someone's class once in a while to give that teacher a bit of a break, or leaving an anonymous note or token of appreciation, will add a great deal of positive energy to the culture of the school and will probably leave you feeling pretty good at the same time.[6] Just remember that good relationships don't happen by accident, and even in a really toxic environment, there are always things you can do to create your own little corner of safety and support.

Activity

1. What have you done to build support relationships with the following groups of people?

   Administration:

   Support staff:

   Other teachers:

   Parents:

   Other school staff:

   Other community resources:

2. How have the relationships you've established contributed to the enjoyment of your job (and your overall mental health)?

   Administration:

   Support staff:

   Other teachers:

   Parents:

   Other school staff:

   Other community resources:

3. In what ways have you involved the following people in your discipline program?

   Administration:

   Support staff:

   Other teachers:

   Parents:

   Other school staff:

   Other community resources:

4. What have you done to maximize the ability of these individuals to help—without making them responsible for solving the problem for you?

5. In what ways have these people supported or contributed to your efforts to create a win-win classroom environment?

   Administration:

   Support staff:

   Other teachers:

   Parents:

   Other school staff:

   Other community resources:

Activity

Think about a situation in which your needs were in conflict with the needs of another adult (in school or out). Regardless of how you actually approached or resolved the conflict, use the following questions to explore the various dimensions of the situation and the possibilities involved:[7]

1. Your needs (what you wanted):

2. The other person's needs (what they wanted):

3. The conflict (how that person's needs interfered with yours):

4. Your initial feelings or reactions:

5. Describe the powering (you win, the other person loses) options you considered or might have considered:

   a. Describe the probable or actual short-term outcomes of your implementing these solutions:

   b. Describe the probable or actual long-term outcomes of your implementing these solutions:

6. What would have been the probable outcomes of simply ignoring the problem?

   a. Short-term:

   b. Long-term:

7. List any other people you talked with about this problem before you actually confronted the person involved:

   a. What was the purpose of these discussions?

   b. In what ways did these discussions help you (or the situation)?

   c. In what ways did (or could) these discussions create new problems?

8. How long did this problem exist before you actually confronted the person directly?

9. If your approach was not immediate, what held you back?

10. Brainstorm a variety of possible win-win solutions in which you and the other person could eventually manage to get what you each wanted. (If that is not practical or possible—say, you're both fighting over the last piece of candy—how can you resolve the conflict in the best interests of all concerned?)

   a. What are the probable short-term outcomes of the win-win solutions you suggested?

   b. What are the probable long-term outcomes?

11. In what ways did your actual approach consider the needs and feelings of the other person?

12. Describe the other person's response:

13. In what ways (or to what degree) were you successful at preventing the situation from becoming no-win?

14. In what ways are you satisfied with the way you handled your feelings about this problem?

15. In what ways do you wish you had behaved differently?

16. In what ways are you satisfied with the way the situation was resolved?

17. If the problem was not resolved to your satisfaction, how could it be better?

18. Describe any new problems created by the solution.

19. How can the new problems—or your dissatisfaction with the solution—now be resolved in the best interests of all involved?

20. How do you plan to handle similar conflicts in the future?

Gift Certificate

This certificate can be a sanity saver for someone you care about. It offers your support and will probably make you feel pretty good, too. Duplicate this certificate and fill it in with the name of the person and what you're willing to do for him or her.

Some possibilities follow:

- Coverage of one recess duty
- A six-pack of his favorite soft drink
- Grading of one assignment (one class, no essay)[8]
- A double-dip ice cream cone after school
- A new, student-made bulletin board courtesy of your class
- Dinner at your house (or her favorite restaurant, your treat)
- Use of your class's computer (or some other equipment) for one full afternoon
- One hour of grunt work (such as laminating, filing, cutting, or cleaning)
- A new poster for his room
- A surprise brown-bag lunch
- A break while you invite her class to watch a movie with yours
- A copy of your emergency activity file
- A puppet show for his class performed by your class
- Help washing her car
- The return of his library books (or some other local errand)
- One evening of house- (or dog- or baby-) sitting
- An hour's sanctuary for any one student she is about to choke
- A partner for racquetball (or tennis, aerobics, jogging, or bridge)
- Company on his next shopping trip
- Others:

Gift Certificate

This certificate entitles

_____

to _____

_____

Date _____ Signed _____

NOTES

1. I use this term to refer to biological parents, stepparents, foster parents, grandparents, or any other guardians or caregivers involved in the lives of our students.

2. The vice principal said that his calls to parents averaged less than twenty seconds each. He would simply call to say something like, "Hey, I was talking to your child's Spanish teacher today and I heard that he's been doing just great with his grammar exercises. I thought you might want to hear that." He shared that the parents quickly understood that he had many other calls to make and didn't have time to chat. He simply wanted to pass on a positive comment he had heard.

3. Paradoxically, I have found that the more responsibility teachers are willing to take for the problems they encounter with their students, and the less parental intervention they demand, the more supportive are the parents. This seems to occur most frequently in classrooms in which systematic, positive contact with parents is a regular part of the teacher's routine.

4. Anecdotal records are brief notes describing a student's language, performance, interests, behaviors, strengths, or interactions, for example, usually with regard to some specific incident or observation. Although fairly subjective, they document your perspective and can be used to indicate the development of a particular problem or issue, as well as progress made. For more information about data collection tools and strategies, see Bluestein, *Being a Successful Teacher* (Torrance, CA: Fearon Teacher Aids, 1989).

5. Triangulating may best be described as going to a third party, or going behind the back of the person to whom we need to be speaking, to try to resolve a conflict or get what we want through a more indirect channel. This approach can, itself, create additional conflict and mistrust.

6. See sidebar, "Gift Certificate," at the end of this chapter.

7. You can also use some of these questions in discussions and activities on conflict resolution and relationship building with your students.

8. Check on your district's privacy policies first.

25

Secrets of Successful Self-Care

I f teaching involved only planning, presentation, and assessment, it would still be an extremely demanding job. But consider the paperwork that requires secretarial skills, the movement and organization that calls for management expertise, the emotional needs that oblige a teacher to serve as a counselor, or the bumps and bruises that invoke the role of nurse. Every facet of teaching, as fulfilling and enriching as it may be, also depletes.

As if that weren't enough, the common habit of setting unrealistic expectations for ourselves can be terribly stress producing in itself. Becoming a great

> Every facet of teaching, as fulfilling and enriching as it may be, also depletes.

teacher is a developmental process that doesn't always jibe with our self-expectations. Even if we've been teaching for years, as long as we're committed to excellence, we'll always be looking for new tricks to try and new ways to grow. But of all the strategies critical to successful teaching, perhaps the most important is self-care. Not surprisingly, this is often the part that, for many of us, comes last on the list—if we think of it at all.

One of the greatest things about teaching, which may also be the most challenging, is the fact that there is always something new for us to deal with—different groups each year, a new student who alters the chemistry of the current group, changes in content and programs, updated equipment and software, different grades or subjects to teach, or strategies, ideas, and innovations that we encounter for the first time. Even for veteran teachers, a lesson or topic that has always proved reliable, successful, inspiring, or fun can inexplicably fall flat. And any time we try something that is new to us, or face a different group of kids, we can run into problems that would have been impossible to anticipate.

Maintaining a positive focus is critical to our mental health, as well as to our ability to perform and continue to grow. While such a focus certainly enhances relationships with students (and others), our ability to see the positive elements of our own teaching behavior can allow us to differentiate between a lesson that bombs and the end of a career!

During my first year, one of my professors from the university came out to observe in my classroom. He and I had worked together in the past; I had a great deal of respect for this man and wanted him to see me doing a good job. Of course he came in on a day that everything possible went wrong. The duplicating machine had broken and one of my handouts wasn't ready. The students didn't understand my instructions and did the activity incorrectly. My emergency plans flopped when I attempted to show a filmstrip[1] and the bulb burned out on the third frame. When I finally got the kids' attention again, one of the blinds let go and dropped with a crash.

By the time the students left, I was in shambles. I sat and sobbed, offered my resignation, and started wondering how I'd do in dental school instead. I actually started cleaning out my desk and suggested that he try to find a replacement who could actually teach. I felt like a complete and utter failure. My supervisor just sat with me, listening and nodding patiently.

Finally, he got up and said, "You know, your flag looks great!"

I stopped, stunned. My flag? I couldn't even reach the flag without a ladder.

"That's a good start. We'll work on the rest. Don't worry, you'll be fine. You've got everything you need to be a great teacher. You just need a little more practice. I'll see you next week." And with that, he came over, gave me a hug, and left.

Now here was a person able to look beyond the mistakes—some of which I could have managed better, others that were completely out of my control and impossible to predict—to the one thing I hadn't messed up. My flag looked great! He had the nerve to believe in me after seeing me at my worst. He certainly could have filled several pages with notes about my failures (although I doubt he'd have been as hard on me as I tended to be on myself), but instead he focused on the one thing I hadn't messed up! Once I recovered, I started noticing that my flag actually did look pretty good. And then my focus started to shift to other things I'd done right, not the least of which were the lessons and materials that were interesting, appropriate, and well sequenced. I might not have noticed these successes if he had mentioned them, but the comment about the flag certainly got my attention—not terribly illustrious beginnings, I'll admit. But the lesson was not lost on me.[2]

BEING OKAY ABOUT BEING IN PROCESS

One of the dangers of coming from an industrial-era background can be seen in a tendency to get caught up in achievement over efforts, product over process, and perfection over everything else. No wonder looking good and impressing authority (product) can seem more important than seeing the opportunities in each experience to become a better teacher (process).

The pressure to "get it right" can be particularly strong for first-year teachers. As National Education Association president Bob Chase notes, "Teaching is the only job where people who are just beginning are expected to do the same thing as people who have been [in the classroom for] 25 years."[3] While some school districts surely appreciate the developmental processes involved in becoming a great teacher, many educators, including some seasoned veterans and administrators, admit to feeling a tremendous lack of support if they don't come up to whatever standards and expectations are held by their administrators, colleagues, or the parents of their students. Add in the differences in these standards and expectations from one group to another, and it's easy to see why few educators feel much support for simply being "in process"—or even having a bad day.

It takes a great deal of freedom and safety to get past the need to look good, and to see failures or mistakes simply as a chance to reevaluate goals and objectives and look for different approaches or more effective strategies. To self-protect, a lot of teachers simply dig in their heels and stick to what they know best, whether it's working for them or not. The emphasis on performance and perfectionism is often at the core of a resistance to changing our own patterns and behaviors, and as long as we can blame things like curricular demands, instructional scripts or restrictions, or "The Rules," for example, we never have to put ourselves at risk by trying something new. It's also easy to see how a priority in which our appearance supersedes our actual effectiveness can tempt us to become rather arrogant or rather hard on ourselves. Both are based in denial—one of our vulnerability, the other of our capability—and both deny our needs to continually grow and develop as professionals.

But even without much support, there are things we can do, shifts we can make in our thinking, to support ourselves. In sorting through the experience with the flag, I realized that if I wanted to focus on my students' strengths and abilities, I would have to learn to do so for myself. I also had to learn that there were times when it was necessary to detach— not only from self-destructive or difficult students, but also from the demands of the job.

Because the planning and preparation of lessons, activities, materials, and environments can consume so much time—especially during the first few years of a teacher's career, or in a new subject or at a new grade level—it's not uncommon for hobbies, recreational reading, or other outside interests (including personal relationships) to take a back seat to work. Teaching requires a great deal of giving on many levels. True, there can be a great deal of satisfaction in putting out so much time, creativity, and physical and emotional energy. However, many teachers reach the end of the day with little to give back to themselves.

Teaching tends to attract helpers and nurturers. Many of us identify heavily with the progress and performance of our students. We don't want to see people we care about fail—especially if we believe that their failure reflects on us. This attachment can create very negative consequences, for both us and the students. When our ability to feel successful depends on other people's behaviors, appearance, values, attitudes, or performance, we expend a great deal of energy trying to control the choices they make. If our sense of our teaching self is too closely connected to our students' behavior and achievement, we may even

> Teaching tends to attract helpers and nurturers. Many of us identify heavily with the progress and performance of our students.

become resentful and punitive when our devotion and commitment don't generate the kind of enthusiasm and cooperation from our students we need to sustain our sense of adequacy. It's easy to see how our attachment to certain specific outcomes can lead us far from our win-win objectives and indeed create the exact kinds of stress and conflict we're trying to avoid.

LETTING GO

One of the most important skills in self-care is learning to separate things we can change, control, or influence from those we can't. Unfortunately, some of the most frustrating experiences in our lives come from events we can't do much about. We get moved to a grade we didn't want to teach. Our normal ride to work takes twice as long because of a two-year construction project. The parents of our students don't read to them (or perhaps are guilty of more serious neglect).

True, we can transfer to a new school or go back and get a degree in a different field. We can leave the house two hours early to avoid rush hour or buy a home closer to where we work. We can make home visits and start a home literacy education project in our spare time. There are always options and alternatives in any situation, but the more removed something is from our direct control, the greater the discrepancy between the energy we'll need to effect change and the amount of change our energy will actually promote. Hard work and few results are the perfect ingredients for frustration and burnout—outcomes we can avoid when we choose, instead, to channel our efforts in a high-impact direction and make constructive choices about the things we can control.

If we've learned anything about win-win interactions, we know that students fall in that great gray area between those things that are completely out of our control (like the weather) and those that we control completely (like how often we floss). Throughout this book, we have seen how the behaviors, attitudes, and language we choose in interacting with our students can make it more likely that they will behave in a certain way, but at no time do we actually control them.

So when we run into disappointments—lessons that fell flat, students who dropped the ball, administrators who simply couldn't see the beauty in what we were trying to do—it's tempting to lump them all into one pile of things that discredit us as instructors. This is not necessary. We can, as we have seen, take care of everything under our control and still have things go wrong.

Somewhere between beating ourselves up for our failures and becoming completely indifferent is a very loving place called "letting go." This is that nice middle ground at which we realize that regardless of our efforts, the final choice rests with the other person. We sometimes come to this place when we've tried everything and realized that our attempts to control others have endowed us with more responsibility, self-righteousness, anger, and resentment than we can comfortably bear.

Every now and then we will run into students who appear committed to their own destruction or failure, children whose self-concepts are so low or so fragile that they feel safest when engaged in patterns that deliberately attract negative adult attention. Some students expend a great deal of energy trying to convince us that they aren't worth the bother. Others can spend an entire year hiding behind mistrust—of us as well as their own potential for success—regardless of our devotion and encouragement.

In many instances, our love, acceptance, faith, patience, and persistence win out. However, when our efforts fail, or when our efforts take more from the individual we're trying to support, from ourselves, or from the rest of the class than they actually contribute, it helps to remember that the ultimate responsibility for changing self-defeating behaviors and attitudes lies with the person who practices them—child or adult. We can provide a safe and nurturing environment in which this kind of healing can occur. We can make success possible. We can offer caring, acceptance, respect, and opportunities to make positive choices and experience the true empowerment of which the student may be capable. We keep on trying—and we give ourselves credit for trying. And we also let go. We disengage from results over which we have little control. Now, not only are the students still worthwhile and valuable despite their negative beliefs and behaviors, but also so are we.

HEALTHY INTERDEPENDENCE

Our professional self-concept can be rather fragile at times. If the bulk of our experiences have been with factory-era authority relationships, we have years of practice judging ourselves against other people's opinions and reactions. If approval from others is a high priority, we become extremely vulnerable to the power-oriented teacher who doesn't sanction our methods, the parent who wanted his child in a different fourth grade, or the fact that the other geometry teacher is twenty pages ahead of us. Learning to hear, respect, and operate from our own internal vision, guidance, or standards promises a great deal of freedom; however, doing so may require some relearning and refocusing, as well as relinquishing old beliefs that no longer work in our behalf.[4]

Taking care of yourself also means identifying which challenges deserve your time and attention and determining whether you even need to get involved. Wherever you teach, you will find people who work differently from you. And while at times you may find the differences annoying, your involvement is not called for unless the other adult somehow keeps *your* approach from working.

I'm often asked, in workshops and interviews, what to do about other teachers who are not committed to win-win principles or relationships. I typically respond, "Nothing." If someone wants new ideas or suggestion for making changes in order to achieve more positive goals, and they come to you for help, if you have the information, time, and inclination, by all means share what you've got. But I have found that people are generally resistant to suggestions that require major changes in their belief systems or behaviors until they are either curious or dissatisfied enough to be receptive to this information. People who are invested in *not* changing, either because they firmly believe in what they're doing or because they aren't ready to question beliefs they've always held, will certainly see your best intentions to help as controlling and invasive. Until they are open to the possibility of doing things differently, even the most inquisitive will simply be looking for an opportunity to vent or complain. (You'll be able

> Your assistance may not be welcome, even when it's requested, if your response is not the one the other person wants to hear.

to tell when this happens by how often they counter your suggestions with "Yeah, but. . . .") Further, your assistance may not be welcome, even when it's requested, if your response is not the one the other person wants to hear.

The more win-win your orientation becomes, the more sensitive you'll become to other people's win-lose approaches. Most of us sincerely want to keep people from hurting one another, and it will be a matter of conscience at which point you become involved. Even when you believe that another teacher's behavior is unprofessional, destructive, or hampering student success, it's usually just a judgment call. One person's teaching style is another person's hurtful behavior. That line can be pretty fine. I recommend extreme caution in confronting another teacher. The cost of unsolicited intervention, particularly when it comes in the form of judgments or criticisms, can be high. Little growth is likely to occur in an atmosphere of suspicion, resentment, or defensiveness. Often, the best way to help someone move forward is simply to move forward yourself. Your success and self-confidence will be far more inspiring than your advice or admonitions.

The same holds true when you encounter situations in which, for example, two colleagues are in conflict with one another, a teacher you care about is having problems with the principal, or you are working with someone who can't quite get it together. Situations like these can engage you almost by accident. Whether you're hooked by conflicting values or just trying to help, your involvement puts you at risk for creating additional stresses and problems for yourself. Taking responsibility for these kinds of problems, even when your help is desired and appreciated, can take a tremendous toll on your energy and goodwill. Few things in life are more exhausting—physically, emotionally, psychologically, or spiritually—than the pressure of feeling as if the whole system would fall apart if it weren't for you.

Healthy interdependence requires boundaries. You can be supportive of another teacher and still recognize where this responsibility begins and ends. You can listen,

---

The best help is often giving others the space and support they need to solve their own problems.

---

model, reflect, acknowledge, provide information and materials, and help the other person think through possible solutions—when you are willing and able—without assuming responsibility for the problem. These strategies neither attempt to control others nor do they attempt to impose your value system on them.

Further, these behaviors offer alternatives to rescuing, saving, or fixing others, which frees you to be there for them without becoming enmeshed or assuming the burden of their conflicts. Remember, the best help is often giving others the space and support they need to solve their own problems.

SURVIVING NO-WIN SITUATIONS

Detachment is critical if you ever become involved in a no-win situation. When unable to resolve a conflict to your satisfaction, you may need to involve arbitration. Unfortunately, when you turn a problem over to someone else, you almost always turn over the responsibility for a solution to that person as well. The advantage is that the third party can usually see things more clearly and objectively and may suggest options that didn't occur to either party. The disadvantage is that a mediator may solve the problem as quickly and conveniently as possible, or in accordance with his or her own agenda. Further, an outside person may have difficulty remaining objective, avoiding power decisions, or sticking with relevant issues. There is always the chance that the third party will make things worse, so select your arbitrator cautiously.

Sometimes persistence can overcome a seemingly no-win situation. Even with the support of your principal, custodian, and the students' parents, it may still be hard to convince those in repair services that you and your students really need to have the heater fixed. But when they realize that they will no longer be bothered by three calls a day once the heater works, you are more likely to get results. Be pleasant if you choose to be persistent and, if possible, always make a point of telling the other people involved what's in it for them to cooperate.

Unfortunately, there may be problems you simply can't resolve. No-win situations may result from a loss of perspective or a personality conflict. One teacher told of an observation in which he was rebuked by his principal for doing an activity that was not in the teacher's guide to the adopted textbook. The principal asked that he use the guide exclusively, which he did, although under protest. However, in the following observation, he came under attack for being unoriginal! He asserted, "I'm trying to follow your suggestions, but it seems that I can't do anything without being criticized. Is there something I'm not understanding?" The principal condescendingly responded that he was being too sensitive. When pressed to elaborate her expectations, she refused further discussion.

What options does this teacher have? He may try several different approaches, depending on his need for approval, his tenure and mobility within the system, his confidence and documentation, his career goals, his sense of humor, and his ability to enjoy positive outcomes of teaching despite the principal's demands. He may choose to enlist parents, colleagues, and the union to fight. He might continue to persuade the principal to give him more specific information—or at least attempt to understand his approach. He might agree with the principal to her face and devote his energy to beating or sidestepping the system for as long as he can get away with it. He may go with the flow to try to keep the principal off his back to whatever degree that is possible. As it turned out, the deliberate lack of support and intent to undermine the teacher's confidence and credibility made it clear that he would not be in for a long-term relationship with this principal. In such a painful no-win situation, seeking a position elsewhere turned out to be the most emotionally cost-effective option.

When our jobs—for whatever reasons—become a stressful bundle of obstacles and conflicts, we may need to reevaluate if the payoffs and benefits are more need fulfilling than the negative aspects of the work. The times we are most vulnerable to burnout, fatigue, depression, and poor self-concept are times when no other options seem available (low sense of personal empowerment).

One of the most powerful behaviors we can engage in for our own self-protection is the conscious act of exploring our options. Consciously choosing to stay in a situation in which we are well aware of the challenges, lack of support, or other, more negative realities can eliminate constant disappointment and an exhausting sense of being victimized. Sometimes it can help relieve some of the pressures in even the most negative situations to simply realize that we're not trapped—we just haven't found a more satisfying option yet.

MAKING "SELF" MATTER

In any teaching situation, there are a number of things we can do to take care of ourselves. Self-care starts with a belief in its legitimacy. Traditional factory-era upbringing applauded self-sacrifice and denounced self-care, confusing it with selfishness, and leaving us with a lot to unlearn. *Selfishness* either fails to consider the needs of others or simply disregards them, but *self-caring* behavior leaves plenty of room for caring and giving—in a way that will not leave us feeling depleted, violated, or angry.

> Self-care starts with a belief in its legitimacy.

Self-care involves our ability to meet our own needs. Of all the ingredients of healthy and positive relationships, it is perhaps the most important, for lacking an ability to take care of ourselves will inevitably compromise the quality of any relationship we have with others. Self-care reduces the chances that we will feel resentful, self-righteous, or disempowered—feelings which often result from self-sacrifice—and enhances the quality of love and care we can give others.

Self-care requires a belief in our own deservingness, acknowledging that it is not just for other people. Until we believe we deserve to be treated with respect, for example, modeling self-respect and maintaining boundaries with others will certainly be quite difficult. And it's equally challenging to effectively coach children to make self-caring choices if we have a hard time appreciating what we see in the mirror or making constructive choices on our own behalf.

One of the best ways to take care of ourselves is to avoid or minimize our exposure to negative people, information, or influences. Even in a positive and supportive environment, this can be tough! Start by noticing how you feel after you're around certain people or experiences. Does more than a few moments' contact with a particular individual leave you feeling drained or depressed? Do you find certain kinds of music uplifting or energizing while others make you edgy or downhearted? Do you walk out of the teachers' lounge some days wondering why you ever went into this profession?

Any person or experience can have an impact on our energy.[5] On days that you find watching the news or reading the paper to be devastating, switch channels or turn to the comics. Read or listen to inspirational material, either exclusively or in between more disquieting matter. Watch for that sense of obligation to spend time with people who are toxic and exhausting for you, even if they care about you, need you to be there for them, or happen to be related to you. Learn to say no, even at the risk of rejection or criticism. (Do you really want someone actively involved in your life who does not respect you, your boundaries, or your right to take care of yourself? Being rejected or abandoned by toxic or abusive people is actually not a bad thing!) Be selective about the people on whom you bestow the gift of your time, energy, and friendship.

Perhaps hardest of all, learn how to ignore or defuse criticism from others. You have a right to your enthusiasm, dedication, commitment, optimism, preferences, personality, beliefs, and priorities, without having to defend them and without being subjected to ridicule, judgments, or put-downs. Sometimes the best way to avoid a potential conflict is to simply agree with the other person. Watch what happens when you respond by saying something like "You could be right," "No kidding!" or "I appreciate your concern," and then changing the subject or walking away, which communicates that you don't care to discuss the issue further.

> Sometimes the best way to avoid a potential conflict is to simply agree with the other person.

Note that we're talking about criticism, not reasonable requests to cooperate. There's a difference between "Please turn down the music you're playing in your room," and "I can't believe you let your kids listen to music that loud!" Recognize, however, that many people are more comfortable criticizing and judging than they are asking for what they want. Regardless of how you interpret their comments or respond, the point here is to not get hooked emotionally, to whatever degree that is possible, and respectfully disengage.

This strategy is certainly less stressful, time-consuming, and taxing than becoming defensive, making excuses, trying to interpret what the other person is saying, making accusations, or explaining yourself to secure the other person's approval. Unless the strategies you use in your classroom interfere with someone else's teaching, it really is no one else's business why you allow your students to sit where they want for certain activities, offer choices about work sequence or materials, individualize subjects everyone else teaches to whole groups, or spend an extra week on the Civil War.

STRIVING FOR BALANCE

We need interests and diversions in our lives besides teaching to give us balance and perspective. Author and educator Jenny Mosley encourages teachers to create "golden moments" for ourselves, time out to replenish, reward, refresh, and reenergize ourselves.[6] Activities that are also stress-reducing can serve us best. Being good at what we do comes easier when we're in shape physically and mentally. Taking a class, pursuing a hobby, practicing relaxation techniques, exercising, reading some good fiction, joining a sports team, listening to motivation tapes, or learning something we've never done before can help us develop as vital, dynamic, and well-rounded people.[7]

Set goals for yourself to acknowledge your power, potential, and capability, not to mention your optimism. Write out your goals, specific and concrete, including numbers, names, and dates. The process strengthens your commitment and determination as well as the probability that you'll realize your objectives. Go back to your list from time to time to see how much you've accomplished. Acknowledge the progress you've made and continually update and revise your list.

If you are working in a particularly supportive environment, you may be getting a good bit of positive feedback about the work you're doing. Unfortunately, it's likely that you don't get many strokes from your colleagues (who, incidentally, probably need them just as badly). It's certainly reasonable to ask for positive feedback, especially when you can be specific about the kinds of information that would be helpful to you. Whether or not you get the support you need, you certainly increase the odds by asking for what you want. Better yet, you can make a habit of recognizing and appreciating others—for your own sake as well as theirs; however, don't take this route unless you can do so without an agenda or expectation for getting something back in return.

Regardless of the quality of the support networks you build, the bottom line in responsibility for self-care is self. Fortunately, even in an extremely negative, nonsupportive workplace, you can still draw support from within. Learn to offer recognition and feedback to yourself. This behavior is a great way to practice focusing on the positive and will help you perceive a failure, mistake, or a bad day simply as an excuse to help you refine or set new goals for yourself. To pat yourself on the back, use the same process my professor employed, looking for what you did right. If you've ever found yourself lying awake in bed at night, agonizing over the bulletin board you haven't changed in five months, the papers you still haven't graded, or the laundry you forgot to take out of the washer last Tuesday, you're a great candidate for this strategy.

Keep a journal or a tablet next to the bed. Tonight and every night, before you shut your eyes, take a few seconds to make a list of at least three things you did right that day—regardless of the results or anyone else's reaction—or three things for which you feel grateful. Fill the page if you can. The only rule is that you can't qualify what you write or use the word *but*. Simply put down what you did well, what you tried for the first time, what you appreciate about yourself or your life, or what you feel good about—even if it's only "my flag looked great."

Best wishes for success with your process and happiness in your work!

Educators at Risk

Characteristics of educators at risk:[8]

- Feels personally responsible for a student's successes and failures
- Measures personal success by student behavior and achievement, or by approval from others
- Has an overwhelming need to avoid conflict and generate approval from others (which can manifest as attention seeking, maintaining status quo, or even rebelliousness)
- Compromises student needs to avoid rocking the boat, either with administrators, parents, or other students
- Believes that the job would be easier to perform if only the students, their parents, the administration, or the system would change
- Has difficulty setting and maintaining boundaries between self and other people
- Has difficulty setting and maintaining boundaries between self and job

(Continued)

(Continued)

- Deals with problems by shaming, blaming, complaining, manipulating, ignoring, or dumping them on someone else
- Feels threatened by another teacher's progress or success
- Feels as if "things would completely fall apart if it weren't for me"
- Swings from chaos, helplessness, and victimization to moral superiority and self-righteousness
- Often rescues students by ignoring misbehavior, offering inappropriate second chances, or failing to impose previously stated consequences
- Protects a student from failure or negative consequences in an effort to feel successful, valuable, or powerful
- Overidentifies with, and even adopts, another person's feelings
- Appears to be "fine" and "in control"
- Probably denies that any of the above are personally relevant

These patterns[9] can ultimately interfere with a teacher's ability to do the following:

- Interact with students without violating their dignity or self-worth
- Interact with school staff effectively
- Meet students' academic and learning-style needs
- Behave consistently within the framework of his or her own values
- Feel worthy and successful
- Detach from the job
- Take care of himself or herself

Other contributing factors:

- A tradition of dysfunctionality (which now feels normal)
- A scarcity of healthy, functional role models
- The lack of a healthy, functional system to support people trying to operate in healthy, functional, and self-caring ways
- The very human tendency to resist change

Some assumptions on reducing risk factors:

- It is possible to adopt healthy patterns of behavior, even in unhealthy and unsupportive environments.
- The system is not likely to change all by itself, nor is it likely to take care of (or support) a teacher's needs regardless of that teacher's enthusiasm, instructional skills, dedication, good intentions, or wishful thinking.
- Change happens best in supportive environments. Teachers tend to function effectively, grow professionally and personally, and avoid stress and burnout when they can create a support network for themselves, either in or out of school—preferably in both environments.
- Change is most effective when individuals take responsibility for their own growth, rather than attempting to change or blame others.
- Change is most effective when encouraged rather than coerced.
- As individuals change, the system will change.

Activity: Things I Do Well

In the spaces that follow, identify the things you already do well. Select categories that apply to your interests and to your life, such as Planning and Organization, Instruction, Interpersonal Skills, Hobbies, Taking Care of My Body, Relaxation, Driving, Housekeeping, Sports, Personal Appearance, or whatever is meaningful and important to you. There's space for seven different categories—feel free to duplicate these sheets and add more! Start with where you are and write only good stuff! Try for two or three specific talents or accomplishments in each category. Note: The harder this activity is for you to do, the more you need to do it!

Category:

Category:

Category:

Category:

Category:

Category:

Category:

Category:

Activity: New Behaviors I Would Like to Achieve

Using the same or different categories, now identify goals—new behaviors you would like to achieve at some point. Be as specific as possible and start each goal statement with the words "I can. . . ." or "I will. . . ." (For example, instead of saying, "I want to spend less time working at home on planning and paperwork," write, "I will leave school empty-handed by 4:00 twice a week." Instead of expressing your desire to lose a few pounds, write, "I can get into my gray pants again.") Make more copies of these pages if necessary.

Category:

Category:

Category:

Category:

Category:

Category:

Category:

Activity: Sanity Savers (My Favorite Things)

Make a list of things you can do to relax, relieve stress, release negative feelings, and gain perspective. What do you enjoy doing? What makes you feel happy and alive? Brainstorm ideas you can go back to after a long day. Note: The best sanity savers are those that do not depend on another person's availability or cooperation. Also, please avoid listing alternatives that are ultimately self-destructive or those that will hurt someone else. Use extra paper if you'd like; continue to revise and add to this list.

Activity: Self-Recognition

Starting with today, use a blank calendar or notebook to recognize what is going well for you. Keep it on your desk to be the last thing you do before you leave school, or next to your bed to be the last thing you do before you go to sleep. For each day, write down at least three things you did great, or three things for which you're grateful. Do not qualify or use the word *but*. Stay positive. You're doing fine![10]

Postassessment

Chances are, if you've made it this far, you've considered some new ideas, practiced new strategies, and reflected on the process. If you've been working through the ideas and activities in this book for a few weeks, you might want to take another look at the self-assessment in Chapter 2. As with the earlier assessment, select the statement that most closely resembles your own beliefs or attitudes.

Use the following Reflection form to compare your responses to your pretest choices. Although you may notice several differences immediately, many of the goals suggested in this book require changes that need time and practice before they feel truly integrated. Check back again in another few months or even a year and take this survey again. Use your answers to focus on new goals for growth.

Best wishes for success with your process and happiness in your work!

Reflection Form

Date _____

Areas of greatest growth:

What I'd like to improve or work on next:

NOTES

1. Filmstrip: A length of film containing a succession of images intended for projection one frame at a time with or without recorded sound. (Definition courtesy of ITS.MARC Web site, Library Corporation, available at http://www.itsmarc.com/crs/bib2594.htm). This instructional resource was common and popular back in the early 1970s when I started teaching.

2. I don't think I even appreciated the value of this wonderful gift at the time. The fact that I am still a part of this profession is an enormous testament to this man, and I truly believe that he is, today, a part of every word I write or speak on behalf of teachers and kids.

3. Quoted in Barbara Kantrowitz and Pat Wingert, "Teachers Wanted," *Newsweek* (Oct. 2, 2002): 37–42.

4. Control issues, approval seeking, rescuing, and the desire to manage what other people think of us are among the topics discussed in greater detail in Melody Beattie's *CoDependent No More* (New York: Harper-Hazelden, 1987) as well as other resources on codependency and family systems. Although the term *codependent* originated in work with families of alcoholics and has unfortunately been overused, misapplied, and misunderstood (and has long since worn out the trendy fascination it once held), the dynamics of codependency can occur in any situation and are especially common in the helping professions. Therefore, the behavioral characteristics associated with these interaction and relationship dynamics put many educators, counselors, directors, and administrators at risk. (See sidebar, "Educators at Risk.")

5. For more information about self-care, particularly as it applies to physical well-being, read Caroline Myss, *Anatomy of the Spirit* (New York: Harmony Books, 1996). This outstanding book also addresses maintaining (and reclaiming) one's energy—or spirit—as well as healing and releasing old hurts, and the willingness to change. Also check out Joel Levey and Michelle Levey, *Living in Balance: A Dynamic Approach for Creating Harmony & Wholeness in a Chaotic World* (Berkeley, CA: Conari Press, 1998) and Donna Eden, *Energy Medicine* (New York: Jeremy P. Tarcher/Penguin, 1998). See the "Recommended Reading" section of this book for more resources on self-care.

6. Jenny Mosley, *Golden Moments for Busy Teachers* (Wiltshire, UK: Positive Press, 2003).

7. If you're feeling extremely stressed out, depressed, or stuck; if you have difficulty feeling deserving of self-caring choices (or feel guilty when you set boundaries or say "no"); if you feel particularly vulnerable to other people's judgments or opinions of you; or if you feel tempted to engage in negative or self-destructive behaviors, please consider joining a support group, talking to a counselor, or taking advantage of your employee assistance program if one exists. Find a place, preferably outside your immediate work world, where it will be safe to explore and express your feelings, restructure belief systems, seek alternative behavior patterns, and rethink your goals and directions.

8. The term *Educators at Risk* refers to being at risk for lots more stress, frustration, and conflict than you would like. This list was developed from a handout originally titled "Codependency in the Classroom." In searching for a more generic title, I've borrowed the idea of "Educators at Risk" from Orville Dean, educator and consultant, in Medina, Ohio.

9. We're probably all guilty, to some degree, of all of these patterns from time to time. This list is simply a sample of the ways at-risk factors can show up in the classroom. These patterns become problematic when they become *typical* of a teacher's feelings and behaviors.

10. Be sure to add to this list on a daily basis and commit to at least one month for starters. Many people report significant changes in their perspective, attitude, and peace of mind and continue to use this strategy to reinforce their progress, commitment, and sense of gratitude.

Epilogue

Creating a Win-Win Reality

Much of what we do or value in schools is simply the product of what has been done or valued in the past. Certain practices and mythologies have come to represent a reality that often goes unquestioned. Yet despite their lack of veracity, many of these myths persist as real, and in the process hurt and limit students, teachers, and the profession.

So much of the reality we've come to accept is steeped in win-lose, scarcity thinking that we lose track of what really matters and what is truly possible. Let's turn this pattern around. What if the best intentions to not leave any child behind translated not to misguided efforts to push every child into the same mold, but instead to helping each child achieve his or her own potential and develop the skills and talents each was given? What if we dumped old standbys like comparative and competitive grading, ranking students, arbitrary benchmarks, and the bell curve, and created opportunities for individual growth and success? What if we quit believing in a world of scarcity and struggle and started focusing on abundance and possibilities instead?

I'm wondering what would happen if we all just quit buying into this reality. How much freedom would we all experience if we started to respond to limiting myths by asking, "So what?" Imagine the possibilities: So what if these kids have never been any good in math? So what if the kids in this community have no support at home? So what if our scores dropped again this semester? (Or better still: So what if our test scores went *up* 40 points?) Getting hung up on these "realities" restricts our vision and detracts from what is truly possible and what is truly worth honoring in an educational setting.

Rather than a reality mired in problems and failure, we need a reality based on what schools *could* be. I am convinced that as we as individuals change our beliefs, our behaviors, and our interaction patterns, so will we see changes in the system. I don't believe that solutions will come from politics, from force, or from the system itself, and I don't see our obsession with testing or our lust for high scores leading to positive changes in relationships and interactions. Nonetheless, I do believe with every fiber in my being in the possibilities of a win-win school culture, because I see evidence of these strategies working all the time. (And I'm also convinced that as the teachers adopt win-win strategies and build the quality of their relationships, power dynamics, and instructional interactions, the tests and performance goals will take care of themselves.)

In my office I have a postcard with a quote by Margaret Mead that reads, "Never underestimate the power of a few committed people to change the world. Indeed it is the only thing that ever has." Even if only for your own sanity, choose optimism over pessimism. Choose a promise over a threat. Choose to see what's good in every student and to teach to the place in each child that, deep down, wants to succeed. For by these acts of grace will we change our reality, and we will change our schools—one heart at a time.

Resource A

Win-Win Ideas for Administrators

The model described in this book offers a wide range of practical and effective strategies to help educators shift from overwhelmingly familiar patterns of negativity, reactivity, and win-lose power dynamics to more positive and productive ways of interacting with students of any age. Although originally conceived as a discipline model, this approach has evolved to embrace a far more broad set of issues. Nonetheless, efforts by individual teachers to create win-win classrooms will invariably accompany a sharp decline in discipline problems—and a decrease in failure and negative social interactions, as well—which can ultimately contribute to improvements in the overall culture of your school.

Consider yourself fortunate if you are working with teachers who are already committed to using win-win strategies in working with their students (and hopefully, with one another). They will make your job much easier. These are teachers devoted to developing strong, assertive authority relationships with their students, communicating with parents on a regular basis, and building success with *all* of their students. They work diligently to engage even the most defiant, defeated, and indifferent youngsters. They handle their own conflicts responsibly and independently, and will see you as a resource, not a rescuer when things go wrong. (In contrast, notice how often teachers who use more traditional, win-lose strategies ask that you intervene when their approach proves frustrating and ineffective or actually escalates the problems they are having.)

You will probably notice that the attitudes of win-win teachers are generally more positive than those of their authoritarian counterparts, and that these teachers are also able to create an atmosphere that encourages growth and learning without the stress and need for external control typical in so many win-lose classrooms. By focusing on the connections between choices and outcomes, your win-win teachers will help students become personally accountable for their actions and behaviors. As a result, you will probably see a greater degree of student initiative, independence, self-management, and consideration for others' needs than in a win-lose classroom, where students are more inclined to do only what is required to get by or stay safe. Win-win teachers are also clear about their limits and boundaries and secure enough with their authority to encourage empowerment among their students.

Yet, creating a win-win classroom can be quite a challenge for any teacher, and those unfamiliar with win-win management models may have a hard time seeing how adopting more positive behaviors can pay off for them. As is often the case in the life of an administrator, your job will involve *selling* these ideas, giving teachers good enough reasons for wanting to change what, in many instances, will be deeply ingrained habits and ideas. And just as important as providing alternatives to habitual yet ineffective patterns, you will need to create high trust relationships with your teachers to assure them that they are safe to move in a different direction.

These changes do not happen in a vacuum. For better or worse, your behavior sets the pattern for the entire school, affecting the school climate and classroom communications.[1] This may mean facing down your own win-lose programming, as well as the pressures you may feel to encourage teacher behaviors that are better suited to a factory economy than to the needs of the current information-age workplace. If you are asking teachers to adopt new behaviors and improve their teaching skills, your subsequent behaviors—including the feedback you give, the resources you provide, and your willingness to advocate for the changes they are trying to make—must be congruent with these requests. Fearful and suspicious teachers will generally devote more time to their own survival and self-protection than to creating a new educational paradigm. I am always delighted to have teachers tell me about the wonderful things their principals do and about the positive impact this relationship has on the teachers' loyalties, attitudes, and commitments, and on the climate of the school in general. But unfortunately, this is not always the case, and clearly, the changes suggested in this book are far more likely to happen when teachers do not bear the additional burden of a nonsupportive, inconsistent, or hostile administrator.[2]

By the same token, administrators regularly recount their experiences with rigid and negative teachers who are reluctant to budge on long-ingrained attitudes and teaching behaviors, even when these patterns are creating problems and poor results for them. (Sadly, feedback I've received over the years suggests that this tendency is not confined to "old school" veterans but is increasingly common with beginning teachers.) While there may be burned-out, tired, and inflexible teachers in any school, many administrators have been pleasantly surprised when they stopped trying to "get rid of the dead wood around here" and started nurturing the resources they had.

Just as we (hopefully) do with the kids, see what happens when you can cultivate an attitude that allows you to value and accept your staff exactly where they are now. Recognize their strengths and build on what they do well. Help them remember why they came to this profession in the first place. Encourage them to keep their focus on the things that are really important and to recapture a sense of purpose and intention that can easily get buried under the pressures of political agendas. Model the flexibility, enthusiasm, commitment, and simple pleasantness you'd like to see them exhibit with their kids. Invite your staff to stretch beyond their comfort zones and provide the safety and support necessary for them to take these risks. Involve teachers in decisions you may have previously made alone. Empowered teachers, those who feel they have input in decisions that affect them, have a greater stake in—and are more likely to commit enthusiastically to—the success and welfare of the organization.

You might find it useful to start with staff members who are most open to change, perhaps those who have already indicated a commitment to win-win objectives, if not the actual skills to reach them. Allow their successes to be the invitation and inspiration for others. Provide the information they need about effective adult behaviors for achieving a variety of interactive goals. Your support will encourage these teachers to take risks and try new approaches and will help build confidence needed for attempting new techniques. Keep in mind that implementing successful changes in the classroom takes time and effort—and a great deal of courage and faith. A win-win focus involves relearning and retraining; schoolwide or individually, this process could take a number of years to fully implement.

Beware of the difficulties inherent in attempting to mandate across-the-board attitude changes or in adopting any particular discipline or instructional program schoolwide or districtwide. Be especially wary of packages that offer quick fixes or simple formulas for managing or reacting to children's behavior (or getting through the curriculum), regardless of the amount of pressure you feel from your community or staff.[3] Relationship building—the key to minimizing problems in school—is a process. So many of the changes necessary in making a transition from industrial-age beliefs and behaviors to those of an information-age model occur at a very personal level—and on a very individual basis. You probably won't have much success compelling these changes or trying to establish "win-win strategies" as a uniform discipline code, for example. (Adults aren't much different from kids when it comes to being told what to do, especially if such directives prescribe how to feel or what to tolerate.) Work with your core group and anyone who cares to join in, and focus your energies on creating a school climate in which win-win interactions are the norm.

As an administrator, begin to think of new ways to motivate, empower, value, inspire, and build commitment with your staff, perhaps by

- accommodating staff members' needs for input and choice when making administrative decisions that concern them.
- giving them opportunities to suggest topics and resources for inservice and staff development programs.
- presenting options for scheduling, room assignment, or grade level whenever possible.
- providing the most direct channels possible for access to supplies, resource personnel, and yourself.
- modeling the beliefs, behaviors, language patterns, and attitudes you would like your teachers to adopt.
- providing resources, research, and information about success-oriented strategies that have been proven to work in other settings.
- providing similar information for parents and the community to reduce the possibility that your staff will come under attack for using nontraditional strategies (although this is less likely to come from parents whose children are engaged, enthusiastic, and experiencing success).
- building strong relationships with parents and community. (Research suggests that kids learn best in schools where teachers feel respected and connected to their colleagues and the community.[4])
- resisting the tradition of evaluating teachers according to their ability to keep kids quiet and still.
- encouraging and supporting the use of brain-friendly strategies throughout the school.
- allowing and encouraging professional discretion in differentiating instruction, content selection, placement, and requirements in order to challenge individual students appropriately, using your district curriculum (or test criteria) as a guide.
- encouraging the kind of assessment, record-keeping, and documentation that will make it possible for you to advocate for the instructional decisions the teachers make.
- encouraging teachers to focus on their students' successes, give positive feedback, and offer opportunities for "do-overs" and self-correction, for example.
- resisting the traditions (and enduring presence) of the bell curve or the expectation that all teachers have at least some percentage of failing students in their classes.
- refusing to insist that teachers present the same content on the same day.

- avoiding the use of teacher-proof curricular programs.
- allowing alternative, noncompetitive grading and record keeping, such as anecdotal records, portfolios, rubrics, skill mastery checklists, and so forth.
- discouraging dependence or victim behavior by helping teachers explore and evaluate available options for dealing with student behavior problems (rather than solving problems for them, assigning punishment, or using the office as a dumping ground for uncooperative or disruptive kids).
- encouraging staff to not sweat the small stuff, to pick their battles carefully, focus on solutions, and ask for what they want directly (requesting desirable behaviors rather than labeling negative behaviors and attitudes).
- reducing the number of rules and the emphasis on rules (and especially their negative consequences); increasing the number of desirable outcomes on a contingency basis (to give teachers greater leverage for building cooperation).
- encouraging staff to help students learn to respectfully and appropriately self-manage the privileges they desire (having cell phones in school, using mp3 players, choosing their clothing, bringing water bottles or snacks to class, for example) rather than outlawing these privileges and requiring teachers to micromanage student behavior.
- offering acceptance, feedback, and support while encouraging teachers to solve their problems themselves.
- resisting the habit of getting in the middle of—and taking responsibility for—squabbles between kids and teachers, even if that's always been your job.
- refusing to punish students for infractions you did not witness.
- helping teachers resolve conflicts with other staff members or parents without assuming responsibility for the solution of the problems.
- encouraging the development or creation of a reward-oriented school environment, helping teachers find ways to increase the number of positive options they can offer to students.
- modeling a shift in your emphasis, away from negative consequences of undesirable behavior (either teacher or student) and toward the positive outcomes of doing what you're asking.
- providing resources or support necessary to help teachers develop success-oriented instruction and routines (to make success possible for students at a variety of ability levels).
- being visible in nonconflict arenas and visiting every classroom, as often as possible, to offer feedback or just help out.
- finding something positive to say about every member of your staff.
- making time to regularly acknowledge the contributions your staff members make (including casual, informal verbal, or written messages of recognition and appreciation).
- encouraging (not requiring) your staff to do the same for one another.
- using motivators and rewards to show appreciation, recognize special achievements, or just break up routines.
- identifying and changing negative, reactive school policies.
- helping staff clarify their intentions, develop a mission and sense of purpose, and remember what brought them to the profession; helping staff keep the big picture in mind.
- encouraging individuals to set their own goals for professional growth and providing whatever support is necessary to the degree that this is possible; making the school a professional learning community.

- evaluating school policies and practices in the context of your mission and intentions and encouraging the staff to do the same with their own behaviors.
- working to change any negative aspects of the school's culture which may be undermining staff morale and productivity.
- allowing time for new skills to develop and mature.
- encouraging staff to connect with kids, with one another, and with the community.
- encouraging (not requiring) your staff to report positive student behavior (and, if possible, sharing these reports with the students' parents).
- maintaining regular and positive communication with the community; directly contacting parents from time to time to let them know something positive you saw or overheard regarding their children.
- being willing to learn and grow outside your own comfort zone. (Remember, "like the queen on a chessboard, the teacher with the most moves has the most options and the greatest degree of influence."[5])
- taking care of yourself; learning to let go, delegate, set, and maintain boundaries.

As you model cooperative interactions with students, parents, and staff, you will set the tone for the entire school. The payoffs for you and the other adults in your building are considerable. But in terms of learning, behavior, commitment, and self-concept, the real winners are the students.[6]

NOTES

1. David N. Aspy and Flora N. Roebuck. *Kids Don't Learn from People They Don't Like* (Amherst, MA: Human Resource Development Press, 1977).

2. I have honestly lost count of the number of teachers over the years who have told me that they were encouraged to try new approaches and then received reprimands or poor evaluations for their efforts, even when the strategies worked. I can only begin to imagine the impact of this betrayal on the climate in their classrooms.

3. See Resource C for a list of characteristics of positive, healthy, win-win classroom relationships, including a checklist of specific behaviors that can reflect or create these characteristics. Feel free to use the checklist as a goal sheet for yourself and your staff, to communicate to parents the kind of relationships your school is committed to building, or to evaluate the components of any discipline, curriculum, or instructional program or approach being recommended or considered for your school. Additionally, you will find a copy of a survey to assess, "Is Your School an Emotionally Safe Place?" on my Web site at http://www.janebluestein.com/handouts/survey.html. This survey can provide additional feedback and a sense of focus and direction in your efforts at restructuring the culture of an individual classroom or your entire school or district.

4. Barbara Kantrowitz and Pat Wingert. "Teachers Wanted," Newsweek (Oct. 2, 2000): 37–42.

5. Bob Garmston and Bruce Wellman, quoted in Louise Stoll, "Enhancing Schools' Capacity for Learning." Paper presented at Innovations for Effective Schooling Conference, Auckland, NZ (August 1999).

6. You can use the aforementioned suggestions as a checklist or self-assessment, rating yourself on each item on a scale that works for you, or identifying specific goals you want to set for yourself. You can also use the list to request feedback from your staff, perhaps asking them to circle the five skills they appreciate most or think you do best, adding suggestions to the list, or identifying one or two items they would appreciate.

Resource B

Magic Sentences

M*agic sentences* (or key phrases) are simply practical ways to use language to prevent, minimize, or de-escalate conflicts with kids. Different sentences will be useful in different situations.

Great first draft. Use when kids turn in work that is incomplete, illegible, or incorrect. Invites kids to redo, complete, clean up, or self-correct their work.

We'll try again later. For times when you withdraw a positive consequence (ask kids to sit somewhere else, stop reading the story, etc.). This keeps the door open for kids to try again and make better choices at a later time.

This isn't working. An excellent way to interrupt disruptive or off-task behavior without attacking or criticizing.

I know you wish you could. . . . Validates a child's desire to do something (not go to a particular class, go to the nurse or go home, hit a classmate, not take a test, etc.) when that option is not available or not negotiable.

That won't work for me. A simple, nonattacking way to reject a student's suggestion when it proposes something inappropriate or inadequate for your objectives. You can validate the worth of the proposal ("Interesting idea" or "Oh, that *does* sound like it would be fun") and, if appropriate, even offer to look for opportunities to offer that suggestion at another time.

Think of a solution that will work for both of us. Transfers responsibility to a dissatisfied student to find a solution that will work for him or her *and* for you (and not become a problem for anyone else).

Can you live with that? Affirming a commitment after coming to an agreement.

Tell me what you just agreed to (do). Confirms the student's understanding of an agreement, making sure you and the student are on the same page.

Humor me. When you ask for something that seems unreasonable, when you ask for something just because it's important to you, or when you have to give seemingly needless instructions, for example. This works best when mutually respectful relationships have been established.

Because we're all different and everyone gets to succeed. When questioned about why different students are on different pages, have different assignments or different requirements, or are being taught in different ways.

Equally appropriately challenged. A win-win definition of *fair* (as opposed to fair meaning "same"); it allows different kids to be on different pages, have different assignments or different requirements, or to be taught in different ways so that all students can achieve success and make progress regardless of differences in cognitive development, prior achievements, or learning styles.

We don't say that here. Nonattacking response to a student's hurtful or offensive language.

My door is open. An invitation to come and talk. Indicates an awareness of a troubled student's situation without being nosy or invasive. Most effective in a high trust relationship and emotionally safe environment.

We don't need to talk about that. A way to disengage from gossip or toxic interchanges. Also "That's none of my business" or "I appreciate your concern." Change the subject immediately to make it clear that you do not wish to continue the discussion.

Resource C

Characteristics of Healthy Relationships

U se this checklist to evaluate patterns in your current relationships with children and adults. If you have implemented (or are considering) a specific discipline or behavior management model, does it encourage relationships in which the following are true?[1]

Proactivity

Teacher behaviors include the following: recognizing and, whenever possible, accommodating the student's need for unconditional acceptance, safety, belonging, success, limits, fun, recognition, and control (power), without allowing anyone else's needs to be violated; anticipating; doing something before (there is a problem); letting the student know limits or conditions—and payoffs—ahead of time. An alternative to reactivity.

____ I focus on prevention—not reaction.

____ I attempt to anticipate my students' needs, as well as what could possibly go wrong, before implementing a new program or assignment.

____ I attempt to meet student needs in healthy, constructive, and positive ways.

____ I let my students know what they need in order to experience success *before* there is a problem or before the problem gets worse.

Win-Win Power Dynamics

Teacher behaviors include the following: respecting students' needs for power and limits, as well as the need to establish teacher authority without violating students' needs (that is, getting one's needs for power and autonomy met without violating anyone else); accommodating students' needs for power and autonomy within limits, and without disempowering oneself. An alternative to win-lose (powering or permissiveness).

____ I can motivate cooperative behavior without powering, threatening, humiliating, or using conditional approval.

____ I am more interested in encouraging cooperation than compliance, even though the outcome behaviors usually look about the same.

279

___ I want to empower my students within limits that do not disempower or disturb others.

___ I use my authority to set limits, to offer choices, and to decide what is and is not negotiable within those limits.

Success Orientation

Teacher behaviors include the following: helping a student be successful by giving clear directions, setting boundaries, offering opportunities to choose and negotiate, requesting age-appropriate behaviors and responses, accommodating curricular and learning style needs, giving opportunities to self-manage, and staying in present time (teaching according to a student's current academic needs, rather than anticipating demands of other teachers or grade levels in the future or circular mandates). An alternative to unrealistic expectations, misunderstandings, instruction or environments poorly matched to students' needs, and setups for failure, passivity, or rebelliousness.

___ I give clear directions.

___ I set clear, proactive, and win-win boundaries.

___ I attempt to meet student cognitive and curricular needs.

___ I attempt to accommodate student preferences and learning styles.

___ I am willing to allow students adequate movement, hydration, tactile or oral-motor stimulation, and so on, to accommodate neurological and physiological needs.

___ I present information in a variety of ways to accommodate students' modality preferences.

___ I allow students to correct errors and make improvements on their assignments and resubmit corrected work for full credit (or an improved grade).

___ I give students opportunities to self-manage.

___ I stay in the present, responding to actual needs of students (rather than anticipated needs or requirements of future teachers).

Positivity

Teacher behaviors include the following: being able to distinguish the child's worth from his or her behavior, particularly when the child is misbehaving; focusing on what the child is doing right and building on strengths; creating a reward-oriented environment in which consequences are positive outcomes and incentives received or experienced as a result of cooperation; communicating positively (using promises instead of threats, emphasizing positive outcomes instead of punishment, for example); offering positive feedback that focuses on what the students are doing right; maintaining a sense of humor. An alternative to negativity and punitive orientation.

___ I can separate my students' behavior from their worth.

___ I state boundaries as promises rather than threats.

___ My classroom is reward oriented.

___ I think of consequences as the positive outcomes for cooperation or completion.

___ In evaluating my students' work, I look for the positive (what the student is doing right) and build on that.

___ The majority of the feedback I give my students is positive, focusing on what they're doing right.

___ I try to maintain my sense of humor.

Avoiding Double Standards

Teacher behaviors include the following: interacting and communicating with a child in ways that one would use in talking to another adult, maintaining congruence between one's own behaviors and those expected of the student, responding to a student's behavior in ways similar to what would be inspired by the same behavior if it were demonstrated by an adult, being willing to accept the fact that students require meaningful, positive outcomes for their efforts, just as adults do.

___ I model the kinds of behavior I would like my students to exhibit.

___ I model the kinds of language, tone of voice, and attitude toward my students that I would like them to use in their interactions with me.

___ I avoid talking to students in ways I would not talk to adults.

___ In terms of motivation, I recognize that students desire (and deserve) to experience meaningful outcomes as a result of the behaviors they choose, just as adults do.

___ I avoid making a big deal over issues and incidents that involve my students just because they aren't adults (things I would never address if they were said or done by another adult).

Boundaries

Teacher behaviors include the following: connecting in positive ways what you want with what the student wants; motivating and reinforcing cooperative behavior with outcomes other than adult approval or avoidance of negative adult reactions (shaming, criticism, abandonment, etc.); withholding or withdrawing positive consequences until the student holds up his or her end of the bargain; being consistent in immediately following through and intervening in breaches in conditions or limits of a boundary, avoiding warnings or delayed consequences; intervening in negative behavior without using punishment; reinforcing positive behavior with recognition instead of praise.

___ I offer students a variety of meaningful positive consequences to motivate or encourage cooperative behavior.

___ I can recognize positive student behavior without reinforcing dependence and people pleasing.

___ I avoid giving warnings, as well as delayed or meaningless consequences. (When a student misbehaves, I am willing to withdraw privileges immediately.)

___ I avoid asking for excuses. (I am willing to withhold privileges and rewards until students come through on their end regardless of their excuses.)

___ I have built in some proactive flexibility (such as requiring ninety-five percent of all homework assignments, rather than one hundred percent, or giving students until the end of the day to get work finished) so I can accommodate occasional problems that may arise without compromising my boundaries or asking for excuses.

Supportiveness

Teacher behaviors include the following: responding to a student's problems or feelings with acceptance, support, and validation; providing outlets for students' feelings that will allow them to deal with their feelings without hurting themselves or others; helping students seek solutions to problems without enabling, fixing, dismissing, or judging the children's problems or feelings; resisting the inclination to adopt students' feelings or take responsibility for the solutions to their problems, either directly solving the problems or giving advice or solutions.

___ I recognize that students can't simply leave their feelings at the door, and I do not demand that they do so.

___ I can accept a student's feelings even if I don't understand or agree with them.

___ I am willing to accept a student's feelings without asking him or her to explain or defend them.

___ I have a variety of healthy outlets for students to use to get their feelings out (or be heard) without creating problems for themselves or others.

___ I can listen and validate without giving advice, dismissing the problem, making the student wrong (for having the feelings or for the situation that triggered the feelings), or otherwise interfering with the feelings.

___ I encourage students to stick up for themselves and ask for what they want from others in healthy, positive ways.

___ I ask questions to help students find solutions to problems rather than giving them answers or advice about what they should do.

Integrity and Professionalism

Teacher behaviors include the following: maintaining congruence between personal values and behavior; listening and responding to inner guidance and personal values; acting within a personal value system despite potential or actual criticism from others; making decisions based on what is best for a particular student or group of students, rather than simply, automatically following tradition; being able to withstand judgment, criticism, and ridicule, if necessary, without becoming defensive, apologetic, or reactive; maintaining documentation to support decisions, when necessary.

____ I make choices based on my priorities and my students' needs regardless of possible reactions from others.

____ I understand that the best choice (for my students, for myself, for good educational practice) may not be the most popular choice (or even sanctioned by my colleagues).

____ I am able to deal with criticism without becoming defensive, apologetic, or reactive, and without explaining in an attempt to secure approval for what I'm doing.

____ The choices I make about how and what I teach are supported by student assessment.

____ The choices I make about how and what I teach are supported by current research.

____ I minimize potential conflict with documentation and communication with my administrators and my students' parents.

Communication

Teacher behaviors include the following: taking responsibility for feelings, without attempting to make others responsible; expressing feelings in nonhurtful ways; being able to depersonalize and resolve conflict; maintaining regular, positive contact with students' parents, working with administrators, support staff, and parents without projecting blame or expecting (or demanding) that they take responsibility for solving problems you may be having with a particular student or group.

____ I can ask for what I want without talking about my feelings.

____ I avoid using my feelings as a way to control or change others.

____ I avoid using my feelings to suggest that they are the result of someone else's behavior.

____ I take responsibility for solving problems that arise in my classroom.

____ I communicate positively and responsibly with parents on a regular basis.

____ I use administrators, support personnel, and parents as resources without attempting to make them responsible for my problems.

____ When I slip up and say or do something hurtful, I take responsibility for my behavior (rather than blaming it on something the student has done).

____ When I make a mistake or fail to keep my word, I avoid making excuses and do what I need to do to make things right.

____ I am able and willing to directly ask for what I want.

Self-Care

Teacher behaviors include the following: identifying personal needs and feelings, setting boundaries, taking time for self, self-validating, and getting help when necessary; being able to distinguish between self-care and selfishness; feeling deserving of self-caring behaviors and decisions; using mistakes and failures as opportunities for new goals, strategies, or growth; utilizing support resources while maintaining responsibility for solving one's own problems; being able to self-forgive.

____ I model a commitment to personal growth.

____ I am able to ask for what I want, clearly, directly, and assertively.

____ I know how to set boundaries and am willing to do so to take care of myself.

____ When things get to be too much for me, I am willing to reach out for help without making others responsible for my feelings or state of mind.

____ I have developed a strong support network and am willing to use it.

____ I minimize or avoid contact with negative, toxic people and experiences.

____ I use my mistakes and errors as opportunities for new learning rather than as excuses for beating myself up.

____ I have a variety of outlets and resources outside the classroom for personal enrichment, relaxation, stress management, and fun.

____ I acknowledge what I'm doing right and give myself space to grow and keep getting better!

NOTE

1. Is your classroom (or school) an emotionally safe place? Visit http://www.janebluestein .com/handouts/survey.html for a free copy of a survey you can use to assess, in greater detail, the emotional climate of your classroom, school, or district.

Recommended Reading

The books listed in this section include resources that were referenced in the text of *The Win-Win Classroom* as well as materials on related topics. I have tried to include a wide range of resources (and viewpoints) for educators, counselors, administrators, and other school staff, not only for their own personal and professional development, but also for use with or by students as well. While the majority of the titles were published fairly recently, I make no apologies for the oldies-but-goodies I've included. They are a part of my own history, a part of what shaped the content of this book, and generally are as relevant now as they were when they were written.

The titles are loosely grouped into categories. (Many items include a range of content that could be classified in several different categories.) Because Web addresses change as frequently as they do, I have not included many in this book (other than a few footnotes to reference specific content). Please check my Web site at http://www.janebluestein .com/links/index.html for links to sites with information and resources relevant to topics discussed in this book.

BEHAVIOR MANAGEMENT, CLASSROOM MANAGEMENT, CLASSROOM CLIMATE, MOTIVATION, AND MENTORSHIP

Albert, Linda. *Cooperative Discipline.* Circle Pines, MN: American Guidance Service, 1996.

Aspy, David N., and Flora N. Roebuck. *Kids Don't Learn From People They Don't Like.* Amherst, MA: Human Resource Development Press, 1977.

Bailey, Becky. *There's Got to Be a Better Way: Discipline That Works.* Oveido, FL: Loving Guidance, 2003.

Bluestein, Jane. *Building Responsible Learning Behavior Through Peer Interaction.* Doctoral dissertation, University of Pittsburgh, PA, 1980.

Bluestein, Jane. *Mentors, Masters and Mrs. MacGregor: Stories of Teachers Making a Difference.* Deerfield Beach, FL: Health Communications, 1995.

Bluestein, Jane. *TeacherTapes: Being a Successful Teacher.* Albuquerque, NM: ISS Publications, 1998.

Bluestein, Jane and Lynn Collins. *Parents in a Pressure Cooker, Teacher Workbook.* Rosemont, NJ: Modern Learning Press, 1999.

Clark, Jean Illsley. *Time-In: When Time-Out Doesn't Work.* Seattle: Parenting Press, 1999.

Gibson, Janice T. *Discipline Is Not a Dirty Word.* Brattleboro, VT: Lewis Publishing, 1983.

Ginott, Haim. *Teacher and Child.* New York: Scribner Books, 1993.

Jones, Frederic H. *Positive Classroom Discipline.* New York: McGraw-Hill, 1987.

Loomans, Diane, and Karen Kolberg. *The Laughing Classroom.* Tiburon, CA: H. J. Kramer, 1993.

Marshall, James. *The Devil in the Classroom: Hostility in American Education.* New York: Schocken Books, 1985.

Marshall, Marvin. *Discipline Without Stress, Punishments or Rewards: How Teachers and Parents Promote Responsibility and Learning.* Los Alamitos, CA: Piper Press, 2001.

Marston, Stephanie. *The Magic of Encouragement: Nurturing Your Child's Self-Esteem.* New York: Pocket Books, 1990.

McLaughlin, Cathrine Kellison. *The Do's and Don'ts of Parent Involvement: How to Build a Positive School-Home Partnership.* Torrance, CA: Innerchoice Publishing, 1993.

Mendler, Allen N.. *Power Struggles: Successful Techniques for Educators.* Rochester, NY: Discipline Associates, 1997.

Miller, Alice. *For Your Own Good: Hidden Cruelty in Child-Rearing and the Roots of Violence.* New York: Farrar, Straus & Giroux, 1990.

Miller, Alice. *Thou Shalt Not Be Aware: Society's Betrayal of the Child.* New York: New American Library, 1986.

Murray, Margo. *Beyond the Myths and Magic of Mentoring.* San Francisco: Jossey-Bass, 1991.

Moorman, Chick, and Nancy Moorman Weber. *Teacher Talk: What It Really Means.* Saginaw, MI: Personal Power Press, 1989.

Nelsen, Jane. *Positive Discipline.* New York: Ballantine Books, 1987.

Ohme, Herman. *101 Ways for Teachers to Motivate Students.* Palo Alto: CA Education Plan, 1991.

Osborn, D. Keith, and Janie Dyson Osborn. *Discipline and Classroom Management.* Athens, GA: Education Associates, 1977.

Phillips, Vicki. *Empowering Discipline.* Carmel Valley, CA: Personal Development Publishing, 1998.

Rogers, Spence, Jim Ludington, and Shari Graham. *Motivation & Learning: A Teacher's Guide to Building Excitement for Learning & Igniting the Drive for Quality.* Evergreen, CO: Peak Learning Systems, 1997.

Stipek, Deborah, and Kathy Seal. *Motivated Minds: Raising Children to Love Learning.* New York: Henry Holt, 2001.

Tobin, L. *What Do You Do With a Child Like This? Inside the Lives of Troubled Children.* Duluth, MN: Pfeifer-Hamilton Publishers, 1991.

TEACHING AND LEARNING, SUCCESS AND ACHIEVEMENT, AND STUDY SKILLS AND ASSESSMENT

Allen, Richard Howell. *Impact Teaching.* Boston: Allyn & Bacon, 2002.

Arends, Richard I. *Learning to Teach.* New York: Random House, 1998.

Beckley, William L. *Creating a Classroom Portfolio System.* Dubuque, IA: Kendall/Hunt Publishing, 1997.

Bloom, Benjamin S., ed. *Taxonomy of Educational Objectives, Handbook I: Cognitive Domain.* New York: Longman, 1956.

Bluestein, Jane. *Being a Successful Teacher.* Torrance, CA: Fearon Teacher Aids (Frank Schaffer Publishers), 1989.

Bluestein, Jane. *Creating Emotionally Safe Schools: A Guide for Educators and Parents.* Deerfield Beach, FL: Health Communications, 2001.

Bluestein, Jane. *Rx: Handwriting: An Individualized, Prescriptive System for Painlessly Managing Handwriting Instruction.* Albuquerque, NM: ISS Publications, 2005. First published 1980.

Davis, Leslie, and Sandi Sirotowitz, with Harvey C. Parker. *Study Strategies Made Easy: A Practical Plan for School Success.* Plantation, FL: Specialty Press, 1997.

Dryden, Gordon, and Jeanette Vos. *The Learning Revolution.* Torrance, CA: Jalmar Press, 1994.

Dunn, Kenneth, and Rita Dunn. *The Educator's Self-Teaching Guide to Individualized Instruction.* Englewood Cliffs, NJ: Parker Publishing, 1975.

Faber, Adele, and Elaine Mazlish. *How to Talk So Kids Can Learn.* New York: Rawson, 1995.

Fay, Jim, and David Funk. *Teaching With Love and Logic.* Golden, CO: The Love and Logic Press, 1995.

Finney, Susan. *Together I Can.* Spring Valley, CA: Innerchoice Publishing, 1991.

Glasser, William. *Schools Without Failure.* New York: Perrenial Library, 1975.

Glasser, William. *Every Child Can Succeed.* Chatsworth, CA: William Glasser, 2004.

Goertzel, Ted, and Joseph Fashing. "The Myth of the Normal Curve: A Theoretical Critique and Examination of Its Role in Teaching and Research," *Humanity and Society,* 5, 1981; reprinted in *Readings in Humanist Sociology,* Bayside, NY: General Hall, 1986. Available from Rutgers University Web site: http://www.crab.rutgers.edu/~goertzel/normalcurve.htm.

Grant, Jim. *I Hate School.* Rosemont, NJ: Modern Learning Press, 1986.

Harmin, Merrill. *Strategies for Active Learning.* Edwardsville, IL: Inspiring Strategies Institute, 1995.

Lazear, David. *Seven Ways of Teaching.* Arlington Heights, IL: SkyLight Training & Publishing, 1991.

Lewis, Byron, and Frank Pucelik. *Magic of NLP Demystified.* Portland: Metamorphous Press, 1990.

Ohanian, Susan. *One Size Fits Few: The Folly of Educational Standards.* Portsmouth, NH: Heinemann, 1999.

Ohanian, Susan. *What Happened to Recess and Why Are Our Children Struggling in Kindergarten?* New York: McGraw-Hill, 2002.

Ohme, Herman. *"Learn How to Learn" Study Skills.* Palo Alto: California Education Plan, 1986.

Perkins, David. *Smart Schools: Better Thinking & Learning for Every Child.* New York: Free Press/Simon & Schuster, 1992.

Rogers, Spence, and Shari Graham. *The High Performance Toolbox: Succeeding With Performance Tasks, Projects and Assessments.* Evergreen, CO: Peak Learning Systems, 1997.

Shalaway, Linda. *Learning to Teach.* Cleveland: Edgell Communications (Instructor Books), 1989.

Silberman, Mel. *Active Learning: 101 Strategies to Teach Any Subject.* Boston: Allyn & Bacon, 1996.

Stoll, Louise. "Enhancing Schools' Capacity for Learning." Paper presented at Innovations for Effective Schooling Conference, Auckland, NZ (August 1999).

LEARNING STYLES, BRAIN-RELATED TOPICS, AND SPECIAL NEEDS

Armstrong, Thomas. *The Myth of the ADD Child: 50 Ways to Improve Your Child's Behavior and Attention Span Without Drugs, Labels or Coercion.* New York: Dutton, 1995.

The Australian Journal of Learning Disabilities, June 2004, Vol. 9, No 2: 14–22.

Bleuer, Jeanne, Susanna Palomares, and Garry Walz. *Activities for Counseling Underachievers.* Torrance, CA: Innerchoice Publishing, 1993.

Bower, Gordon H. "How Might Emotions Affect Learning?" In *The Handbook of Emotion and Memory: Research and Theory,* edited by Sven-Ake Christianson. Hillsdale, NJ: Lawrence Erlbaum, 1992.

Budd, Linda S. *Living With the Active Alert Child.* Seattle: Parenting Press, 1993.

Burke, Kay. *The Mindful School: How to Assess Authentic Learning.* rev. ed. Arlington Heights, IL: IRI/SkyLight Training and Publishing, 1994.

Caine, Renate Nummela, and Geoffrey Caine. *Making Connections: Teaching and the Human Brain.* Menlo Park, CA: Addison-Wesley, 1994.

Caine, Renate Nummela, and Geoffrey Caine. *Education on the Edge of Possibility.* Alexandria, VA: Association for Supervision and Curriculum Development, 1997.

Carter, Rita. *Mapping the Mind.* Berkeley: University of California Press, 1998.

Cherry, Clare, Douglas Godwin, and Jesse Staples. *Is the Left Brain Always Right?* Torrance, CA: Fearon Teacher Aids, 1989.

Cummings, Rhoda, and Gary Fisher. *The School Survival Guide for Kids With LD.* Minneapolis: Free Spirit Publishing, 1991.

Dauten, Dale. "Lighting Deserves a Look," *Albuquerque Journal* (Jan. 25, 2000).

Davis, Joel. *Mapping the Mind: The Secrets of the Human Brain and How It Works.* Secaucas, NJ: Carol Publishing Group, 1997.

Dennison, Paul E., and Gail E. Dennison. *Brain Gym, Teacher's Edition.* Ventura, CA: Edu-Kinesthetics, 1996.

Faculty of New City School. *Celebrating Multiple Intelligences.* St. Louis, MO: New City School, 1994.

Fogarty, Robin. *Brain Compatible Classrooms.* Arlington Heights, IL: SkyLight Training & Publishing, 1997.

Gardner, Howard. *Frames of Mind: The Theory of Multiple Intelligences.* New York: Basic Books, 1983.

Gazzaniga, Michael S. *Mind Matters.* Boston: Houghton Mifflin, 1988.

Gazzaniga, Michael S. *The Social Brain: Discovering the Networks of the Mind.* New York: Basic Books, 1985.

Greenspan, Stanley I., with Beryl Lieff Benderly. *The Growth of the Mind.* Reading, MA: Addison-Wesley, 1997.

Hannaford, Carla. *Smart Moves: Why Learning Is Not All in Your Head.* Arlington, VA: Great Oceans Publishers, 1995.

Hannaford, Carla. *The Dominance Factor.* Arlington, VA: Great Oceans Publishers, 1997.

Heacox, Diane. *Up From Underachievement.* Minneapolis, MN: Free Spirit Publishing, 1991.

Hersey, Jane. *Why Can't My Child Behave?* Alexandria, VA: Pear Tree Press, 1999.

Hirsh-Pask, Kathy, and Roberta Michnick Golinkoff. *Einstein Never Used Flash Cards.* Emmaus, PA: Rodale Press, 2003.

Howard, Pierce. *The Owner's Manual for the Brain.* Austin, TX: Leornian Press, 1996.

Jensen, Eric. *Brain-Based Learning.* San Diego: The Brain Store, 1996.

Jensen, Eric. *Brain Compatible Strategies.* San Diego, CA: The Brain Store, 1997.

Jensen, Eric. *Super Teaching.* San Diego, CA: The Brain Store, 1998.

Johnson, Steven. "Don't Fear the Digital." *Time* (March 27, 2006): 56.

Jones, Frederic H. *Positive Classroom Instruction.* New York: McGraw-Hill, 1987.

Joyce, Bruce, and Marsha Weil. *Models of Teaching.* Englewood Cliffs, NJ: Prentice Hall, 1980.

Kaufeldt, Martha. *Begin With the Brain.* Tucson, AZ: Zephyr Press, 1999.

Kaufeldt, Martha. *Teachers, Change Your Bait! Brain-Compatible Differentiated Instruction.* Norwalk, CT: Crown House Publishing, 2005.

Kline, Peter. *Why America's Children Can't Think: Creating Independent Minds for the 21st Century.* Makawao, Maui, HI: Inner Ocean Publishing, 2002.

Kotulak, Ronald. *Inside the Brain: Revolutionary Discoveries of How the Mind Works.* Kansas City, MO: Andrews McMeel Publishing, 1997.

Kranowitz, Carol Stock. *The Out-of-Sync Child.* New York: Berkley Publishing Group, 1998.

LeDoux, Joseph. *The Emotional Brain.* New York: Simon & Schuster, 1996.

Levine, Mel. *A Mind at a Time.* New York: Simon & Schuster, 2002.

Lillard, Paula Polk. *Montessori Today.* New York: Schocken Books, 1996.

"The Many Effects of Daylight," *Pure Facts,* newsletter of the Feingold Association of the United States (March, 2000): 1-5.

Markova, Dawna, and Anne R. Powell. *The Open Mind.* Berkeley, CA: Conari Press, 1996.

Martin, Gail. The Charlotte Reporter, reported in The Irlen Institute Newsletter, June 2005, Vol. XV, No. 2: 8.

McCutcheon, Randall. *Get Off My Brain: A Survival Guide for Lazy Students.* Minneapolis, MN: Free Spirit Publishing, 1985.

McMurchie, Susan. *Understanding L.D.* Minneapolis, MN: Free Spirit Publishing, 1994.

Mitchell, Craig, with Pamela Espeland. *Teach to Reach.* Minneapolis, MN: Free Spirit Publishing, 1996.

Moberg, Randy. *TNT Teaching.* Minneapolis, MN: Free Spirit Publishing, 1994.

Neville, Helen, and Diane Clark Johnson. *Temperament Tools.* Seattle, WA: Parenting Press, 1998.

Ostrander, Sheila, and Lynn Schroeder, with Nancy Ostrander. *Superlearning.* New York: Delacorte Press, 1979.

Parry, Terence, and Gayle Gregory. *Designing Brain Compatible Learning.* Arlington Heights, IL: Skylight Publishing, 1998.

Promislow, Sharon. *Making the Brain Body Connection.* West Vancouver, BC: Kinetic Publishing, 1999.

Sousa, David A. *How the Brain Learns.* Reston, VA: National Association of Secondary School Principals, 1995.

Sprenger, Marilee. *Becoming a "Wiz" at Brain-Based Teaching.* Thousand Oaks, CA: Corwin Press, 2001.

Sylwester, Robert. *A Celebration of Neurons.* Alexandria, VA: Association for Supervision and Curriculum Development, 1995.

Vitale, Barbara Meister. *Unicorns Are Real.* Torrance, CA: Jalmar Press, 1982.

Vitale, Barbara Meister. *Free Flight: Celebrating Your Right Brain.* Torrance, CA: Jalmar Press, 1986.

Waas, Lane. *Imagine That.* Torrance, CA: Jalmar Press, 1991.

Wallis, Claudia. "The Multitasking Generation," *Time* (March 27, 2006): 48–55.

Williams, Mary Sue, and Sherry Shellenberger. *How Does Your Engine Run?* Albuquerque, NM: TherapyWorks, 1996.

Winebrenner, Susan. *Teaching Kids With Learning Difficulties in the Regular Classroom.* Minneapolis, MN: Free Spirit Publishing, 1996.

HEALTHY RELATIONSHIPS, HEALING, SELF-CARE, AND INSPIRATION

Algozzine, Bob. *Teacher's Little Book of Wisdom.* Merrillville, IN: ICS Books, 1995.

Beattie, Melody. *CoDependent No More.* New York: Harper-Hazelden, 1987.

Bluestein, Jane, Judy Lawrence, and S. J. Sanchez. *Daily Riches: A Journal of Gratitude and Awareness.* Deerfield Beach, FL: Health Communications, 1998.

Bradshaw, John. *Bradshaw on: The Family.* Deerfield Beach, FL: Health Communications, 1988.

Brown, Les. *Live Your Dreams.* New York: Avon Books, 1992.

Childre, Doc, and Howard Martin. *The HeartMath Solution.* San Francisco: Harper San Francisco, 1999.

Clark, Jean Illsley, and Connie Dawson. *Growing up Again.* San Francisco: Harper & Row, 1989.

Collins, Lynn, and Barbara McDuffie. *Blind Spots: Your Psychological Speed Bumps.* Xlibris, 2005.

Cox, Fran, and Louis Cox. *A Conscious Life: Cultivating the Seven Qualities of Authentic Adulthood.* Berkeley: Conari Press, 1996.

Eden, Donna. *Energy Medicine.* New York: Jeremy P. Tarcher/Penguin, 1998.

Glass, Lillian. *Toxic People: 10 Ways of Dealing With People Who Make Your Life Miserable.* New York: St. Martin's Griffin, 1995.

Levey, Joel, and Michelle Levey. *Living in Balance: A Dynamic Approach for Creating Harmony & Wholeness in a Chaotic World.* Berkeley, CA: Conari Press, 1998.

Lloyd, Ken. *Jerks at Work: How to Deal With People Problems and Problem People.* Franklin Lakes, NJ: Career Press, 1999.

Loeb, Paul Rogat, ed. *The Impossible Will Take a Little While.* New York: Basic Books, 2004.

Mosley, Jenny. *Golden Moments for Busy Teachers.* Wiltshire, UK: Positive Press, 2003.

Muller, Wayne. *Legacy of the Heart: The Spiritual Advantages of a Painful Childhood.* New York: Simon & Schuster, 1992.

Myss, Caroline. *Anatomy of the Spirit.* New York: Harmony Books, 1996.

Wright, Esther. *The Heart and Wisdom of Teaching.* San Francisco: Teaching From the Heart, 1997.

Wright, Esther. *Why I Teach: Inspirational True Stories From Teachers Who Make a Difference.* Rocklin, CA: Prima Publishing, 1999.

PROBLEM SOLVING, CONFLICT RESOLUTION, BULLYING ISSUES, VIOLENCE, AND SAFETY

ABC News Web site. "Recent Incidents of Thwarted School Violence." April 24, 2006, http://abc news.go.com.

Agassi, Martine. *Hands Are Not for Hitting.* Minneapolis, MN: Free Spirit Publishing, 2000.

Alexander, Titus. *Citizenship Schools.* London: Campaign for Learning, 2001.

Aronson, Elliot. *Nobody Left to Hate: Teaching Compassion After Columbine.* Henry Holt, 2000.

Beane, Allan L. *The Bully-Free Classroom.* Minneapolis, MN: Free Spirit Publishing, 1999.

Beaudoin, Marie-Nathalie, and Maureen Taylor. *Breaking the Culture of Bullying and Disrespect, Grades K–8: Best Practices and Successful Strategies.* Thousand Oaks, CA: Corwin Press, 2004.

Bluestein, Jane, and Eric Katz. *High School's Not Forever.* Deerfield Beach, FL: Health Communications, 2005.

Bosch, Carl. *Bully on the Bus.* Seattle, WA: Parenting Press, 1988.

Cantor, Ralph, Paul Kivel, and Allan Creighton. *Days of Respect.* Alameda, CA: Hunter House, 1997.

Coloroso, Barbara. *The Bully, the Bullied, and the Bystander.* New York: Harper Resource, 2003.

Cowan, David, Susanna Palomares, and Dianne Schilling. *Teaching the Skills of Conflict Resolution.* Spring Valley, CA: Innerchoice Publishing, 1992.

Cowan, David, Susanna Palomares, and Dianne Schilling. *Conflict Resolution Skills for Teens.* Torrance, CA: Innerchoice Publishing, 1994.

Crary, Elizabeth. *Kids Can Cooperate.* Seattle, WA: Parenting Press, 1984.

Crary, Elizabeth. *Children's Problem-Solving Series* (six books). Seattle, WA: Parenting Press, 1996.

Creighton, Allan, with Paul Kivel. *Helping Teens Stop Violence.* Alameda, CA: Hunter House, 1992.

Dental Plans.com. "Reporting Trouble Works! Prevents School Violence." Presented by HealthNewsDigest.com, 2005, and reported on the DentalPlans.com Web site.

Drew, Naomi. *Learning the Skills of Peacemaking.* Torrance, CA: Jalmar Press, 1995.

Drew, Naomi. *The Peaceful Classroom in Action.* Torrance, CA: Jalmar Press, 1999.

Drew, Naomi. *The Kids' Guide to Working Out Conflicts.* Minneapolis, MN: Free Spirit Publishing, 2004.

Duvall, Lynn. *Respecting Our Differences.* Minneapolis, MN: Free Spirit Publishing, 1994.

Freiberg, Jo Ann. "Elements of Respect: Translating Respect Into a Playground Code of Conduct" (handout).

Karres, Erika V., *Mean Chicks, Cliques, and Dirty Tricks: A Real Girl's Guide to Getting Through the Day With Smarts and Style.* Avon, MA: Adams Media, 2004.

Kaufman, Gershen, and Lev Rafael. *Stick Up for Yourself.* Minneapolis, MN: Free Spirit Publishing, 1990.

Kehayan, Alex. *Partners for Change.* Torrance, CA: Jalmar Press, 1992.

Kincher, Jonni. *Psychology for Kids.* Minneapolis, MN: Free Spirit Publishing, 1995.

Kivel, Paul, and Allan Creighton. *Making the Peace.* Alameda, CA: Hunter House, 1997.

Lantieri, Linda, and Janet Patti. *Waging Peace in Our Schools.* Boston: Beacon Press, 1996.

Olweus, Dan. *Bullying at School.* Oxford, UK: Blackwell Publishers, 1993.

Payne, Lauren Murphy, and Claudia Rohling. *We Can Get Along.* Minneapolis, MN: Free Spirit Publishing, 1997.

Quarles, Chester L. *Staying Safe at School.* Thousand Oaks, CA: Corwin Press, 1993.

Romain, Trevor. *Bullies Are a Pain in the Brain.* Minneapolis, MN: Free Spirit Publishing, 1997.

Saunders, Carol Silverman. *Safe at School.* Minneapolis, MN: Free Spirit Publishing, 1994.

Shakeshaft, Charol, Laurie Mandel, Yolanda M. Johnson, Janice Sawyer, Mary Ann Hergenrother, and Ellen Barber. "Boys Call Me Cow." *Educational Leadership* 55, no. 2 (October 1997).

Strauss, Susan, with Pamela Espeland. *Sexual Harassment and Teens.* Minneapolis, MN: Free Spirit Publishing, 1992.

Sullivan, Keith, Mark Cleary, and Ginny Sullivan. *Bullying in Secondary Schools: What It Looks Like and How to Manage It.* London: Paul Chapman Publishing, 2004.

Thompson, Michael, and Catherine O'Neill Grace. *Best Friends, Worst Enemies: Understanding the Social Lives of Children.* New York: Ballantine, 2001.

Williams, Linda K., Dianne Schilling, and Susanna Palomares. *Caring and Capable Kids: An Activity Guide for Teaching Kindness, Tolerance, Self-Control, and Responsibility.* Torrance, CA: Innerchoice Publishing, 1996.

PREVENTION, DEPRESSION, STRESS MANAGEMENT, DROPOUT, SUBSTANCE ABUSE, AND GANGS

Arkin, Elaine Bratic, and Judith E. Funkhouser. *Communicating About Alcohol and Other Drugs: Strategies for Reaching Populations at Risk.* Rockville, MD: U.S. Department of Health and Human Services, Office for Substance Abuse Prevention, 1990.

Arthur, Richard, with Edsel Erickson. *Gangs and Schools.* Holmes Beach, FL: Learning Publications, 1992.

Burns, E. Timothy. *From Risk to Resilience.* Dallas, TX: Marco Polo Publishers, 1996.

Dennison, Susan. *Creating Positive Support Groups for At-Risk Children.* Torrance, CA: Jalmar Press, 1997.

Flach, Frederic. *Resilience: Discovering a New Strength at Times of Stress.* New York: Fawcett Columbine, 1988.

Fox, C. Lynn, and Shirley E. Forbing. *Creating Drug-Free Schools and Communities.* New York: HarperCollins, 1992.

Hipp, Earl. *Fighting Invisible Tigers.* Minneapolis, MN: Free Spirit Publishing, 1995.

Laik, Judy. *Under Whose Influence?* Seattle, WA: Parenting Press, 1994.

Portner, Jessica. *One in Thirteen: The Silent Epidemic of Teen Suicide.* Beltsville, MD: Robins Lane Press, 1999.

Redenbach, Sandi. *Autobiography of a Drop-Out: Dear Diary.* Davis, CA: Esteem Seminars Publishing, 1996.

Sheldon, Carolyn. *EQ in School Counseling.* Torrance, CA: Innerchoice Publishing, 1996.

Thornburgh, Nathan. "Dropout Nation," *Time* (April 17, 2006).

EMOTIONAL AND PERSONAL DEVELOPMENT, CHARACTER DEVELOPMENT, SELF-WORTH, AND EMOTIONAL SUPPORT

Adderholdt-Elliott, Miriam. *Perfectionism: What's Bad About Being Too Good?* Minneapolis, MN: Free Spirit Publishing, 1987.

Adler, Alfred. *Understanding Human Nature.* Center City, MN: Hazelden Foundation, 1999.

Akin, Terri, Gerry Dunne, Susanna Palomares, and Dianne Schilling. *Character Education in America's Schools.* Torrance, CA: Innerchoice Publishing, 1995.

Benson, Peter, Judy Galbraith, and Pamela Espeland. *What Kids Need to Succeed.* Minneapolis, MN: Free Spirit Publishing, 1995.

Benson, Peter L., Judy Galbraith, and Pamela Espeland. *What Teens Need to Succeed: Proven, Practical Ways to Shape Your Own Future.* Minneapolis, MN: Free Spirit Publishing, 1998.

Bernstein, Daryl. *Kids Can Succeed.* Holbrook, MA: Bob Adams, 1993.

Bloom, Benjamin S., ed. *Taxonomy of Educational Objectives, Handbook II: Affective Domain.* New York: David McKay, 1964.

Bluestein, Jane, and Eric Katz. *High School's Not Forever.* Deerfield Beach, FL: Health Communications, 2005.

Borba, Michele. *Building Moral Intelligence: A Parent's Guide to Teaching the Seven Essential Virtues.* San Francisco: Jossey-Bass, 2001.

Borba, Michele. *Esteem Builders.* Torrance, CA: Jalmar Press, 1989. (Also *Home Esteem Builders* and *Staff Esteem Builders*, 1994 and 1993.)

Branden, Nathaniel. *The Power of Self-Esteem.* Deerfield Beach, FL: Health Communications, 1992.

Branden, Nathaniel. *The Six Pillars of Self-Esteem.* New York: Bantam Books, 1994.

Capacchione, Lucia. *Creative Journal for Teens: Making Friends With Yourself.* Franklin Lakes, NJ: New Page Books, 2002.

Crary, Elizabeth. *Dealing With Feelings Series* (six books). Seattle, WA: Parenting Press, 1994.

Dahlstrom, Lorraine M. *Writing Down the Days: 365 Creative Journaling Ideas for Young People.* Minneapolis, MN: Free Spirit Publishing, 2000.

Elchoness, Monte. *Why Can't Anyone Hear Me?* Ventura, CA: Monroe Press, 1989.

Elchoness, Monte. *Why Do Kids Need Feelings?* Ventura, CA: Monroe Press, 1992.

Elias, Maurice J., et al. *Promoting Social and Emotional Learning: Guidelines for Educators.* Alexandria, VA: Association for Supervision and Curriculum Development, 1997.

Evans, Patricia. *Teen Torment: Overcoming Verbal Abuse at Home and at School.* Avon, MA: Adams Media, 2003.

Fassler, David G., and Lynne S. Dumas. *Help Me, I'm Sad.* New York: Viking, 1997.

Freedman, Joshua, Anabel Jensen, Marsha Rideout, and Patricia Freedman. *Handle With Care: Emotional Intelligence Activity Book.* San Mateo, CA: Six Seconds Publishing, 1998.

Fox, C. Lynn. *Let's Get Together.* Torrance, CA: Jalmar Press, 1993.

Goldstein, Arnold P. *The Prepare Curriculum: Teaching Prosocial Competencies.* Champaign, IL: Research Press, 1999.

Goleman, Daniel. *Emotional Intelligence.* New York: Bantam Books, 1995.

Johnson, Kendall. *Trauma in the Lives of Children: Crisis and Stress Management for Counselors, Teachers, and Other Professionals.* 2nd ed. Alameda, CA: Hunter House, 1998.

Johnson, Kendall. *School Crisis Management.* Alameda, CA: Hunter House, 1993.

Kroen, William C. *Helping Children Cope With the Loss of a Loved One: A Guide for Grownups.* Minneapolis, MN: Free Spirit Publishing, 1996.

Krueger, David W. *What Is a Feeling?* Seattle, WA: Parenting Press, 1993.

Lantieri, Linda. *Schools With Spirit: Nurturing the Inner Lives of Children and Teacher.* Beacon Press, 2001.

Lewis, Barbara A. *What Do You Stand For? A Kid's Guide to Building Character.* Minneapolis, MN: Free Spirit Publishing, 1998.

Lickona, Thomas, *Educating for Character: How Our Schools Can Teach Respect and Responsibility.* New York: Bantam Books, 1991.

Lickona, Thomas. *Character Matters.* New York: Touchstone, 2004.

McDaniel, Sandy, and Peggy Bielen. *Project Self-Esteem.* Torrance, CA: Jalmar Press, 1990.

Moorman, Chick. *Spirit Whisperers: Teachers Who Nourish a Child's Spirit.* Saginaw, MI: Personal Power Press, 2001.

Packer, Alex. *How Rude! The Teenagers' Guide to Good Manners, Proper Behavior and Not Grossing People Out.* Minneapolis, MN: Free Spirit Publishing, 1997.

Palomares, Susanna, Sandy Schuster, and Cheryl Watkins. *The Sharing Circle Handbook.* Spring Valley, CA: Innerchoice Publishing, 1992.

Payne, Lauren Murphy. *Just Because I Am.* Minneapolis, MN: Free Spirit Publishing, 1994.

Peterson, Jean Sunde. *Talk With Teens About Self and Stress.* Minneapolis, MN: Free Spirit Publishing, 1993.

Peterson, Jean Sunde. *Talk With Teens About Feelings, Family, Relationships and the Future.* Minneapolis, MN: Free Spirit Publishing, 1995.

Piaget, Jean. *Judgment and Reasoning in the Child.* Totowa, NJ: Littlefield, Adams, 1976.

Piaget, Jean. *The Moral Judgment of the Child.* New York: Free Press Paperbacks (Simon & Schuster), 1997.

Pipher, Mary. *Reviving Ophelia: Saving the Selves of Adolescent Girls.* New York: Ballantine Books, 1994.

Racosky, Rico. *dreams+action=Reality.* Boulder, CO: Action Graphics Publishing, 1996.

Ryan, Kevin, and Karen E. Bohlin. *Building Character in Schools: Practical Ways to Bring Moral Instruction to Life.* San Francisco: Jossey-Bass, 1999.

Schilling, Dianne. *Getting Along: Activities for Teaching Cooperation, Responsibility, Respect.* Torrance, CA: Innerchoice Publishing, 1993.

Schilling, Dianne. *50 Activities for Teaching Emotional Intelligence. Level I: Elementary School.* Torrance, CA: Innerchoice Publishing, 1996. (Also *Level II: Middle School* and *Level III: High School,* 1996, 1999.)

Schilling, Dianne, and Susanna Palomares. *Helping Teens Reach Their Dreams.* Torrance, CA: Innerchoice Publishing, 1993.

Wilber, Jessica. *Totally Private and Personal: Journaling Ideas for Girls and Young Women.* Minneapolis, MN: Free Spirit Publishing, 1996.

LEADERSHIP, DEVELOPMENT OF SCHOOL CULTURE, AND HISTORICAL AND CULTURAL CONTEXT

Alexader, Titus, and John Potter, eds. *Education for a Change: Transforming the Way We Teach Our Children.* London: Routledge Falmer, 2005.

Aspy, David N., and Flora N. Roebuck. *Kids Don't Learn From People They Don't Like.* Amherst, MA: Human Resource Development Press, Inc., 1977.

Blankstein, Alan M. *Failure Is Not an Option.* Thousand Oaks, CA: Corwin Press, 2004.

Bluestein, Jane. *Creating Emotionally Safe Schools: A Guide for Educators and Parents.* Deerfield Beach, FL: Health Communications, 2001.

Cowan, David. *Taking Charge of Organizational Conflict.* Spring Valley, CA: Innerchoice Publishing, 1995.

Deal, Terrence E., and Kent D. Peterson. *Shaping School Culture: The Heart of Leadership.* San Francisco, Jossey-Bass, 1999.

Fox, Matthew. *The Reinvention of Work.* New York: HarperCollins, 1994.

Gatto, John Taylor. *Dumbing Us Down: The Hidden Curriculum of Compulsory Schooling.* Gabriola Island, British Columbia, Canada: New Society Publishers, 2005.

Garfield, Charles. *Peak Performers.* New York: William Morrow, 1986.

Gordon, Thomas. *L.E.T.: Leader Effectiveness Training.* Toronto, Ontario, Canada: Bantam Books, 1980.

Hawley, Jack. *Reawakening the Spirit at Work.* New York: Simon & Schuster, 1993.

Hyland, Bruce, and Merle Yost. *Reflections for Managers.* New York: McGraw-Hill, 1994.

Kantrowitz, Barbara, and Pat Wingert. "Teachers Wanted," Newsweek (Oct. 2, 2000): 37–42.

Kozol, Jonathan. *Savage Inequalities: Children in America's Schools.* New York: Crown Publishers, 1991.

Liebig, James E. *Merchants of Vision.* San Francisco: Berrett-Koehler Publishers, 1994.

McGinnis, Alan Loy. *Bringing Out the Best in People.* Minneapolis, MN: Augsburg Publishing House, 1985.

Naisbitt, John. *Megatrends: Ten New Directions for Transforming Our Lives.* New York: Warner Books, 1982.

Naisbitt, John. *Megatrends 2000.* New York: William Morrow, 1990.

Naisbitt, John, and Patricia Aburdene. *Re-Inventing the Corporation.* New York: Warner Books, 1985.

Ouchi, William G. *Making Schools Work.* New York: Simon & Schuster, 2003.

Peters, Thomas J., and Robert H. Waterman, Jr. *Thriving on Chaos: Handbook for a Management Revolution.* New York: Alfred A. Knopf, 1987.

Pulliam, John D., and James Van Patten. *History of Education in America.* 6th ed. Englewood Cliffs, NJ: Prentice Hall, 1995.

Purkey, William Watson, and David Strahan, "School Transformation Through Invitational Education," *Research in the Schools* 2, no. 2 (1995): 1–6.

Schaef, Ann Wilson. *When Society Becomes an Addict.* San Francisco: Harper & Row, 1987.

Senge, Peter. *The Fifth Discipline.* New York: Currency Doubleday, 1990.

Sizer, Theodore. *Horace's Hope.* Boston: Houghton-Mifflin, 1996.

Toffler, Alvin. *The Third Wave.* New York: William Morrow, 1980.

Wheatley, Margaret J. *Leadership and the New Science: Learning About Organization From an Orderly Universe.* San Francisco: Berrett-Koehler Publishers, 1994.

Wilson, Kenneth G., and Bennett Daviss. *Redesigning Education.* New York: Henry Holt, 1994.

Wright, Ronald. *A Short History of Progress.* New York: Carroll & Graf Publishers, 2004.

Youngs, Bettie B. *Stress Management for Administrators.* Torrance, CA: Jalmar Press, 1993.

PARENTING AND CHILD DEVELOPMENT

Bluestein, Jane. *Parents, Teens & Boundaries: How to Draw the Line.* Deerfield Beach, FL: Health Communications, 1993.

Bluestein, Jane. *The Parent's Little Book of Lists: Do's and Don'ts of Effective Parenting.* Deerfield Beach, FL: Health Communications, 1997.

Bluestein, Jane, and Lynn Collins. *Parents in a Pressure Cooker.* Rosemont, NJ: Modern Learning Press, 1989.

Borba, Michele. *Parents Do Make a Difference.* San Francisco: Jossey-Bass, 1999.

Dyer, Wayne W. *What Do You Really Want for Your Children?* New York: Avon Books, 1985.

Gibbs, Nancy. "Being 13," *Time* (Aug. 8, 2005): 40–44.

Glenn, H. Stephen, and Jane Nelsen. *Raising Self-Reliant Children in a Self-Indulgent World.* Rocklin, CA: Prima Publishing & Communications, 1988.

Hine, Thomas. *The Rise and Fall of the American Teenager.* New York: Bard, 1999.

Markova, Dawna, and Anne R. Powell. *Learning Unlimited: Using Homework to Engage Your Child's Natural Style of Intelligence.* Berkeley, CA: Conari Press, 1998.

Neufeld, Gordon, and Gabor Maté. *Hold Onto Your Kids.* New York: Ballantine Books, 2005.

Radencich, Marguerite, and Jeanne Shay Schumm. *How to Help Your Child With Homework.* Minneapolis, MN: Free Spirit Publishing, 1997.

Scott, Jonathan T. *Fathering From Love: How to Rediscover One of Life's Greatest Treasures.* Sierra Madre, CA: Proud Parent Publishing, 2006.

Index

CORWIN PRESS

The Corwin Press logo—a raven striding across an open book—represents the union of courage and learning. Corwin Press is committed to improving education for all learners by publishing books and other professional development resources for those serving the field of PreK–12 education. By providing practical, hands-on materials, Corwin Press continues to carry out the promise of its motto: **"Helping Educators Do Their Work Better."**